Secure Recovery

Approaches to recovery in forensic mental health settings

**Edited by
Gerard Drennan
and Deborah Alred**

Routledge
Taylor & Francis Group

LONDON AND NEW YORK

First published 2012
by Routledge
2 Park Square, Milton Park, Abingdon, Oxon, OX14 4RN

Simultaneously published in the USA and Canada
by Routledge
711 Third Avenue, New York, NY 10017

Routledge is an imprint of the Taylor & Francis Group

British Library Cataloguing in Publication Data
A catalogue record for this book is available from the British Library

Library of Congress Cataloging in Publication Data
Secure recovery: approaches to recovery in forensic mental health settings / edited by
Gerard Drennan and Deborah Alred.
  p. cm.
  Includes bibliographical references and index.
  1. Mentally ill prisoners—Mental health services—Great Britain. 2. Prisoners—Mental
  health services—Great Britain. 3. Mentally ill offenders—Rehabilitation—Great Britain.
  I. Drennan, Gerard. II. Alred, Deborah.
  RC451.4.P68S43 2012
  365'.60874—dc23

ISBN 13: 978-1-84392-837-9 (hbk)
ISBN 13: 978-1-84392-836-2 (ppr)
ISBN 13: 978-0-203-12917-3 (ebook)

Typeset in Times New Roman
by Cenveo Publisher Services

Contents

Foreword

Daily life for individuals incarcerated in forensic or correctional settings is typically characterised by moments of frustration and despair. Frustration because they are perceived by members of the community, and sometimes treatment staff, as simply bearers of risk rather than as fellow human beings, when they are so much more than that. Despair because their lives are gradually emptied of all that makes them meaningful: valued activities, hope, purpose, and a sense of identity. Instead, there is an increasing preoccupation with risk assessment, with those around them constantly monitoring their behaviour for signs that they are likely to harm others or themselves. It is little wonder that the men and women confined to forensic hospitals or prisons have become physically, and metaphorically, invisible to others and to themselves.

While strength-based approaches to intervention have been with us for as long as mental health services have existed, they have often been impotent in the face of communities determined to prioritise safety over the wellbeing of offenders and patients. However, there is now a growing recognition that it is possible to reduce the risk of reoffending by helping individuals build richer and more fulfilling lives. This book represents an important step forward on the path toward more constructive ways of working with people with mental disorders who have committed serious offences. The recovery model is an exciting development and resonates well with the broader positive psychology movement. I congratulate Gerard Drennan and Deborah Alred for having the vision and the initiative to edit this marvellous book on the application of the recovery model to the field of forensic mental health. In my view, it is likely to prove to be a landmark work and set the agenda for practice and research for the next twenty years. Quite simply, it is a gem of a book.

Professor Tony Ward
School of Psychology
Victoria University of Wellington
PO Box 600, Wellington, New Zealand
Email: Tony.Ward@vuw.ac.nz

Preface

In the narrative tradition of recovery, we want to introduce this collection with a brief account of how a recovery orientation emerged in our forensic service. Many of the chapters in this book tell similar stories of service user recovery and service development to support recovery. Ours is a story of a relatively small forensic mental health service that has begun to change how we respond to the needs of the men and women of Sussex who, through the combination of their mental health difficulties and offending behaviour, became forensic service users. It is a story of a service that set out to improve its approach to forensic psychiatric rehabilitation through embracing recovery principles and finding that what began to emerge was something quite different and unexpected. When we came to consider what difference a recovery orientation could make to how we approached our task we found ourselves considering a fundamental reconceptualization of how we worked with our service users.

As the leads for occupational therapy and psychology in the Sussex Partnership Forensic Service, in 2007 we recognised the need to rejuvenate the in-patient interventions programme at the same time as taking on the challenge of the emerging principles of recovery-oriented practice. We had the advantage at the time that the wider Sussex Partnership Trust leadership had endorsed recovery as a principle of service delivery and produced a Trust Board paper to guide local services (Badu, 2007). This paper set out six key tenants of recovery: hope, partnership working, responsibility, strengths, education, supportive environment, and ongoing journey. We were also aware that recent policy papers had endorsed recovery (CSIP, 2007; DoH, 2006, 2007; Hope, 2004; NIMHE, 2005; Royal College of Psychiatrists, 2004). In spite of these endorsements we believed that forensic services were likely to have misgivings about how the concepts of recovery could be applied in secure settings. Concepts such as choice, empowerment and an emphasis on strengths do not sit easily with the imperatives to prioritise risk assessment and offence-focused interventions. In this we recognised that 'there [was] a particular need to work out the implications of recovery thinking in the most difficult circumstances, where choice and responsibility may be most compromised' (CSIP, 2007, p. 26). We held a series of four workshops with service user volunteers and in-patient staff across our service to consider how the needs of our service users and the nature of secure settings could help or hinder the embedding of recovery principles in our treatment model. What emerged in these discussions, virtually from the off, was that enthusiasm for adopting recovery principles for our service users required our staff teams to feel that they too were somehow personally and professionally engaged in a process of recovery. This may have been linked to the fact that the first recovery theme we considered was that of hope. It was rapidly clear that 'both hope and despair are contagious' (CSIP, 2007, p. 26) and that in order to be hope-inspiring for our service users, we would need to be both inspired and hopeful ourselves (Repper and Perkins, 2003).

Our understanding of the implications of being a recovery service was also gradual, although we have often discussed how there is a moment of insight, a 'Eureka moment', when the sea change that is recovery dawns on one. This qualitative shift in thinking is difficult to create, and in the early stages of championing recovery we tried to impress upon our colleagues the scale of the continuing professional development task to understand what a new recovery paradigm means. However, our service was no different to other services in the early stages of adopting recovery principles in that we encountered the response of 'this is what we have always done', and by this we understood that a recovery orientation has a great deal in common with psychiatric rehabilitation approaches. And of course this is quite correct. There are many aspects of recovery that build on and continue a proud tradition of psychiatric rehabilitation (Roberts *et al.*, 2006; Royal College of Psychiatrists, 2004). However, it was interesting and important to note that in the course of the same discussions in the service we also encountered the paradoxical response of 'recovery – never!'. This latter view could be seen as an appreciation of just what a change to forensic services the adoption of recovery principles could be, and no small amount of alarm at this. This too is understandable. Would a service that allowed patients more choice and decision-making as part of their daily experience in some way compromise the security of the environment? Who decides what choices patients have without simple tokenism? The shift from providing a rehabilitation programme to being a resource of support to someone in their own recovery requires subtle but fundamental change. Which patients could this apply to and when will it not work? In psychiatric rehabilitation the focus of the service has the provider consulting and collaborating with the patient but led by the service. Recovery suggests a shift to the patient leading the process as far as they can and drawing on service provider resources to do so. This subtle difference has a fundamental impact and has been referred to as service providers being 'on tap not on top' (Shepherd, Boardman, Slade, 2008). This is a deeply challenging notion for forensic services. In the chapters that follow there will be many illustrations of how this principle has been safely and constructively applied in a range of forensic settings.

With these considerations in mind we believed that distinguishing a recovery-orientation in forensic services from general services was helpful. In our service we took the view that it was important to distinguish between a recovery approach as it might be taken up in general mental health services and how it needs to be interpreted and translated in a secure setting with forensic clients. We named our particular adaptation of recovery principles 'Secure Recovery' and defined this simply in the following terms:

Secure Recovery acknowledges the challenges of recovery from mental illness and emotional difficulties that can lead to offending behavior. It recognizes that the careful management of risk is a necessary part of recovery in our service but this can happen alongside working towards the restoration of a meaningful, safe and satisfying life.

This requires a clarification as this book is entitled Secure Recovery. This collection of papers spans a broad and eclectic selection of recovery practices in a range of settings and with a variety of client groups. There is no sense in which this describes a unitary recovery model, and, indeed, many of our contributors would reject the very idea that there is *a* recovery model for forensic services. In the context of this book the 'secure' in the title refers to the setting – secure services – and the essence of the text is about recovery applied to secure settings. However, it is also intended to denote the ideas of safety, security, containment, dependability and stability as important aspects of recovery for forensic service users.

Our intention in this collection is to highlight that the process of developing recovery in forensic settings can articulate the 'forensic relevance' of a recovery orientation, taking forward the notion that there should be 'no recovery-free zones' (Roberts and Wolfson, 2004). In this way translations of recovery as developed in mainstream mental health settings can be applied in forensic settings. The development of recovery in forensic mental health care can also articulate the impact of 'risk-consciousness' on a recovery orientation – an acknowledgement that there are also 'no risk-free zones'. It is also our hope that this volume will contribute to the creation of practice-based evidence of the value of a recovery orientation across a range of forensic domains and populations, and in this way contribute to the emerging science of recovery. Finally, we believe that the challenges of applying recovery in forensic settings could influence mainstream recovery thinking with what we learn in forensic settings and in this way contribute to the growing understanding of recovery values and philosophy. Support for the relevance and application of recovery concepts in prison and probation populations would be another advance, and we hope that clearly identifying the tasks of 'offender recovery' will contribute towards this.

In the time that this collection has been in production the current government has encouraged a fundamental reconceptualization of the rehabilitation of offenders and the term 'Rehabilitation Revolution' has been coined. An innovative payment-by-results project at Peterborough prison has considerably developed the role of peer mentors, been lauded in the media, and the model has been taken up for national roll-out by the government. The Venture Trust's work with young offenders to inspire hope and self-belief through wilderness courses and creative-writing projects in prisons have also attracted positive media attention. Restorative Justice approaches are also gaining momentum. The current Secretary of State has highlighted the need for renewed attention to meaningful occupation in prison settings as an under-resourced part of offender rehabilitation. There appears to be a growing recognition that the approach to the rehabilitation of offenders needs to change and there are emerging models of what could be done differently. It is our view that the ethos and principles of recovery would provide a conceptual framework around which the need for change in rehabilitation in criminal justice settings could be organised in a coherent way (Alred and Drennan, 2010). This collection and the practice innovations described here could contribute towards developments in the rehabilitation of offenders generally.

How this collection came to be

Starting in May 2008 we convened a seminar group under a banner of 'Recovery in Forensic Settings', with the first seminar taking place at a seventies-style hotel near Gatwick Airport in West Sussex, such was our limited budget. We convened a seminar with the intention of gathering together services who were working to develop recovery-oriented practice and submitting a proposal to the Forensic Division of the British Psychological Society for an edition of the annual *Issues in Forensic Psychology* series to be on the theme of recovery in forensic settings. In the months that followed the proposal was developed and a network of practitioners applying recovery principles with their forensic clients and willing to submit a chapter was developed. It was through the seminar, and the contacts that it helped to establish, that we were able to identify areas of excellence in practice. The diverse range of 'pinnacles' identified in this way were what we drew on in constructing a collection of themes and papers that seemed to us to have a goodness of fit.

Leibrich (1999) described recovery as the 'progressive discovery of solutions', a phrase that captures the heart of this book. The authors, the individuals and groups of practitioners, describe how they have taken on the challenge and adapted recovery principles to meet their unique circumstances. There is much inspirational recovery-oriented practice in other services not represented here. However, each contributor was willing to put down a marker of their starting point and their progress to date. These are not completed pieces of work. What we have here are beginnings and steps along the way. For this reason we have encouraged the authors to take on a reflexive writing style, to situate themselves within the text. We believed that this style of writing would assist in illuminating how recovery practice emerges over time and is not static or completed, but an evolving narrative developed in conjunction with the service users who pass through forensic services. It aims to uncover and articulate the complex, multi-faceted nature of embedding recovery principles in practice and the extent to which this process is shaped by the individuals and the particularities of the services within which they take shape. A recovery approach is individual, contextual and fluid.

It was our intention to have at least one chapter of the book written by a service user. For a range of reasons this was not possible and this degree of integration of practitioner and service user contributions will remain an aspiration. The collection of recovery stories of forensic service users in the booklet

Our Stories: Moving On, Recovery and Well-being, collated by Sarah Allen of the South West London & St. George's Mental Health Trust Forensic Services, is a commendable contribution. Our own approach was to ask each contributor to consider service user contributions to their chapter, to ensure the service user voice and perspective were woven into the fabric of the text and the ideas. Each author has approached this differently. Some have asked service users to read and comment on their chapter, some have incorporated feedback within the chapter or made use of the service user perspective, and some have collaborated with users to develop their chapter. We have also incorporated service user artwork into the cover of this book. We hope that in this way service user voices can be heard throughout the chapters and that the chapters can speak to service users as much as they speak to practitioners.

There are client groups and settings that are regrettably absent from this collection. We did not succeed in obtaining a contribution that considered the particular challenges of recovery in black and minority ethnic groups. We tried and failed to identify a contributor from services for people with learning disabilities. We do not have a chapter from the recently developed specialist services for men with dangerous and severe personality disorders. And we do not have chapters that focus on services for clients with particular offence types, most notably men and women who have sexually offended. We do not have a contribution that highlights the impact of a recovery orientation on community-based forensic services, or one with a specific focus on recovery approaches to substance misuse difficulties. These areas and client groups, amongst others, will await articulation in other forums.

A word on terminology. Earlier discussions about recovery and the development of recovery-orientated services have distinguished between rehabilitation, the professional and service-led process, or what the clinicians did, and recovery, the clinical outcome, or what the patients did (Deegan, 1988; Roberts *et al.*, 2006). The authors in this book have used the term recovery when describing the work they do too. The separation of terminology has largely been dropped. This highlights the developing partnerships and dialogue as clinicians seek to understand the recovery experience and use this developing knowledge to engage with the service user group from which it emerged (Slade, 2009). The integration of recovery terms into professional language reflects the development of services and is considered more fully in Chapter 1, in which we articulate our view about a shift from rehabilitation to recovery.

Throughout the text we have written recovery without a capital letter. In earlier versions we did use a capital letter for recovery because we wanted to highlight recovery as a paradigm that has a whole set of concepts that contribute to an expanded meaning. This expanded meaning includes the fundamental change to what recovery from mental health difficulties means in the service user movement and – as a consequence of the emphasis on hope, empowerment of service users and the agency of service users – the changes to how services are conceptualised, structured and resourced. Weinstein (2010), for example, has recovery written with a capital letter to denote this new meaning. However, when reviewing the text it became clear that a capital letter distinguishing Recovery as a paradigm from recovery without a capital letter signifying the service user experience was an artificial divide and led to more confusion. For this reason we have elected to allow the context of writing to convey the sense of recovery that is implied in each instance. An additional consideration was the many ways in which recovery was referred to in the chapter contributions. Each contributor has written of 'recovery orientation', 'recovery approach', 'recovery model', 'recovery-based practice' and so forth. We have not imposed a 'recovery terminology' on the contributors, choosing instead to let each use the terms that suited their purpose.

We have also been catholic in the terms used to refer to 'patients', 'service users', 'clients', and 'residents'. The term used to refer to those who access services has and continues to be a source of debate (McGuire-Sniekus, 2003) and each service will have their own reasons for the terminology they use. Context is everything and each contributor has used the term that suited their meaning.

Overview

The book is divided into three sections. The first section is made up of four chapters that consider overarching issues: what we mean by recovery, risk, service-user participation and organisational change. We provide an overview of the development of recovery and its relation to psychiatric rehabilitation and describe four aspects of recovery – clinical, functional, social and personal – and, for the first time, the concept of 'offender recovery'. Richard Barker follows on with a consideration of the key issue of risk assessment and management. The credibility of recovery as an approach and how it is taken up in forensic services will be fundamentally shaped by how the questions of risk are addressed and so the importance of articulating this territory cannot be underestimated. Anita Bowser tackles another cornerstone aspect of developing and embedding recovery practice, the rapidly evolving area of service user participation in forensic services. Together with Kate Law we pick up the question of organisational change in forensic settings in response to the invitation and challenge of recovery.

The second section of the book focuses on service user perspectives on their recovery and on applied recovery practice. This comprises six chapters that all highlight in different ways how recovery principles have been adapted to meet the needs of service users in a variety of different secure settings. Estelle Moore, Darren Lumbard, John Carthy and Joe Ayres, and a selection of 19 service users at Broadmoor High Secure Hospital, describe their findings from a series of focus groups specifically undertaken for the purposes of understanding what service users think about recovery and what they have experienced in their highly regulated treatment environments. Patricia Abbott, Anthony Hague and Andre Jedrzejcyk describe their sophisticated and courageous approach to promoting recovery in Ashworth High Secure Hospital amongst men who have cognitive impairments, another client group who might be considered the least likely to be helped by a recovery approach, and yet where a recovery orientation is fundamental to the progress they make. Jay Smith and Veronica Garcia describe the therapeutic environment in a long-stay medium secure ward and how, through attending to the meaning and significance of what happens in the life of a ward, recovery becomes possible for men who could be considered the least likely to make these strides towards a meaningful and safe, or safer, life. Sally Carr and Sue Havers describe the model of rehabilitation that the South Staffordshire and Shropshire Forensic Services have developed to create a recovery-promoting treatment environment across all dimensions of in-patient care. Helen Miles and her colleagues at the Kent Forensic Service describe a multi-layered and systematic interventions programme that is designed around a recovery ethos in order to create multiple sources of inspiration for service users to progress on a recovery journey through their medium secure service. Sarah Birch's chapter describes some of the courage, capacity to tolerate uncertainty, and reflective practice that staff teams can require when deeply committed to facilitating the recovery journeys of women with personality disorder and offending behaviour detained in conditions of medium security. This section of the book concludes with a view from Michael Brookes on the connections between recovery concepts and the strong tradition of democratic therapeutic community within HMP Grendon Underwood. This echoes the link between recovery in forensic mental health service users and the recovery processes necessary for the men and women who find themselves in the mainstream of the criminal justice system to 'go straight' which we introduce in the first chapter.

The final section of the book attends to the key issues of training for, and evaluation of, recovery-based practice. In the first of three chapters, Helen Eunson, Suzanne Sambrook and Diane Carpenter describe how they have embedded recovery concepts in all training undertaken with staff, highlighting that a thoroughgoing adoption of recovery-based practice will see this perspective reflected in all facets of training for forensic practice. Helen Walker and Dave Langton of the Scottish Forensic Service at Carstairs High Secure Hospital use their chapter to present evaluation data from a number of projects underway in their service to measure the impact of recovery practice, with a particular focus on clinical interventions. Finally, Elina Baker and her colleagues at the Langdon Clinic in Devon describe a baseline evaluation of the recovery health of their service at a particular point in the process of their implementation of recovery practice, with the benefit of a comparison with a local non-forensic rehabilitation service.

Throughout these contributions we believe that forensic practitioners will recognise many of the issues and dilemmas that they encounter in their daily practice. The book is designed to be both a resource and an inspiration to practitioners, to increase understanding of contemporary challenges and to suggest ways forward. It may also be of interest to our colleagues working in mainstream mental health services, who may find our discussion of risk and recovery sheds light on some of the dilemmas they encounter. It is our hope too that forensic mental health service users and their carers may find in these chapters a source of information about what they could expect of forensic mental health services, and a source of strength for their recovery journeys. Hope is a central tenet of recovery and we believe this book holds a message of hope. The contributions share the stories of the service users and the staff who work with them. It shows that behind the walls of secure settings, high, medium and low, hope and recovery-based practice can flourish as people undertake their individual transformative journeys.

References

Allen, S. (2010) *Our Stories: Moving On, Recovery and Well-being*. South West London & St. George's Mental Health Trust Forensic Services.

Alred, D. and Drennan, G. (2010) 'Recovery & forensic mental health services: the progressive discovery of solutions'. Presented at the Nacro National Conference: Mental health and crime: Making sustainable change happen, Loughborough, 21st–23rd September 2010.

Badu, V. (2007) *Principles of recovery*. Sussex Partnership NHS Trust: Unpublished paper.

Care Services Improvement Partnership, Royal College of Psychiatrists, Social Care Institute for Excellence. (2007) *A common purpose: Recovery in future mental health services*. Leeds: Social Care Institute for Excellence.

Deegan, P. (1988) 'Recovery: The Lived Experience of Rehabilitation'. *Psychosocial Rehabilitation Journal*, 11(4): 11–19.

Department of Health. (2006) *From values to action: The CNO's review of mental health nursing*. London: Department of Health.

—— (2007) *Capabilities for inclusive practice*. London: NSIP/CSIP.

—— (2010) *See, Think, Act: Your guide to relational security*. London: Department of Health.

Hope, R. (2004) *The ten essential shared capabilities: A framework for the whole of the mental health workforce*. London: Department of Health and Sainsbury Centre for Mental Health.

Leibrich, J. (ed.) (1999) *A Gift of Stories: Discovering How to Deal with Mental Illness*. Dunedin: University of Otago Press and the Mental Health Commission.

McGuire-Sniekus, R. (2003) 'Patient, Client or Service User? A Survey of Patient Preferences of Dress and Address of Six Mental Health Professions'. *The Psychiatrist*, 27: 305–308.

NIHME. (2005) *Guiding Statement on Recovery*. London: Dept. of Health.

Ralph, R. O. (2000) 'Recovery'. *Psychiatric Rehabilitation Skills*, 4(3): 480–517.

Repper, J. and Perkins, R. (2008) *Social Inclusion and Recovery: A Model for Mental Health Practice*. London.

Roberts, G. and Wolfson, P. (2004) 'Rediscovery of recovery: open to all'. *Advances in Psychiatric Treatment*, 10: 37–48.

Roberts, G., Davenport, S., Holloway, F. and Tattan, T. (eds). (2006) *Enabling Recovery: The Principles and Practise of Rehabilitation Psychiatry*. London: Gaskell.

Royal College of Psychiatrists. (2004) 'Rehabilitation and Recovery Now. Council Report (CR121)'. London: Royal College of Psychiatrists.

Shepherd, G., Boardman, J. and Slade, M. (2008) *Making Recovery a Reality (Policy Paper)*. London: Sainsbury Centre.

Slade, M. (2009) *Personal Recovery and Mental Illness*. London: Kings College.

Weinstein, J. (ed.) (2010) *Mental Health, Service User Involvement and Recovery*. London: Jessica Kingsley Publishers.

Contributors

Patricia Abbott is a Consultant Rehabilitation Psychiatrist and Clinical Lead of the Cognitive Rehabilitation Service, Ashworth Hospital, Mersey Care NHS Trust. Patricia has worked in high secure setting for more than 16 years and has published papers and book chapters on recovery in forensic settings.

Deborah Alred is Head of Occupational Therapy within the Secure and Forensic Services at Sussex Partnership NHS Foundation Trust. Deborah trained in Liverpool before working in a wide range of mental health settings. She has worked in forensic mental health services for 15 years. She is co-editor of Forensic Occupational Therapy (2003, Wiley-Blackwell), the first book to focus on occupational therapy in forensic settings. Deborah is undertaking a Ph.D. involving a participatory research study to explore the skills service users most value in their transitions from secure services into the community.

Joe Ayres is Head Occupational Therapist for the South of England Directorate and Chair of Recovery & Social Inclusion for Broadmoor Hospital. He has many years of experience as an Occupational Therapist across a range of specialist high secure forensic services and has published on the contribution of forensic occupational therapy in high secure hospitals.

Elina Baker is a Clinical Psychologist currently working at the Devon Partnership NHS Trust rehabilitation and recovery service in Exeter. She has previously worked in a number of forensic and secure settings, where she has been involved in work to develop user involvement and recovery-based practice and has lead on a number of projects and published several papers in this area.

Richard Barker has worked as a Clinical & Forensic Psychologist in Reaside Clinic Birmingham & Solihull Mental Health NHS Foundation Trust for the past 12 years. As well as working in both male medium and low secure settings he is also Recovery Lead for the men's service. Outside of his NHS work he also has a role as Deputy Course Director for the Centre for Rational Emotive Behaviour Therapy at the School of Psychology, University of Birmingham.

Sarah Birch is a Clinical Psychologist who has worked within the secure women's services of Sussex Partnership NHS Foundation Trust for the past seven years. Sarah has maintained a longstanding interest in working with women who have been diagnosed with personality disorder and in gender issues in mental health generally, and has recently published the findings of a six-year audit of deliberate self-harm in women's services. Sarah is currently training in psycho-analytic psychotherapy.

Anita Bowser trained as an Occupational Therapist in Oxford in the late 1980's. Anita has spent the last 12 years working in forensic mental health and currently manages the occupational therapy teams in medium secure and low secure units in Hampshire. Anita is undertaking a research project on boredom in in-patients in medium secure units and has developed a range of vocational rehabilitation projects within the Hampshire services of the Southern Health NHS Foundation Trust.

Michael Brookes is a Consultant Chartered Forensic Psychologist and currently Director of Therapeutic Communities at HMP Grendon and Visiting Professor to Birmingham City University. Michael started working in secure settings in the 1980's and went on to develop and manage a number of psychology services within the prison estate. Upon transferring to headquarters in 1997 Michael became Head of the Psychology Liaison Unit and also of the HR Planning and HR Strategy teams. Since taking up his current appointment, Michael has published a number of chapters and papers on HMP Grendon's unique custodial therapeutic community environment.

Diane Carpenter trained as a Mental Health Nurse and has worked in a variety of clinical settings since the early 1980's. Diane is currently the academic group lead for the mental health team at the University of Southampton. Diane's first degree was in social policy and her M. Sc was in evidence-based health care. She recently obtained her Ph.D. for a thesis entitled "Above All a Patient Should never be Terrified: An Examination of Mental Health Care and Treatment in Hampshire 1845–1914".

Sally Carr is the Recovery Lead and Specialist Practitioner within the Psychology Specialty at Staffordshire and Shropshire's Medium Secure Unit in Stafford. Sally qualified as a Registered Mental Nurse in 1983 and went on to manage an alcohol service for many years before returning to nursing in 2006. In her current post Sally has presented at a wide variety of national and international confer-ences on the topic of recovery in secure settings.

John Carthy is a Consultant Forensic Nurse at Broadmoor Hospital. John has a specific remit to promote recovery-oriented practice and improve user involve-ment through his role as chair of a multi-disciplinary Learning & Development committee. Since qualifying as a Registered Mental Nurse in 1981 John has worked in a range of secure settings and has teaching affiliations at with Middlesex University, The Tavistock Clinic and the Royal College of Psychiatry.

Gerard Drennan is a Consultant Clinical Psychologist and Head of Forensic Clinical Psychology & Psychological Therapies at Sussex Partnership NHS Foundation Trust. Gerard trained in clinical psychology in South Africa where he completed a Ph.D. on the role of interpreters in mental health settings. He has worked in forensic mental health settings in England for the past 13 years, specialising first in the development of forensic rehabilitation services and then in the development of new services for the recovery of personality disordered offenders. However, since taking up his current post in Sussex Partnership Foundation Trust five years ago he has focussed on the integration of recovery approaches into forensic services in general. He is training in psychoanalytic psychotherapy.

Helen Eunson is the Practice Development Nurse and Training Lead for the Adult Forensic Services, Southern Health NHS Foundation Trust. Helen qualified as a RMN in 1995 in Scotland and has worked in various nursing roles in the Hampshire forensic services. Helen completed an M.A. in 2007, a PgCE in 2009 and has commenced a Professional Doctorate Programme at the University of Portsmouth with a focus on service user involvement in forensic nursing supervision and reflective practice.

Jason Fee is a Consultant Forensic Psychiatrist working on the Recovery and Continuing Care wards at the Butler Clinic Medium Secure Services, Langdon Hospital, Devon Partnership NHS Trust. Jason has played an active role in promoting recovery locally, regionally and nationally through project work, research and teaching. He is currently involved in the Implementing Recovery Organisational Change (ImROC) programme for Devon Partnership NHS Trust.

Veronica Garcia is currently undertaking training as a Consultant Psychiatrist in Psychotherapy at South West London and St. George's Mental Health Trust. Veronica has worked in a wide range of mental health settings and has an enduring interest in forensic psychiatry and rehabilitation.

Anthony Hague is a Modern Matron and Lead Nurse for the Cognitive Rehabilitation Service Ashworth Hospital, Mersey Care NHS Trust, with more than 17 years of experience of work in this environment.

Sue Havers is a Consultant Forensic & Clinical Psychologist and Clinical Director of the Forensic Mental Health Service at South Staffordshire and Shropshire Healthcare NHS Foundation Trust. Sue trained as a clinical psychologist in Liverpool in the late 1980's before going on to work in a wide range of settings. Sue is a regular contributor to the Staffordshire Doctoral Training in

Clinical Psychology and has presented papers on the recovery approach within forensic settings at various professional conferences.

Andre Jedrzejcyk is an Associate Specialist Psychiatrist in the Cognitive Rehabilitation Service, Ashworth Hospital, Mersey Care NHS Trust, with almost two decades of experience of working in this setting.

David Langton was the Nurse Consultant for the Forensic Network in NHS Scotland until his retirement in 2011, a post he had held since 2005, with a remit to support service development throughout Scotland. In a forensic nursing career spanning almost four decades David worked in 2 of the 4 high secure hospitals in the UK in nursing, teaching and management posts. As an active member of the Royal College of Nursing David was the chair of the RCN's Forensic Nursing Forum between 2008 and 2011 and a member of the editorial board of the British Journal of Forensic Practice until 2011.

Kate Law is a Chartered Clinical & Forensic Psychologist. Kate is currently the Lead Psychologist at Farmfield and Sturt House Hospitals, part of the Priory Group, where she leads on implementing recovery approaches and service user involvement, and has previously worked in HM Prison Service and in the Probation Service headquarters, developing national groupwork treatment programmes for offenders. She has given numerous papers and poster presentations at conferences and seminars on recovery and groupwork treatment programmes.

Darren Lumbard is a Principal Clinical Psychologist at Broadmoor Hospital, with a specific role to promote the principles of assertive rehabilitation and recovery. Darren has worked at Broadmoor Hospital since qualifying in clinical psychology 10 years ago and has special interests in DBT and in the delivery of groupwork for violent offenders. Darren also has teaching commitments on a number of forensic and clinical psychology professional training courses.

Dr Helen Miles is a Chartered Principal Clinical Psychologist working at the Trevor Gibbens Medium Secure Unit, Kent Forensic Psychiatry Services, Kent & Medway NHS & Social Care Partnership Trust. She is also an honorary lecturer with the Institute of Psychiatry, Kings College London and the University of Kent at Canterbury. She has worked in forensic secure services for the past nine years and has a special interest in forensic addictions and recovery in secure settings, publishing research in these areas in various peer reviewed journals. Dr Miles had the invaluable assistance of the following colleagues at the Trevor Gibbens Unit in the preparation of this chapter; Tom Foulds (Nursing Team Leader), Sonia Griffin (Ward Manager and Nursing Recovery Lead), Carol Guinan (Assistant Psychologist), Dr Tracy King (Chartered Senior Clinical Psychologist), Anna Murphy (Occupational Therapist), Kate Pellowe (Senior Occupational Therapist), Miriam Pucyutan (Occupational Therapist) as well as service users from the secure services in Kent.

Estelle Moore is a Consultant Clinical & Forensic Psychologist and Lead for the Centralised Groupwork Service, Newbury Therapy Unit, Broadmoor Hospital, West London NHS Trust. Estelle has worked for over 15 years in a high security hospital, ten of which have included responsibility for the design and the delivery of recovery-oriented group treatment programme that provides a holistic understanding of the past, present and future needs of mental health service users with a history of serious offending. Estelle has published chapters and peer reviewed journal articles in the areas of expressed emotion, personality disorder and the evaluation of group therapies.

Suzanne Sambrook is a Consultant Clinical Psychologist working within the low secure unit of the Wessex Adult Forensic Service. Her areas of specialist interest are in working with complex trauma and developing recovery-based interventions with service users.

Jay Smith is a Consultant in Forensic Rehabilitation and Jungian Analyst. Jay has developed psychiatric rehabilitation services in East London in general adult mental health and in forensic settings over the past 20 years. Jay has written and published on the role of the treatment environment and the therapeutic milieu over many years.

Helen Walker is currently Educational Project Manager for NHS Education for Scotland and part-time Practice Education Co-ordinator for the School of Forensic Mental Health. Helen is also undertaking a Ph.D. with the University of the West of Scotland. Helen has published journal articles on a number of clinical initiatives, most of which are linked to either training or impact of psycho-education for forensic patients in high secure services. Much of her work within the School of Forensic Mental Health has centred on the development and implementation of a range of short courses, in particular the New to Forensic education programme.

Zeffa Warren is a Clinical Psychologist working in Devon Partnership NHS Trust secure services at Langdon Hospital. Her interests include promoting recovery in forensic services and current project areas are sexual expression in forensic services and terminology used when referring to people using the service.

Contributions to chapter 14 were also made by Alexis Clarke (Trainee Clinical Psychologist, University of Plymouth), Emma Laughton (person who has used services and member of Saplings, East Devon Mental Health Self Advocacy Project) and Elaine Hewis (person who has used services and consultant trainer in mental health, Exeter, Devon).

1 Recovery in forensic mental health settings

From alienation to integration

Gerard Drennan and Deborah Alred

'Contemplating the loss of reason as pre-eminent in the catalogue of human afflictions; and believing that the experience of the Retreat throws some light on the means of its mitigation, and also that it has demonstrated, beyond all contradiction, the superior efficacy, both in respect of cure and security, of a mild system of treatment in all cases of mental disorder, an account of that experience has long appeared to me, due to the public.'

(Tuke, [1813] (1996), p. vi)

In this chapter we introduce and describe the evolution of recovery in mental health services. We make the case for why we consider that the development of recovery concepts and their implications for practice is an emergent and new paradigm in mental health work generally, and forensic mental health work in particular, and that the interpretation of recovery principles in forensic mental health settings requires an adapted approach to how they are promoted in mainstream services. We will review four facets of recovery – clinical, functional, social and personal recovery – and introduce 'offender recovery' as a fundamental additional recovery task for forensic service users. In order to set out our case for recovery in forensic settings we will make links with the development of desistance in the arena of offender rehabilitation. Finally, we will suggest that a new synthesis of the elements drawn from mental health and criminal justice settings offers a way of understanding the complex recovery tasks forensic patients need to address in order to navigate a return from a state of alienation from family, society, the care system and all too often themselves, to a state of integration in which a safe and satisfying life becomes possible.

From psychiatric rehabilitation to recovery

The recovery movement as we have come to know it today benefited in the UK from the 2007 publication of a Joint Position Paper by the Care Services Improvement Partnership (CSIP), the Royal College of Psychiatrists and the Royal College of Nursing entitled 'A Common Purpose'. This paper set outs what was meant by recovery, the importance of embracing its concepts and the many ways in which this process would challenge service providers to rethink what it meant to be a service delivery organisation. Recovery as a guiding principle brought with it a set of themes rather than hard and fast directives for service change. Recovery emphasised values in practice, the fundamental importance of hope, a shift away for emphasising pathology to an emphasis on strengths and wellbeing. Meaning in life, choice, empowerment and a positive sense of personal identity were other key elements for someone to be in recovery.

Roberts and Wolfson's (2004) publication of 'The rediscovery of recovery: open to all' in *Advances in Psychiatric Treatment* also made a key contribution to the recognition of new meaning to the term recovery, although they were sanguine about whether this was a new paradigm as they traced the origins of these concepts back to the establishment of 'moral treatment' at the Quaker Retreat in York, described by Samuel Tuke's grandson (Tuke, [1813] 1996). Roberts and Wolfson (2004) describe moral treatment as based on kindness, compassion, respect and hope of recovery. There were many elements at the Retreat that would be recognisable to today's practitioners, notably the therapeutic use of occupation, resulting in a varied programme of outdoor activities, gardening, farming, exercise and indoor activities such as dressmaking, reading, writing and maths (Wilcock, 2001).

Jacobson (2004), in her historical and anthropological analysis of the emergence of recovery in the USA, suggests that Tuke distinguished between 'cure' and 'recovery', and that he preferred the word 'recovered' – the above quote notwithstanding – because of the emphasis on recovery of social function and humility in recognising that their approach supported natural healing processes rather than effecting a cure directly. The recovery principles of the Retreat considered the potential for recovery to lie in the individual, the extent to which they could rediscover a sense of control and their 'desire for esteem' (Tuke, [1813] (1996), p. 157, quoted in Jacobson, 2004, p. 34).

The word recovery has therefore been a feature of health and mental health practice for a considerable time, and indeed the word recovery is ubiquitous in our culture, with everything from the economy to the environment needing to recover. Reference to the goal of recovery has also been prominent in the paradigm of psychiatric rehabilitation as it developed in the last three decades. In their seminal texts on the psychiatric rehabilitation model, William Anthony, Robert Liberman and colleagues in America (Anthony and Liberman, 1986; Anthony, Cohen and Farkas, 1990; Pratt *et al.*, 1999) and Wing, Bennett and Shepherd in the UK (Shepherd, 1984; Watts and Bennett, 1991) encouraged practitioners to recognise that they were not only 'doing rehabilitation' but also achieving what they called therapeutic benefits for the patient. While not without its critics (BPS, 2000), the psychiatric rehabilitation model did seek to be progressive through addressing the clinical and social aspects of rehabilitation. The model set out four dimensions to the negative impact of severe mental illness. These were impairment, dysfunction, disability and disadvantage. Impairment was defined in terms of the traditional symptoms of mental illness, such as hallucinations and delusions. Dysfunction was defined as the restriction or loss of ability to perform an activity or tasks such as activities of daily living, work skills and social skills.

Disability was defined as the incapacities that resulted in unemployment, home-lessness, and other social roles. Finally, disadvantage was defined as the lack of opportunity to engage in an activity or role as a result of discrimination, poverty, and so on (Anthony *et al.*, 1990). In this model, recovery from severe mental illness was seen as multi-faceted and incorporated a range of social elements.

The sophistication of the psychiatric rehabilitation model lay in its comprehen-siveness. Besides formal medical treatment, it conceptualised the need to address psychosocial rehabilitation through skills training, interventions to promote social inclusion, and service user empowerment. Even the importance of hope, a cornerstone of recovery, is present in many early rehabilitation texts and in prac-tice (Bachrach, 1992; Geller, 2000; Watts and Bennett, 1983; Menninger, 1959). However, it has been our experience in trying to develop recovery in our forensic service that the degree of common language between the psychiatric rehabilita-tion model and recovery has led to a difficulty in conveying how recovery as a paradigm could mark a fundamental break with the psychiatric rehabilitation model. In spite of texts that have provided clarification of the meaning of recov-ery as distinct from rehabilitation (e.g. Repper and Perkins, 2009; Shepherd, 2006) this has arguably not yet penetrated into mainstream understanding and so Lloyd *et al.* (2008), Meehan *et al.* (2008), Slade *et al.* (2008) have all noted the ongoing confusion in terminology.

Recovery: a new paradigm?

Accounts of the emergence of new concepts of recovery, and recovery as a distinct set of meanings, trace its genealogy throughout the history of mental health services through a number of sources. The critique of the medical model and the 'modernisation' agenda that it suggests can be seen in the Normalisation movement starting in the 1970s (Flynn and Nitsch, 1980; Brown and Smith, 1992), deinstitutionalisation in the 1980s (Geller, 2000; Maclean, 2000) and the Consumer/Survivor movement in more recent times (Deegan, 1988, 1993; Mead and Copeland, 2000).

However, it is Patricia Deegan's (1988) paper that is most often attributed with being the first mouthpiece of a groundswell of change. Patricia Deegan, a psychologist diagnosed with schizophrenia, described her experience as a journey of personal recovery and linked this to the empowerment discourse that had emerged from physical disability empowerment. The shift in any recovery vision was towards the recognition that all the efforts to 'treat' on the part of the health-care system were of limited value, if not iatrogenically harmful, if they did not progress a service user on a personal recovery journey.

Anthony (1993), in another seminal paper, takes up the contrast between a traditional rehabilitation approach and a recovery-orientated approach at the level of the organisation by proposing:

> recovery-orientated system planners see the mental health system as greater than the sum of its parts. There is the possibility that efforts to affect the

impact of severe mental illness positively can do more than leave the person less impaired, less disabled, and less disadvantaged. These interventions can leave a person not only with 'less', but with 'more' – more meaning, more purpose, more success, and more satisfaction with one's life. The possibility exists that the outcomes can be more than the specific service outcomes of, for example, symptom management and relief, role functioning, services accessed, entitlements assured, etc. While these outcomes are the raison d'etre of each service, each may also contribute in unknown ways to recovery from mental illness.

(Anthony, 1993, p. 530)

And further that:

Recovery-oriented health systems must structure their settings so that recovery 'triggers' are present....The mental health system must help sow and nurture the seeds of recovery through creative programming....Helpers must have a better understanding of the recovery concept in order for this recovery-facilitating environment to occur.

(Ibid, p. 534)

In Jacobson's (2004) anthropological account of the introduction of recovery into mental health services in Wisconsin, she observed the many facets or 'complexes of meaning' of the concept that she encountered, and described this as a kaleidoscope. One of the older meanings is that of *recovery-as-evidence*, referring to the history of treatment and institutional care with all the applied knowledge and scientific evidence of what can bring about recovery. Jacobson (2004) also identified *recovery-as-experience*, in which she included the recovery stories of service users, carers and services themselves. Jacobson goes on to describe *recovery-as-ideology*, which refers to when the coming together of economic factors, the evidence base for treatment, and experiences of recovery give rise to support for certain service models and specific approaches to treating mental illness. Jacobson suggested that when a third aspect of recovery – *recovery-as-ideology* – became established in the minds of professionals it became a driving force for mental health system reform. Inevitably, political factors have entered into the recovery arena and so Jacobson identified two further aspects – *recovery-as-politics* and *recovery-as-policy*. In Jacobson's account of what she saw in Wisconsin, it was clear that the development of recovery during a period of economic downturn had a significant impact on how services responded to the challenge represented by the experience and evidence of recovery. This is surely very pertinent for UK forensic services at the start of this decade.

It is also important for our purposes here to highlight that all of these different ways in which recovery has meaning expand the concept of recovery from simply being an aspect of a person's response to illness to potentially a form of political struggle with roots in the anti-psychiatry, critical psychiatry and survivor movements; to a set of principles by which mental health services can be modernised and reformed and, as a result, a model for service delivery. The chapters in this volume will describe how this kaleidoscope of meaning in the recovery paradigm has found expression in UK forensic settings.

Meanings of recovery for the person

Over and above the ways in which Jacobson has described the meanings of recovery, there are four principal meanings of recovery for the individual person, and we have summarised these below.

Clinical recovery

This is usually the first and most commonsensical meaning of recovery. It applies to all disease and illness conditions and refers to the absence of the signs and symptoms of these illnesses or diseases. In mental illness this could mean the absence of disturbances of perception or belief, suicidal feelings or impulses, inappropriately elated mood, disorganised thinking and a whole raft of other similar such indicators of mental health disturbance.

In this sense, clinical recovery implies a return to a state of health that preceded the onset of clinical symptoms; however, clinical recovery can be full or partial. After a long period in the history of madness, when there was considerable scepticism about the prospect of clinical recovery in conditions such as the schizophrenias, longitudinal studies reignited hope for clinical recovery, when the potential for recovery was measured in decades (Harding *et al.*, 1987; Harrison *et al.*, 2001; Jobe and Harrow, 2005). It is very important that the goals of clinical recovery remain a hope and aspiration, for the sake of the service user and their carers. Indeed, much of the energy and enthusiasm for recovery in services and carers of people with severe and enduring forms of mental illness was reignited by discoveries of clinical recovery in patients with whom this had not been expected or anticipated (Bellack, 2006; Davidson *et al.*, 2006).

The notion of clinical recovery can be controversial for patients who suffer from the features of personality disorder, since sufferers will often respond that they cannot 'return' to a state of wellness as this state had never previously existed for them.

The notion of clinical recovery is controversial for another reason. Clinical recovery is the aspect of a broader approach to recovery from mental illness or emotional disturbance that is most likely to be described in outcomes defined by others, whether they be professional or non-professional, and this may detract from self-acceptance processes (Repper and Perkins, 2003) and valuing the transformative power of such personal experiences (Repper, personal communication).

Functional recovery

Functional recovery (Lloyd *et al.*, 2008) does not require the absence of all experiences associated with illness. Rather, the achievement in this dimension of recovery is the restitution of functional capabilities for undertaking life tasks, whether daily routines of living or more demanding tasks such as holding down a job, staying in a partnership or parenting. Getting on with life and enjoying what it has to offer does not require the complete absence of discomfort. So mental health service users may still experience hearing voices, have feelings of paranoia, conduct compulsive rituals or have urges to self-harm, and may yet lead full and enriching lives. This form of recovery is most closely linked to the aims and objectives of skills training in the psychiatric rehabilitation paradigm. However, there is much overlap with social recovery.

Social recovery

This aspect of recovery has been embedded in the psychosocial rehabilitation approach to recovery from mental illness from the outset. However, the tenets of social recovery have moved on to be synonymous with the vast sweep of issues linked to social inclusion. Repper and Perkins (2003) have made a substantial contribution to the field and set out in considerable detail the indivisible link between recovery, taken as a whole, and the means of social inclusion. Their position on the social exclusion of mental health service users is more social polemic than simply identifying social exclusion as characteristic of what mental health service users experience. They argue convincingly that social exclusion results from discrimination in society directed towards the mentally ill and that the impact on service users is devastating. These impacts extend from simple facts of daily living that include ostracisation, loneliness, harassment and rejection.

The impact of unemployment is deeply felt too, not only through the grim realities of poverty, but also for psychological reasons. For mental health service users, finding employment can be more difficult than if they had been to prison. The impact for forensic service users, as Mezey and Eastman (2009) have observed, is that they have the worst of both worlds. The challenge to overcome stigma, including self-stigma, is all the more difficult for forensic service users and the professionals who seek to support them. Access to housing, education, meaningful social roles, employment, community involvement, recreational facilities, and social networks outside of professional carers are all fraught with difficulty and the potential for failure.

The recovery movement has also highlighted the extent to which mental health service users are disenfranchised as citizens (Sayce, 2003) and socially excluded (Boardman *et al.*, 2010). They invariably do not see themselves as potentially valued members of the community who have rights, who can also have a voice and be heard by local government and policy-makers (Mezzina *et al.*, 2006a). Boardman *et al.* (2010) highlights the loss of social capital for those suffering from mental illness and makes the link with recovery-oriented practice and work as a means of restoring social networks and community participation. Social dimensions to recovery encompass not only the societal level but also the importance of informal or non-professional social networks of support amongst friends, family and peers (Mezzina *et al.*, 2006b; Ridgway, 2001). 'Facilitating integration in this way requires the mental health service system to re-envision its role from that of a treatment and rehabilitation provider to that of a broader community resource, responsible for catalysing and expediting people's access to opportunities, arenas and resources' (Lloyd *et al.*, 2008, p. 325).

Personal recovery

> a deeply personal process of changing one's attitudes, values, feelings, goals, skills and/or roles. It is a way of living a satisfying, hopeful, and contributing way of life even with limitations caused by illness. Recovery involves the development of new meaning and purpose in one's life as one grows beyond the catastrophic effects of mental illness.
>
> (Anthony, 1993, p. 527)

This passage from Anthony's 1993 paper setting out recovery as a new vision for mental health services in the 1990s, is most often quoted as a definition of recovery; however, it is clearly more specifically addressed to the facet of recovery that has now come to be known as *personal recovery*. It is difficult to define the concept of personal recovery because it is, as Anthony writes, a deeply personal experience, unique to each individual and open-ended, more like a process and a journey. This is why some writers have opted instead to think of a 'map' or a collection of themes or characteristics, based on the accounts of service users who can describe their lived experience.

The journey of personal recovery is one in which personal growth is what matters most to the person 'in recovery'. In order for this to happen, the illness experience, the life crisis, the experience of loss, 'hitting rock bottom', comes to be seen as an opportunity. In psychotherapy, symptoms can be seen as messengers, without which we would not realise there was something wrong and to be understood. The paediatrician and psychoanalyst Winnicott (1984) understood this in relation to delinquency as a sign of hope and Motz (2009) has written of deliberate self-harm in similar terms. However, for these moments or experiences to become turning points, or for small steps to become watersheds, there is a fundamental need for hope in the future and in possibility to take root. Hope is of central significance if a recovery journey is to begin and to be sustained – 'if recovery is about one thing it is about the recovery of hope' (CSIP, 2007, p. 5). Personal recovery can be seen as a journey from alienation and despair to the discovery of meaning and purpose (Coleman, 1999; Ralph, 2005; Ridgway, 2001). In a forensic setting, service users usually have to grapple with and come to terms with detention as an opportunity for recovery. From the point of view of a mainstream setting, recovery can seem impossible while detained under the civil or criminal sections of the MHA (O'Hagan, 2003). Roberts *et al.* (2008) acknowledge that detention under the Mental Health Act can create the possibility of recovery that would otherwise not exist in community settings. One Sussex service user discharged into the community after 11 years in Broadmoor High

Security Hospital following a conviction for attempted murder and detention under the MHA category of Psychopathic Disorder expressed gratitude that 'Broadmoor made me stop and let my life catch up with me.'

In order for a life crisis to become an opportunity for positive life changes the person needs to become an active participant in their recovery. Clinical, functional and social recovery can all, to some extent, take place without the full participation of the service user but personal recovery cannot progress if the service user remains a passive recipient of care. This implies another key theme or characteristic of personal recovery, that the service user begins to regain active control over their care and treatment, and ultimately their life. This entails the empowerment and choice aspect of recovery. Even regaining more control can require a service user to accept and cope with the reality of ongoing distress, dysfunction, and disability.

A key feature of personal recovery is the regaining of a positive sense of identity (CSIP, 2007; Slade, 2009). To do this, a person in recovery may need to rediscover a sense of self lost in the course of an illness or long admission to hospital, heal a damaged or distorted sense of self that predates an illness episode or an episode of care, or create anew a sense of self from new experiences and growth. The recovery paradigm has moved on our understanding of what is involved in the process of personal recovery. Various authors have identified stages of recovery (Andresen *et al.*, 2003; NIMHE, 2004; see Slade, 2009 for an overview). These stages map onto the dimensions of identity – individual, social, cultural, interpersonal, spiritual and sexual – in a number of ways. Slade (2009) has described four domains of Personal Recovery (hope, identity, meaning, and personal responsibility) and set these out in a Personal Recovery Framework.

What is also important to highlight here is that being clear about the pivotal importance of personal recovery suggests clear tasks and roles for mental health workers if they are to support this aspect of the process. Slade (2009) has summarised these as four key tasks: the task of supporting hope; the task of supporting identity; the task of supporting meaning; and the task of supporting personal responsibility. These tasks can be defined as competencies specific to facilitating personal recovery. They are not the same tasks or professional competencies that are required for clinical, functional or social recovery. Approached in this way, a new focus on the personal recovery of mental health service users implies an additional set of competencies in mental health workers, that may challenge the competencies they relied upon when approaching psychosocial rehabilitation. Many writers in the field of recovery have identified hope, optimism and a belief in recovery as fundamental to support a service user to recover. This can be a challenging starting point for staff teams at the beginning of a forensic patient's admission following a serious offence. However, when carers can maintain hope, optimism and belief in the possibility that meaning in life is not beyond reach, in spite of all that may have happened, and that each person can (re)discover a sense of value and worth in themselves, this is a powerful factor in supporting personal recovery. The recovery paradigm invites us to consider the holding and instilling of hope as an explicit and priority task in mental health services (Hogan, 2003;

Maddock and Hallam, 2010; SAMHSA, 2005) and a core skill required of helpers (Landeen, Byrne and Pawlick, 1995; NIMHE, 2005; Repper and Perkins, 2003; Russinova, 1999; Shepherd, Boardman and Slade, 2008; Slade, 2009). A psychology of hope has arisen in the USA (Snyder, 2000) and the rise of Positive Psychology (Resnick and Rosenheck, 2006; Seligman and Csikszentmihalyi, 2000) contributes to the momentum and science behind this development. In the psychiatric survivor movement the concept of hope is one of consciousness-raising and deeply political, as antidote to the despair that mental health services can be seen to engender (Jacobson, 2004, p. 67).

Many facets, one process

Divisions of recovery into different types or categories are inevitably artificial. In most circumstances a recovery process will involve a combination of elements with different priorities at different stages. Onken, Dumont, Ridgway *et al.* (2001) concluded that recovery arose as a 'product of the dynamic interaction' amongst:

the characteristics of the individual (the self/whole person, hope/sense of meaning and purpose);
the characteristics of the environment (basic material resources, social relationships, meaningful activities, peer support, formal services, formal service staff);
and the characteristics of the exchange (hope, choice/empowerment, independence/interdependence).

Jacobson and Greenley (2001) describes similar processes in terms of the 'internal conditions' and 'external conditions' that promote recovery. We will consider below the aspect of recovery suggested by the process of turning away from offending behaviour.

Opportunities for recovery-oriented services in the UK

A recovery-orientated revision of mental health services in the USA appears to have taken root rapidly in the early 1990s, possibly due to the charismatic and credible leadership of respected proponents of the psychiatric rehabilitation model, such as Anthony (1993), who set out a 'vision'. Jacobson (2004) has suggested that the rise of recovery as a new service model could also be attributed to the momentum it could give to the drive to reduce the cost of care through deinstitutionalisation, promoting care in the community and self-help.

Two decades on from this era in the United States and we find ourselves at a time of uncertainty over global financial recovery and intense pressures on governments to guarantee the safety of the public from real and imagined risks. The manner in which the capital carried by each of the recovery discourses is deployed will impact on how it manifests as a social movement, a system reform or a service model. The task for forensic mental health services in the UK is to navigate towards a recovery vision in this particular historical and cultural context. The wider mental health care and Department of Health policy context is one in which documents voicing support for recovery in mainstream services have not until recently been taken up with the enthusiasm that the USA, Australia, New Zealand or Scotland have shown. The trickle down to services has often progressed little beyond the renaming of 'rehabilitation' services (Lester and Gask, 2006), with a few notable exceptions (Kelly, Wellman and Sin, 2009). It has been our experience that the scale of the task of introducing recovery as a paradigm and a new clinical philosophy has meant that change has been slow and incremental. The scale of the task and the requirements for a root-and-branch reform of services have been succinctly set out in two recent Sainsbury Centre for Mental Health papers (2009, Shepherd *et al.*, 2010; see Chapter 4 in this volume). However, the need for a coherent and informed understanding of recovery in secure settings has never been more timely. There is currently a rapid increase in the demand for forensic mental health places and a significant expansion of services at medium and low secure levels. The NHS needs to greatly increase their collaboration with criminal justice agency partners to respond to the Bradley Report (DoH, 2009) and consequently will be treating and managing increasing numbers of service users with mental health and offending needs. The changing risk profile of mental health forensic service users has resulted in the publication of new security standards and the recent publication of *See, Think, Act*, DoH guidance on relational security (DoH, 2010). All of these developments represent an opportunity to ensure that recovery principles are embedded at the heart of services, whether it be in their architectural design, their staffing or their service models.

However, there are developments within criminology and the wider criminal justice system that we want to suggest should also be taken into account when considering the place of recovery in forensic mental health services.

Developments in the rehabilitation of offenders

Criminologists and clinicians working with offender populations in prisons and probation have recently described the rise of 'desistance from offending' as an approach to working with men and women who commit crime (Farrall and Calverley, 2005; Gadd and Jefferson, 2007; Maruna, 2005; Smith, 2006). In a helpful parallel with the discussion of psychiatric rehabilitation above, Ward and Maruna (2007), in an opening chapter entitled 'How did "Rehabilitation" become a dirty word?' highlight the decline of this paradigm in their field. 'No one but an academic simpleton will even use the word "rehabilitation" without apprehension' (Richard Korn, 1992, quoted in Ward and Maruna, 2007). They go on to argue that in probation and prison circles rehabilitation is seen as a dated, outmoded, anachronistic term associated with bureaucrats, windowless prison basements, an extreme medical model and a sexist stereotype of a naïve do-good social worker (p. 3). This is a strongly worded position and arguably not shared by many in the UK as it was during this period that Reasoning and Rehabilitation, a cognitive-behavioural, manualised group programme, was a cornerstone of the offender behaviour programmes employed in UK prisons. Nevertheless, 're-entry' became a buzzword in criminal justice circles in the United States in about 2000, when Jeremy Travis famously warned 'they all come back'. In the UK 'resettlement' has competed with 'reintegration' as key terms. Ward and Maruna (2007) note that 'recovery' has also surfaced due to the link between addiction, mental health and offending. In the academic criminology literature 'desistance from crime' has become the current term (Farrall and Calverley, 2005; Kazemian, 2007).

Ward and Maruna (2007) go on to suggest that the 'what works' paradigm in offender rehabilitation implied a strong empirical approach to reducing offending, with the use of randomised controlled trials of interventions, experiments, meta-analyses, and 'dosages' of treatment relevant to specific client types. With the 'what helps' model in the desistance paradigm, all the above are useful but the issue of agency is given a central position. This has arisen, again in parallel to aspects of the recovery perspective, from qualitative research data from interviews with ex-offenders about what helped them. This highlighted that much 'desistance' occurs outside of the formal aspects of the criminal justice system. Offenders described the importance of work, and relationships, as motivators for desisting from further offences. If the provider could support the offender to work towards the issues they regarded as priorities – housing, work and relationships – rather than providing 'expert' offender management systems, then they would focus their efforts differently. Similarly, the 'what works' paradigm targets 'offender deficits', whereas the desistance approach seeks to promote strengths (i.e. strong social bonds, pro-social involvements, and social capital) linked with desistance through research and reformed-offender narratives. Clinical experience and research with offenders highlight that they almost universally hate the term 'rehabilitation'. Morgan Freeman's character in the film *The Shawshank Redemption* refers to rehabilitation as a 'made-up, bullshit' word. Offenders talk of 'going straight, self-change, recovery and even redemption'. Ward and Maruna (2007) reference other writers making the point that 'cognitions, behaviours, [and] resocialisation' are not enough. Rehabilitation needs to make sense to the client and to be clearly relevant to the possibility of a better life. Interestingly, Ward and Maruna (2007) and Robinson and Crow (2009), who also critique rehabilitation concepts, opt to retain the term rehabilitation.

Ward and Maruna (2007) go on to outline a 'model of rehabilitation' that they have developed called the 'Good Lives Model' (GLM). This model has been developed over a number of years by Ward and colleagues in New Zealand with specific reference to work with sex offenders and has been taken up in a number of UK services. This has now been developed to consider its applicability with forensic service users in New Zealand (Barnao, Robertson and Ward, 2010) and in Dangerous and Severe Personality Disorder Services in England. It is very helpful for our purpose in considering the principles of recovery in relation to a population of service users whose mental health needs are complicated by the addition of offending behaviour, that there is a current emergence of models of working with offending itself that endorses such similar principles.

Recovery in forensic settings: service and individual aspects

It would be entirely wrong to suggest that questions of risk are unique to forensic mental health work when issues of risk also present significant challenges in mainstream services (Bonney and Stickley, 2008). The inquiries that follow adverse events in mainstream mental health settings are no less exacting than in forensic settings (Scott-Moncrieff, Briscoe and Daniels, 2009). Davidson *et al.* (2006) noted that risk was one of the cardinal concerns about recovery amongst clinicians in the USA. However, the fact that a forensic service user has already committed a crime, and usually this would need to be serious enough to meet a threshold for access to a forensic service, has a profound impact on the way in which that person's care is approached by services. Not only are the characteristics of the individual forensic patient important, but the characteristics of the treatment and security environment that are required to contain groups of forensic patients together are also important. The risks of further serious harm to others, concerns about coordinated activities to undermine security and escape are just some of the features of the forensic mental health environment. It is because of the importance of this different starting point that we believe that recovery constitutes a profound challenge to forensic services. In this respect we do not share the view that 'there is a minimal difference between recovery processes within forensic psychiatry compared to generic services' (South London and Maudsley NHS Foundation Trust and South West London and St George's Mental Health NHS Trust, 2010, p. 35), as welcome as a positive position statement from an influential group of UK psychiatrists is. We will highlight two main reasons for our view, one related to recovery as a service model (or in Jacobson's terms 'recovery-as-policy') and the other related to the nature of the personal journey of recovery for mental health service users who have committed a serious offence (or 'recovery-as-experience').

In the preceding sections we have set out the argument as to why recovery as a paradigm is a challenge to psychiatric rehabilitation. However, in forensic settings it has long been acknowledged that the tasks of psychiatric rehabilitation also require a consideration of the forensic aspects of the service user (Cox, 1978). Lindqvist and Skipworth (2000) use the term forensic psychiatric rehabilitation; however, what differentiates forensic from mainstream rehabilitation has not been clearly described.

If recovery rightly involves meaningful organisational change in terms of how positive risk-taking, trust and choice for service users (Shepherd *et al.*, 2010; Slade, 2009) are approached, then the implications for forensic services are very considerable. Hospital managers would need assurances that this was done in a careful and thought-through manner. It is not only management but the clinical staff also who need to understand that a naïve interpretation of recovery principles could be hazardous to the public, to the service user themselves and even to their own professional careers.

Roberts *et al.* (2008) acknowledge difference in the arena of choice with detained service users when they suggest that, rather than the 'maximal choice' that could be applied with mainstream service users, 'optimal choice' could be the approach that is more applicable when service users are detained under the Mental Health Act. Significant adaptations would be considered necessary with regard to positive risk-taking (DoH, 2007b) and trust (DoH, 2010), as examples. Our point is that the implementation of recovery as a service model and system reform in forensic services cannot be undertaken on the basis of a direct equivalence with general mental health settings, but rather on the basis of an interpretation and a culturally-informed translation of the principles. To not do so would invite criticism in a media and public climate that has a relatively low level of tolerance of the recovery needs of forensic service users (Meehan *et al.*, 2008).

Anyone living in the UK will be familiar with newspaper headlines decrying the 'wasted tax-payers' money' when reporting on rehabilitation activities or the quality of life provision in secure settings. Albeit in a prison setting, the Secretary of State famously intervened in recent times to put a stop to the funding of stand-up comedy clubs when this was decried by the media. In another recent example that prompted a public and media outcry, a service user who had been convicted for the manslaughter of his wife, treated and successfully discharged into the community, was prohibited from training to become a London cabbie through public demonstrations. These examples serve to illustrate that the use of recovery principles in forensic settings and with forensic service users must be done with an awareness of the public and political climate within which they will be judged (Scott-Moncrieff *et al.*, 2009). They also highlight the 'deep' social exclusion that men and women who become forensic service users are likely to have experienced before and after their contact with services (Carolan, 2007; Levitas *et al.*, 2007; Mezey and Eastman, 2009).

Having reviewed the emerging literature on recovery, it struck us that there were aspects of the needs of forensic service users that appeared to be missing. Key texts on recovery in UK mental health services tend to make no reference at all to dual diagnosis with respect to personality disorder (CSIP, 2007; Slade, 2009). We have addressed the implications of this in more detail elsewhere (Drennan and Alred, in preparation). Meaden and Farmer (2006) are a notable exception in observing that traditional rehabilitation efforts may fail, and staff alienation may increase, when personality disorder is also a part of the clinical picture. Substance misuse issues can feature in recovery texts, but typically not a consideration of the complexity of facilitating recovery when the service user has attracted a psychiatric label of borderline or anti-social personality disorder, far less the controversial psychopathic disorder. Department of Health documents refer to recovery in individual terms as a goal for service users (NIMHE, 2003a, 2003b) but do not address recovery as a wellspring of system reform or as a service model. Yet a significant number of forensic service users will be detained as a consequence of personality disorder alone or as a co-morbid condition with a mental illness diagnosis. It is a common clinical understanding that forensic patients often require longer treatment in conditions of security due to the 'residual' personality disorder or personality dysfunction that remains when the symptoms of mental illness have been treated. It is these very features that are implicated in the development of 'malignant alienation' in staff teams (Watts and Morgan, 1994; Whittle, 1997) that have been linked to adverse outcomes such as suicide and reoffending in forensic service users. Gudjonsson *et al.* (2010) have highlighted that staff teams in forensic services may have reservations about the applicability of recovery approaches to service users with personality disorder, and an initial validation of a brief recovery measure (Recovery Journey Questionnaire) (Green *et al.*, 2011) fared less well when applied to those with personality disorder. While we are of the view that recovery, properly under-stood, has a clear role for those diagnosed with personality disorder and trauma-related conditions (see Birch and Brookes in this volume), this does require considerably more elaboration.

A further clinical consideration is the role of aggression and violence. Anger and aggression are almost ubiquitous issues for forensic service users. It might be assumed that this is only overtly expressed and uncontrolled aggression, but there are also a significant minority whose aggression is submerged until a set of circumstances triggers a catastrophic breakthough of repressed anger and associ-ated violence, often mixed with considerable levels of deliberate self-harm and suicidality. Within the recovery literature, Roberts (2006) has written evocatively about the helpful meanings and metaphors expressed in 'madness'. However, much writing on the narratives of mental illness and the personal meanings that unfold from this tend not to address when 'madness' also involves murderousness or other forms of violent and even sadistic ideation. The index of Roberts *et al.* (2006), a recent significant contribution to the recovery literature in the UK, does not contain the words 'aggression' or 'violence', and yet these issues are funda-mental to what the service user may need to recovery from and what staff teams must be capable of bearing in their engagement with forensic patients. Similarly, Repper and Perkins (2003) emphasise the risk to service users of being inappro-priately stigmatised by public perceptions of 'violent psychiatric patients'. Forensic service users are in that minority of service users who have acted to harm someone and where the perceived risk of violence is not simply a misat-tribution based on prejudice, however stigmatising nevertheless (Mezey and Eastman, 2009).

If recovery is to become safely embedded in forensic settings then there is a need to fundamentally reconceptualise how we approach the provision of serv-ices. The organisation's approach to staff recruitment, induction, training and appraisal would need to be revisited. There is a need for new staff roles and posts, new organisational roles for service users, new approaches to care planning, new approaches to programming for interventions, or even what constitutes an inter-vention, changes to the language we use in our reports, how we describe our services in information packs and finally how we evaluate the quality of service provision and measure outcomes for service users. These aspects are expanded upon elsewhere (see Drennan, Law and Alred in this volume) but this entire book is only a start in setting out how services could implement a recovery orientation through service models adapted to reflect both a recovery orientation and a forensic awareness.

'Offender recovery'

Just as mental illness or the effects of personality disorder need to be recovered from, so the reality of the offence poses a recovery task. This is not the same as recovery from mental health problems, although they may interact in important ways. Recovery from the fact of the offence is profoundly important and, in many cases, more difficult. Recent research based on interviews with service users at a London forensic service has also drawn attention to this aspect of the recovery task (Mezey *et al.*, 2010). This aspect of recovery – 'offender recovery' – refers to the subjective experience of coming to terms with having offended, perceiving the need to change the personal qualities that resulted in past offending, which also create the future risk of reoffending, and accepting the social and personal consequences of having offended.

There are many dimensions to this recovery task that are similar to personal recovery. There is a need to take responsibility for offending and to come to terms with the effect it has had on self-identity. This can involve shame, shock and alienation from oneself as having acted violently. For patients in forensic settings, this can mean that they need to disentangle themselves from a criminal identity. For others it is incorporating a crime into a non-criminal identity. Many patients will say, 'I am not a violent person' and yet they have to come to terms with having acted violently. The extent of the trauma to oneself that the offence has caused can itself be an obstacle to recovery. The self can be experienced as damaged, scarred, perverted, false, empty, meaningless and lost. Acknowledging that acts perpetrated to harm someone else were also deeply harmful to oneself is a very difficult task. Crucially, to do so can be highly protective against further offending (Klaasen and O'Connor, 1998). Psychosis can be sustained as a defence against knowing what one has done, as can other non-psychotic forms of denial that inhibit a capacity to think and empathise instead of acting out internal conflicts.

The mainstream recovery literature refers to service users with mental illness who need to rebuild identity apart from the negative and stigmatising identity conferred on them by a diagnosis or 'the event' of mental illness (Slade, 2009). A forensic service user needs to move beyond the identity conferred on them by their manner of offending, so they may need to move beyond 'high risk violent offender', 'sex offender', and beyond 'the event' of their offence. The ex-Broadmoor service user referred to above struggles with a sense that he does not deserve a life after what he did 22 years previously. A service user who provided helpful comments on a draft of this chapter described this as 'you can't bear to see yourself as the world might see you'. Thus, there is a significant task of redefinition of the self in the wake of the offending, and the rediscovery of a positive sense of self in spite of what one did. In other words, the meaning of hope and life following an offence is crucial to counter despair and chronic alienation (Hillbrand and Young, 2008). It is possible to have a full clinical recovery and for the mental health aspects of personal recovery to have been addressed, and yet if this aspect of the work of recovery is not attended to the negative effects can be very significant, long-term and even catastrophic.

However, as difficult as it is to 'recover' from an offence that is acknowledged as such, it is often the case that the offence is denied, minimised, justified and rationalised. This can be underpinned by a great number of psychological mechanisms that protect the self from knowing about what drives it to transgress interpersonal and societal boundaries through an offence. 'Offender recovery' from a position of denial and self-justification is a much longer journey.

A recovery journey for someone with an offending history may require the person to re-examine the attitudes and beliefs that they hold on the basis of socialisation by peers or even by family members. This aspect of recovery is often addressed explicitly through offender rehabilitation programmes and emphasises the conscious elements of belief systems that underpin offending. However, when offending arises as a result of deep-seated psychological disturbances based on early childhood trauma, the challenge of recovery is that much more difficult as it involves processes that address what may be unconscious aspects of offending. The person whose vulnerability to offending is based on psychological constellations that arose in the context of severe neglect, or physical or sexual abuse, will need to gain some degree of understanding of and tolerance for feelings of hatred towards others, sadistic thoughts and feelings, pathological control over others, a profoundly disturbed capacity for empathy and overwhelming desires for revenge that can all culminate in a capacity for murderousness or 'perversity' of various types. These aspects of 'offender recovery' are embodied in the work of forensic psychotherapy as it addresses the neurotic, psychotic and criminal motivations for offending behaviour (Aiyegbusi and Clarke-Moore, 2009; Cordess and Cox, 1996; de Zulueta, 2006; Hyatt-Williams, 1998; Jones, 2004; Pfafflin and Adshead, 2004; Welldon and van Velsen, 1997).

However, there are also a whole host of social aspects to 'offender recovery'. There is a need to come to terms with the views of one's family, the views of the victim or the victim's family and the wider social community. There may be restrictions on returning to a local area and the ongoing monitoring of one's life in the community. Typically, ongoing social supervision will involve the monitoring not only of medication, but also the monitoring of one's personal relationships, social circle, work context, internet access and personal habits. The perpetrator of a violent crime may live in fear of community or family retribution and their access to the community may draw comment in local or national press. Mezey et al. (2010) identified discharge from hospital as an important indicator of recovery progress but also a potential destabiliser, at least in part for these reasons. These are aspects of the 'deep' social exclusion that are in addition to the social exclusion that may result from mental illness (Mezey and Eastman, 2009).

A participant in a recent workshop at the Birmingham Forensic Service described this aspect of recovery as a form of 'moral' recovery, in a new echo of the 'moral treatment' philosophy of the York Retreat. The desistance literature refers to 'redemption', 'self-change' or 'going straight'. Maruna (2001) refers to how a 'recovery story' for a so-called desister needs to work as a 'redemption script' (p. 87) and he outlines the characteristics of these narratives and their associated 'redemption rituals'. The forensic psychotherapy literature identifies the work of mourning that underpins all such processes of growth and maturation. In order for forensic mental health services to meaningfully engage with recovery as a system reform and service model, it will be necessary to properly acknowledge 'offender recovery' as a fundamentally important recovery task for service users who have committed offences, and who are at risk of committing further offences unless this is addressed. While the psychiatric rehabilitation of many forensic mental health service users results in 'offender recovery', it is perhaps surprising that this is all too often not sufficiently attended to. There has been a powerful tendency in forensic mental health services to treat the apparent symptoms of mental illness and to presume that this simultaneously addresses the potential for future offending. On the other hand, an overemphasis on manualised groupwork that encourages compliance and a 'tick-box' rehabilitation production line, without attending to each individual person's life story and the meaning of their offending within it, is another common way in which services fail to appreciate the importance of 'offender recovery' if future offences are to be avoided. While this is sometimes true of forensic psychiatric rehabilitation, even in high secure settings and after lengthy admissions, it is all the more likely to be the case in the prison estate, where there is so little capacity for meaningful individualised attention to the processes that would support and encourage 'offender recovery' in each person. In this way, 'offender recovery' tasks transcend the fences of the forensic hospital and the walls of the prison.

The contribution of recovery developed in forensic settings

This collection of papers, like Roberts *et al.* (2006), contains a mixture of recovery and psychiatric rehabilitation elements. Only time will tell whether this reflects a transitional phase towards the recovery paradigm subsuming the rehabilitation paradigm or a movement towards a new synthesis. Should we be satisfied with Anthony's (1993) suggestion that rehabilitation is what mental health practitioners do and recovery is what service users do? Should we instead be working towards recovery as the overarching model that guides service and treatment models? As practitioners committed to and invested in the development of recovery in mental health services, until recently we believed that what was required was the development of the recovery paradigm as a theory of rehabilitation, in a manner akin to how Ward and Maruna (2007) have articulated the Good Lives Model as a theory of offender rehabilitation. However, perhaps we originally lacked the imagination or the vocabulary to conceive of a theory of recovery that was not subsumed within the notion of rehabilitation. In other words, the vision of a forensic mental health system that transcends a paternalistic or technocratic era to one in which the challenge of what we now know about recovery processes is built into the foundations of forensic mental health services. In time this could demonstrate the 'superior efficacy, both in respect of cure and security' of services that inspire hope, meaning and purpose in service users and the people who support their recovery.

Acknowledgements

We wish to thank Dr Julie Repper, Helen Eunson, Dr Mary Whittle, Jane Cronin-Davis, Richard Shuker, Dr Richard Noon and service users at Sussex Partnership NHS Foundation Trust for their helpful comments and observations on earlier drafts of this chapter.

References

Aiyegbusi, A. and Clarke-Moore, J. (2009) *Therapeutic relationships with offenders: An introduction to the psychodynamics of Forensic Mental Health Nursing.* London: Jessica Kingsley Publishers.

Andresen, R., Oades, L. and Caputi, P. (2003) 'The experience of recovery from schizophrenia: towards an empirically validated stage model'. *Australian and New Zealand Journal of Psychiatry*, 37: 586–594.

Anthony, W. A. and Liberman, R. P. (1986) 'The practice of psychiatric rehabilitation. Historical, conceptual and research base'. *Schizophrenia Bulletin*, 12: 542–545.

Anthony, W. A. (1993) 'Recovery from mental illness: the guiding vision of the mental health service system in the 1990s'. *Psychosocial Rehabilitation Journal*, 16: 11–23.

Anthony, W. A., Cohen, M. R. and Farkas, M. D. (1990) *Psychiatric Rehabilitation.* Boston: Boston University.

Bachrach, L. L. (1992) 'Psychosocial rehabilitation and psychiatry in the care of long-term patients'. *American Journal of Psychiatry*, 149(11): 1455–1463.

Barnao, M., Robertson, P. and Ward, T. (2010) 'The Good Lives Model applied to a forensic population'. *Psychiatry, Psychology, & Law*, 17(2): 202–217.

Bellack, A. S. (2006) 'Scientific and consumer models of recovery in schizophrenia: Concordance, contrasts and implications'. *Schizophrenia Bulletin*, 32(3): 432–442.

Boardman, J. (2010) 'Social exclusion of people with mental health problems and learning disabilities: key aspects'. In J. Boardman, A. Currie, H. Killaspy, and G. Mezey (eds) *Social Inclusion and Mental Health*, pp. 22–45. London: RCPsych Publications.

Boardman, J., Currie, A., Killaspy, H. and Mezey, G. (2010) *Social Inclusion and Mental Health.* London: RCPsych Publications.

Bonney, S. and Stickley, T. (2008) 'Recovery and mental health: a review of the British literature'. *Journal of Psychiatric and Mental Health Nursing*, 15: 140–153.

British Psychological Society. (2000) *Recent advances in understanding mental illness and psychotic experiences: A report by the British Psychological Society Division of Clinical Psychology.* Leicester: BPS.

Brown, H. and Smith, H. (1992) *Normalisation: A reader for the nineties.* London: Routledge.

Care Services Improvement Partnership, Royal College of Psychiatrists, Social Care Institute for Excellence. (2007) *A common purpose: Recovery in future mental health services.* Leeds: Social Care Institute for Excellence.

Carolan, S. (2007) 'Daring to dream: Mental health, recovery and social inclusion'. Enabling recovery through assertive rehabilitation, Broadmoor Hospital Conference, 18 May.

Coleman, R. (1999) *Recovery: An alien concept. Gloucester.* Handsell Publishing 2nd Edition.

Cordess, C. and Cox, C. M. (1996) *Forensic psychotherapy: psychodynamics and the offender patient.* London: Jessica Kingsley Publishers.

Cox, M. (1978) *Structuring the therapeutic process: Compromise with chaos.* Oxford: Pergamon.

Davidson, L., O'Connell, M., Tondora, J., Styron, T. and Kangas, K. (2006) 'The top ten concerns about recovery encountered in mental health systems transformation'. *Psychiatric Services*, 57 (5): 640–645.

de Zulueta, F. (2006) *From Pain to Violence: The Traumatic Roots of Destructiveness.* London: Wiley Blackwell.

Deegan, P. E. (1988) 'Recovery: The lived experience of rehabilitation'. *Psychosocial Rehabilitation Journal*, 11(4): 11–19.

—— (1993) 'Recovery as a journey of the heart'. *Psychiatric Rehabilitation Journal*, 19(3): 91–97.

Department of Health. (2007) *Best Practice in Managing Risk: Principles and evidence for best practice in the assessment and management of risk to self and others in mental health services.* London: Department of Health.

—— (2009) *The Bradley Report: Lord Bradley's review of people with mental health problems or learning disabilities in the criminal justice system.* London: Department of Health.

—— (2010) *See, Think, Act: Your guide to relational security.* London: Department of Health.

Drennan, G. and Alred, D. (in preparation) 'Recovery in UK Forensic Mental Health Services: A long-term, slow-stream project?'.

Farrall, F. and Calverley, A. (2006) *Understanding desistance from crime: Emerging Theoretical Directions in Resettlement and Rehabilitation.* Maidenhead: Open University.

Flynn, R. J. and Nitsch, K. E. (eds) (1980) *Normalization, social integration and human services.* Baltimore: University Park Press.

Gadd, D. and Jefferson, T. (2007) *Psychosocial Criminology.* London: Sage.

Geller, J. L. (2000) 'The last half-century of psychiatric services as reflected' *In Psychiatric Services. Psychiatric Services*, 51(1): 41–67.

Green, T., Batson, A. and Gudjonsson, G. (2011) 'The development and initial validation of a service-user led measure for recovery of mentally disordered offenders'. *The Journal of Forensic Psychiatry & Psychology*, 22(2): 252–265.

Gudjonsson, G., Webster, G. and Green, T. (2010) 'The recovery approach to care in forensic services. Attitudes and impact of staff training on knowledge and attitudes'. *The Psychiatrist*, 34: 326–329.

Harding, C. M., Brooks, G. W. and Ashikaga, T. *et al.* (1987) 'The Vermont longitudinal study of persons with severe mental illness: II. Long-term outcome of subjects who retrospectively met the DSM-III criteria for schizophrenia'. *American Journal of Psychiatry*, 144: 727–735.

Harrison, G., Hopper, K. and Craig, T. *et al.* (2001) 'Recovery from psychotic illness: a 15 and 25 year international follow-up study'. *British Journal of Psychiatry*, 178: 506–517.

Hillbrand, M. and Young, J. L. (2008) 'Instilling hope into forensic treatment: The anti-dote to despair and desperation'. *Journal of the American Academy of Psychiatry and the Law*, 36: 90–94.

Hogan, M. F. (2003) 'Freedom Commission Report: the President's New Freedom Commission: recommendations to transform mental health care in America'. *Psychiatric Services*, 54: 1467–1474.

Hyatt-Williams, A. (1998) *Cruelty, violence and murder: Understanding the criminal mind.* London: Karnac Books.

Jacobson, N. and Greenley, D. (2001) 'What is recovery? A conceptual model and explication'. *Psychiatric Services*, 52(4): 482–485.

Jacobson, N. (2004) *In recovery: The making of mental health policy*. Nashville: Vanderbilt University Press.

Jobe, T. and Harrow, M. (2005) 'Long-term outcome of patients with schizophrenia: A review'. *Canadian Journal of Psychiatry*, 50: 892–900.

Jones, D. (ed.) (2004) *Working with Dangerous People: The Psychotherapy of Violence.* Oxford: Radcliffe Publishing Ltd.

Kazemian, I (2007) 'Desistance From Crime: Theoretical, Empirical. Methodological and Policy Considerations'. *Journal of Contemporary Criminal Justice*, 23: 5–27.

Klaasen, D. and O'Connor, W. A. (1998) 'A prospective study of predictors of violence in adult male mental health admissions'. *Law and Human Behaviour*, 12(2): 143–158.

Kelly, J., Wellman, N. and Sin, J. (2009) 'HEART – the Hounslow Early Active Recovery Team: implementing an inclusive strength-based model of care for people with early psychosis'. *Journal of Psychiatric and Mental Health Nursing*, 16: 569–577.

Landeen, J., Byrne, D. and Pawlick, J. (1995) 'Hope and schizophrenia: Clinicians identify hope-instilling strategies'. *Journal of Psychosocial Nursing*, 33: 15–19.

Lester, H. and Gask, L. (2006) 'Delivering medical care for patients with serious mental illness or promoting a collaborative model of recovery'. *British Journal of Psychiatry*, 188: 401–402.

Levitas, R., Pantazis, C., Fahmy, E., Gordon, D., Lloyd, E. and Patsios, D. (2007) *The multi-dimensional analysis of social exclusion*. Bristol: University of Bristol. http://www.cabinetoffice.gov.uk/media/cabinetoffice/social_exclusion_task_force/assets/research/chapters/0.pdf

Lindqvist, P. and Skipworth, J. (2000) 'Evidence-based rehabilitation in forensic psychiatry'. *British Journal of Psychiatry*, 176: 320–323.

Lloyd, C., Waghorn, G. and Williams, P. L. (2008) 'Conceptualising recovery in mental health rehabilitation'. *British Journal of Occupational Therapy*, 71(8): 321–328.

Maclean, A. H. (2000). 'From ex-patient alternatives to consumer options: consequences of consumerism for psychiatric consumers and the ex-patient movement'. *International Journal of Health Services*, 30: 821–847.

Maddock, S. and Hallam, S. (2010) *Recovery begins with hope*. London: Centre for Mental Health.

Maruna, S. (2001) 'Making Good: How Ex-convicts Reform and Rebuild Their Lives'. Washington, DC: American Psychological Association.

Mead, S. and Copeland, M. E. (2000) 'What recovery means to us: Consumers' perspectives'. *Community Mental Health Journal*, 36(3): 315–328.

Meaden, A. and Farmer, A. (2006) 'A comprehensive approach to assessment in rehabilitation settings'. In G. Roberts, S. Davenport, F. Holloway and T. Tatton (eds), *Enabling Recovery: The Principles and Practice of Rehabilitation Psychiatry*. London: Gaskell.

Meehan, T. J., King, R. J., Beavis, P. H. and Robinson, J. D. (2008) 'Recovery-based practice: do we know what we mean or mean what we know?' *Australian & New Zealand Journal of Psychiatry*, 42: 177–182.

Menninger, K. (1959) 'The Academic Lecture: Hope'. *American Journal of Psychiatry*, 116(12): 481–491.

Mezey, G. and Eastman, N. (2009) 'Choice and social inclusion in forensic psychiatry: acknowledging mixed messages and double think'. *The Journal of Forensic Psychiatry & Psychology*, 20(4): 503–507.

Mezey, G. C., Kavuma, M., Turton, P., Demetriou, A. and Wright, C. (2010) 'Perceptions, experiences and meanings of recovery in forensic psychiatric patients'. *The Journal of Forensic Psychiatry & Psychology*, 21(5): 683–696.

Mezzina, R., Borg, M., Marin, I., Sells, D., Topor, A. and Davidson, L. (2006a) 'From participation to citizenship: How to regain a role, a status, and a life in the process of recovery'. *American Journal of Psychiatric Rehabilitation*, 9: 39–61.

Mezzina, R., Davidson, L., Borg, M., Marin, I., Topor, A. and Sells, D. (2006b) 'The social nature or recovery: Discussion and implications for practice'. *American Journal of Psychiatric Rehabilitation*, 9: 63–80.

Motz, A. (2009) *Managing Self-harm: Psychological perspectives*. London: Routledge.

National Institute for Mental Health in England. (2003a) *Personality Disorder: No longer a diagnosis of exclusion*. London: Department of Health.

—— (2003b) *Breaking the cycle of rejection: Personality Disorder Capabilities Framework*. London: Department of Health.

—— (2004) *Emerging best practices in mental health*. London: Department of Health.

—— (2005) *Guiding statement on recovery*. London: Department of Health.

O'Hagan, M. (2003) *Force in mental health services: International user/survivor perspectives*. Melbourne, Australia: World Federation for Mental Health Biennial Congress.

Onken, S., Dumont, J. M., Ridgway, P. *et al.* (2001) *Mental health recovery: What helps and what hinders? A National Research Project for the Development of Recovery Facilitating System Performance Indicators*. Alexandria, VA: National Association of State Mental Health Programme Directors, National Technical Assistance Center for State Mental health Planning.

Pfafflin, F. and Adshead, G. (2004) *A matter of security: The application of Attachment Theory to Forensic Psychiatry and Psychotherapy*. London: Jessica Kingsley Publishers.

Pratt, C. W., Gill, K. J., Barrett, N. M. and Roberts, M. M. (1999) *Psychiatric Rehabilitation*. San Diego: Academic Press.

Ralph, R. O. (2005) 'Verbal definitions and visual models of recovery: focus on the recovery model'. In R. O. Ralph and P. W. Corrigan, (eds), *Recovery in Mental Illness: Broadening our Understanding of Wellness*. Washington, DC: American Psychological Association.

Repper, J. and Perkins, R. (2003) *Social Inclusion and Recovery: A model for mental health practice*. London: Bailliere Tindall.

—— (2009) 'Recovery and Social Inclusion'. In P. Callaghan, J. Playle and L. Cooper (eds) *Mental Health Nursing Skills*. Oxford: University Press, Oxford.

Resnick, S. G. and Rosenheck, R. A. (2006) 'Recovery and Positive Psychology: Parallel themes and potential synergies'. *Psychiatric Services*, 57(1): 120–122.

Ridgway, P. (2001) 'Restorying psychiatric disability: learning from first person narratives'. *Psychiatric Rehabilitation Journal*, 24(4): 335–343.

Roberts, G. and Wolfson, P. (2004) 'Rediscovery of recovery: open to all'. *Advances in Psychiatric Treatment*, 10: 37–48.

Roberts, G., Davenport, S., Holloway, F. and Tattan, T. (2006) *Enabling Recovery: The Principles and Practice of Rehabilitation Psychiatry*. London: Royal College of Psychiatrists/Gaskell Publications.

Roberts, G. *et al.* (2008) 'Detained – what's my choice? Part 1 Discussion'. *Advances in Psychiatric Treatment*, 14: 172–180.

Robinson, G. and Crow, I. (2009) *Offender rehabilitation: Theory, research and practice*. London: Sage.

Russinova, Z. (1999) 'Providers' hope-inspiring competence as a factor optimizing psychiatric rehabilitation outcomes'. *Journal of Rehabilitation*, 50–57.

Sainsbury Centre for Mental Health Position Paper. (2009) *Implementing Recovery; A new framework for organisational change*. London: SCMH.

Sayce, L. (2003) *From Psychiatric Patient to Citizen: Overcoming Discrimination and Stigma*. Palgrave: USA.

Scott-Moncrieff, L., Briscoe, J. and Daniels, G. (2009) *An independent investigation into the care and treatment of Daniel Gonzales*. http://www.southeastcoast.nhs.uk/publications/documents/090127-Report.pdf

Seligman, M. E. P. and Csikszentmihalyi, M. (2000) 'Positive Psychology: An Introduction'. *American Psychologist*, 55: 5–14.

Shepherd, G. (1984) *Institutional care and rehabilitation*. Boston, MA: Longman.

—— (2006) 'Mapping and Classifying Rehabilitation Services'. In G. Roberts, S. Davenport and F. Holloway (eds) *Enabling Recovery: The Principles and Practice of Psychiatric Rehabilitation*. Royal College of Psychiatrists/Gaskell Publications, London.

Shepherd, G., Boardman, J. and Burns, M. (2010) *Implementing Recovery: A methodology for organisational change*. London: Sainsbury Centre for Mental Health.

Shepherd, G., Boardman, J. and Slade, M. (2008) *Making recovery a reality*. London: Sainsbury Centre for Mental Health.

Slade, M. (2009) *Personal Recovery and Mental Illness: A Guide for Mental Health Professionals*. Cambridge: Cambridge University Press.

Slade, M., Amering, M. and Oades, L. (2008) 'Recovery: an international perspective'. *Epidemiologia e Psychiatria Sociale*, 17(2): 128–137.

Smith, D. J. (2006) *Social Inclusion and Early Desistance from Crime*. Edinburgh: Centre for Law and Society, The University of Edinburgh.

Snyder, R. C. (2000) *Handbook of Hope: Theory, Measures, and Applications*. New York: Academic Press.

South London and Maudsley NHS Foundation Trust and South West London and St George's Mental Health NHS Trust. (2010) *Recovery is for all. Hope, agency and opportunity in psychiatry. A position statement by Consultant Psychiatrists*. London: SLAM/SWLSTG.

Substance Abuse and Mental Health Services Administration. (2005) *National Consensus Conference on Mental Health Recovery and Systems Transformation*. Rockville, MD: Dept. of Health and Human Services.

Tuke, S. [1813] (1996) *Description of the Retreat: An Institution Near York, for Insane Persons of the Society of Friends*. Reprinted with an Introduction by K. Jones. London: Process Press.

Ward, T. and Maruna, S. (2007) *Rehabilitation: Beyond the risk-paradigm*. London: Routledge.

Watts, D. and Morgan, G. (1994) 'Malignant alienation: Dangers for patients who are hard to like'. *British Journal of Psychiatry*, 164: 11–15.

Watts, F. N. and Bennett, D. H. (eds). (1991) *Theory and practice of psychiatric rehabilitation*. Chichester: John Wiley & Sons.

Welldon, E. and van Velsen, C. (1997) *A Practical Guide to Forensic Psychotherapy*. London: Jessica Kingsley Publishers.

Whittle, M. (1997) 'Malignant alienation'. *Journal of Forensic Psychiatry*, 8(1): 5–10.

Wilcock, A. A. (2001) *Occupation for Health Volume 1: A Journey from Self Health to Prescription*. London: British College of Occupational Therapists.

Winnicott, D. W. (1984) *Deprivation and delinquency*. London: Tavistock Publications.

2 Recovery and risk

Accepting the complexity

Richard Barker

'You lot keep talking to me about recovery. How am I going to "recover" when I've got a history of these offences? It's going to be hard enough getting a job as it is, without being branded as both mentally ill and dangerous.'

(Mr B, patient session)

Introduction

Recovery and risk are concepts that often seem to be at odds with each other. In the quotation above a patient expresses his concern about the twin stigmas of a history of offending and a history of mental illness, and the difficulties that these issues bring to his recovery journey. Rightly, he asks how he can recover (and have hope in his recovery), when the emphasis in his care has been upon his risk and his experiences of mental illness. He recognises that achieving his goal (employment) is a task that is fraught with problems and complexities. Moreover, he highlights a central question for secure services in this time of recovery orientation – how do we reconcile the guiding principles of recovery with the issue of risk?

This chapter aims to examine the way that the principles of recovery and the need to manage risk can impede and restrict one another, and to explore ways in which the complexity that arises might be recognised and used to promote both recovery and responsibility. I will also include descriptions of a patient's journey of 'offender recovery' along the way, which will elucidate the particular ways in which risk and recovery can undermine progress, as well as the possible ways in which they may be constructed to support each other. Before going on to explore the complex relationship between risk and recovery, it is important to define clearly what I mean by both recovery and risk in the context of secure services.

Recovery in secure settings

Recovery as a set of principles is well described in various places. In the introductory chapter to this book, Drennan and Alred usefully break down the different facets of recovery into clinical, functional, social and personal, with the addition of offender recovery as a proposed dimension of recovery that applies to recovery within secure services. It is Anthony's oft-quoted description of recovery (1993), though, that points to a number of central components of recovery.

Recovery is

> a deeply personal process of changing one's attitudes, values, feelings, goals, skills and/or roles. It is a way of living a satisfying, hopeful, and contributing way of life even with limitations caused by illness. Recovery involves the development of new meaning and purpose in one's life as one grows beyond the catastrophic effects of mental illness.
>
> (Anthony, 1993, p. 527)

In considering this definition of recovery in a secure context, it is worth breaking the quote down to give some consideration of its points. First, recovery is a journey (or process) of change and adaptation in response to life/circumstance/experience; second, the goal of this process of change is to reach a state of living a more satisfying, meaningful and contributing life – as judged by the individual whose journey it is; third, this process of change occurs within the limitations imposed by life; and finally, this process of change leads to an onward process of growth. The reason I have restated this description of recovery is because, all too often, during discussions with other clinicians, commissioners and patients, their perspective on recovery has been different. Although the process of change/adaptation/growth in recovery may be similar, the experience of recovery is a highly individualistic journey that, if services are to be truly recovery-orientated, must be respected. It is however this very complexity that makes recovery a difficult set of principles to incorporate into a service in a consistent way; indeed, applying it dogmatically may even be counter to recovery. The essential element, though, that can be drawn from Anthony's description of recovery, is that it is a process of change, and that the direction of travel for that change is towards meaning, purpose and positivity. It is this basic principle of recovery that is the most important aspect to hold on to when considering the myriad of different narrative accounts, research papers, governmental guidelines and general discourse on recovery.

When considering both recovery and risk, it is also important to set out the biases and influences that colour individuals' or services' perspectives on these concepts. Later in this chapter we will discuss how the emphasis on risk in secure services exerts an influence on how we deal with recovery. As a psychologist I also have biases that will affect how I see recovery and risk, and these will inevitably be reflected in this chapter. This therefore is the *caveat emptor* (buyer beware) of this chapter – that this view on risk and recovery is just one view, and is influenced necessarily by the perspective of the author. That perspective is drawn from a primary therapeutic model that is derived from a cognitive-behavioural background, specifically Rational Emotive Behaviour Therapy. Within this context, recovery (as defined above by Anthony) might usefully be seen as a process of change and adaptation to life circumstance, but one that has an emphasis on movement from unhealthy or unhelpful emotions and behaviours (e.g. emotions/behaviours that lead to unhelpful distress, make goals less attainable and result in inflexibility and diminished resilience) to healthier emotions and behaviours (e.g. emotions/behaviours that lead to positive growth, make attaining goals more likely, and increase flexibility and resilience). The outcome of this would then ideally be the individual moving towards a more personally satisfying, meaningful life, but with a clear acknowledgment of the limitations and boundaries of life, and the resilience and flexibility to cope with those limitations and challenge them appropriately.

A comparable process of change to this is that of bereavement. Individuals grieve in response to the loss of a loved one and to the absence of that person in their lives. They must undergo a process of adapting to a new reality, and this has a recognised process of change that in most cases leads to the individual moving on in their lives (Kübler-Ross, 2005). Friends and family can support the grieving process, but they cannot *make* the person grieve; rather, this is something that the individual will do for themselves as they reconcile their lives to being without their loved one, and, all being well, find new meaning in their changed existence. Both grief and recovery are reactions to substantial life changes. In both circumstances the process of change will usually result in some movement from disorder to equilibrium. Similarly, in both grief and recovery, support and the right environmental factors will assist the individual in reaching a state of equilibrium sooner, but also in finding new meaning and new purpose as their lives become redefined by those changes.

Using this analogy has been useful in helping others to understand what recovery might mean for the individuals that they are required to support. By using the grief analogy they gain the crucial understanding that you cannot *do* recovery *to* someone, you can only *support them in their recovery*. Recovery is *their* journey, and ultimately their responsibility, and our task is to support them in their endeavours. I acknowledge that this is a view of recovery that is influenced by my own clinical perspective, and might not be shared by other people, but I have endeavoured in this fashion to make this a pragmatic and practical position that can facilitate thinking about recovery in the context of harmful risk behaviours.

Risk in secure settings

Risk in the context of this chapter refers to individuals (or groups of individuals) acting in a harmful way towards others. This might mean in a violent way, but may also include bullying, manipulation for personal gain, intimidation, or other 'challenging' behaviours that may or may not be associated with the individual's distress. Typically, in secure services this may mean some illegal act (even if that does not include violence), or behaviours that indicate a high likelihood of harmful behaviour occurring. The risk may even mean not taking medication, as relapse may all too often be seen as a precursor to more serious acts of risky behaviour. The chapter is not specifically aimed at self-harming behaviours, although this may fall under the rubric of 'challenging' behaviours.

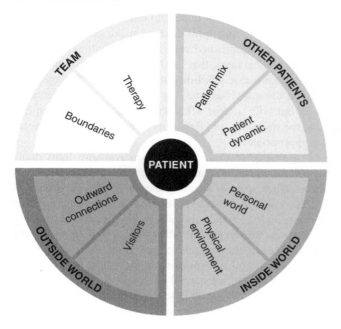

Figure 2.1 Relational security explorer

The elements that make up risk and risk management might be usefully considered in the context of the relational security wheel described in the Department of Health's 2010 guidance *See, Think, Act: Your Guide to Relational Security.* Within that document, security is the process by which risk is managed, and this is divided up into relational security – 'the knowledge and understanding staff have of a patient and of the environment, and the translation of that information into appropriate responses and care'; procedural security – 'the policies and procedures in place to maintain safety and security'; and physical security – 'the fences, locks personal alarms and so on that keep people safe'. These three elements – physical aspects of security and control, policies and procedures, and the management of staff–service user relationships – together encapsulate the way that risk is currently seen within secure services, from the perspective of the Department of Health at least.

Risk in these terms is seen as being managed by the physical and procedural boundaries put in place, but also on a more dynamic basis by the day-to-day interactions of staff and patients. Whilst *See, Think, Act* was written at a time before a recovery focus was widespread amongst secure services, its focus on the quality of the therapeutic relationship is a helpful one in terms of encouraging staff to consider how the quality of that relationship affects security. The difficulty that can arise is when risk and security become so much of a focus of what secure services provide that recovery can come to be seen as a secondary goal, rather than as being the foundation for change, including changing risk behaviour.

Traditional approaches to offender recovery

The pathway into secure mental health services for patients often begins with a referral through court diversion schemes, or with a transfer from a local acute NHS service, another secure hospital along the secure pathway, or as transferred prisoners. Increasingly, it seems people coming into secure services in this manner are restricted hospital patients under the Ministry of Justice (Section 37/41 of the Mental Health Act 1983), adding a further degree of complexity to their care because of the Ministerial oversight that this requires. More pertinently, such individuals have often had difficult and complex developmental histories, previous experiences of institutional care, substance misuse problems and a variety of previous criminal behaviours. For example:

> Mr B has been an in-patient for the past two years, detained under Section 37/41 of the Mental Health Act after developing a psychosis whilst on remand. Prior to his index offence of burglary he had a significant criminal history, including a sexual offence, theft and other burglaries that appeared unrelated to the symptoms of his psychosis. Whilst he has now clinically recovered, he is trapped in the service by a need to demonstrate that his risk has been reduced. However, because his risk has been formulated as being largely unrelated to his mental health problems (apart from the possible presence of antisocial personality traits) he remains detained in hospital because he cannot demonstrate a reduction in his risk solely by a reduction in clinical symptoms or by agreeing to take medication.

In Mr B's case, he had already reached the point of clinical recovery, in the sense that he is largely free of the symptoms of psychosis, but as he pointed out to me when discussing his pathway out of the service, 'I'd be much better off in prison, because they would tell me what courses I need to do to get on and get out.' In returning to the principle of recovery noted in the quotation from Anthony (1993), Mr B has the capacity to change and adapt to life circumstances and is willing to be involved in what he has to do to meet his goal, but at that point in his journey lacked clarity on what was required of him to move forward.

As a restricted hospital patient he remains subject to review by the Ministry of Justice. Moreover, his pattern of significant offending prior to the development of his experiences of mental illness means that when judged according to commonly used assessments of risk, he appears to remain at high risk of reoffending. His risk assessment details a high psychopathy score (as measured by the PCL-R; Hare, 2003), multiple areas of concern on framework of structured professional judgement on risk (HCR-20; Webster *et al.*, 1997), and when scored using an actuarial measure of his risk (Violence Risk Appraisal Guide; Quinsey *et al.*, 1998) has a more than 75 per cent likelihood of committing a violent offence in the next seven years. Whilst he acknowledges his offending behaviour, his view on these aspects of his risk assessment is that such information is stigmatising and prejudicial, and that it is unfair that this is the rubric by which he is judged. As a consequence, Mr B's reaction to this has at times been one of avoidance, disengagement and resentment, in turn giving rise to frustrations and reducing capacity to cope. This disempowers him further and increases the potential for him to be perceived as denying the consequences of his offences. At other times he has openly acknowledged 'playing the game', attending group sessions for the purpose not of gaining knowledge but of giving the appearance of engagement in risk-related work.

From the perspective of the clinical team working with clients like Mr B, similar frustrations develop. Mr B's disengagement from services, avoidance or distancing from his social/personal recovery arises from both the pragmatics of his legal situation and also a culture that has been focused on markers of risk reduction that may not necessarily reflect Mr B's actual risk. Traditional views on risk assessment have largely been based upon the old adage that 'the past predicts the future'. This reductionist view undermines the complexity of behaviour, and the dynamic nature of behaviour in this context. Thus, it has been the case in the past that the simple progress of time without incident, an appearance of engagement and going on escorted and unescorted leave without incident, were taken as evidence of a stable mental state and a consequential reduction in risk.

Yet risk assessment and risk management theories have moved on significantly over the past few decades, moving from simple reductionist heuristics about risk to more complex, individualised approaches that reflect the balancing of static risk factors and dynamic factors, strengths and protective factors. Risk assessment today incorporates multifaceted approaches that combine structured professional judgements, strengths and protective factors, actuarial information and detailed formulations about the individual. Moreover, risk approaches tend to focus much more upon risk management and risk reduction, rather than chasing tenuous predictions about risk.

Risk has historically had a far greater focus than recovery in secure services, mainly because of the nature of the service provision. The *raison d'être* of secure services is to provide the management of risk, thus the control and management of risk exerts a powerful influence on the culture, atmosphere and everyday practice in secure services. When patients first enter our services, often in positions of considerable distress from their experiences, the amount of support provided to them is commensurate with their distress. Along with that support, though, is the need to provide a safe environment that will facilitate their clinical recovery. Yet, because their distress also brings with it a heightened potential for risky behaviours, boundaries are necessarily and rightly imposed, for their safety and for the safety of other people. But it cannot be denied that along with this security comes a culture of control and anxiety about lack of control, and this powerful influence continues to be exerted throughout an individual's stay within and beyond secure services.

In the light of this cultural emphasis, the assessment and observation, and indeed formulation, of an individual's emotions and behaviours become overtly weighted towards perceptions of risk and risk behaviours. Another patient complained to me, 'I cannot have a bad day; if I get pissed off or angry, it's to do with my mental state or people think I'm going to be violent – I'm not, I'm just having a bad day.' Yet, when one considers the base-rates for violent behaviour by mentally disordered offenders, they are far lower than those of other offender groups, and indeed much lower than individuals with substance misuse problems (Slade, 2009).

It seems logical to suggest that the bias towards risk-focussed assessment seems driven by the considerable consequences that can occur when security fails. Society is increasingly driven by a blame culture that is highly reactive to mistakes and failures. Consequentially, the top-down nature of organizational structures matches the pervading concern that mistakes and failures must not occur. This influences policy and local guidelines, practices, perceptions and behaviours. As this influence filters down to the front line it naturally results in heightened anxiety about the prospect of failure; this burden in turn, if not recognised, leads to a typical response to any unavoidable threat – the urge to attempt to control, in order to reduce the chance of the 'bad thing' happening. In secure services, if not kept in check, this can translate at times to defensive practice, over-control and custodial thinking. Moore (1995) describes humorously the concept of 'repetitive doubt syndrome', in which clinicians make decisions on the basis of tenuous risk judgements, which all too often infringe the rights of patients and satisfy nobody, but in order to cope with the anxiety about risk, clinicians develop 'an artificial sense of certainty about our decisions; suspicions harden into theories, anecdotes ossify as rules and prejudices become accepted as indicators which guide practice and reduce anxiety' (Moore, 1995, p. 3).

Clearly harmful behaviours are to be avoided, but how far should the process by which risk is managed in secure services influence the longer-term recovery of patients? Does it in fact reduce risk? Or does the emphasis towards risk and away from recovery result in some patients becoming stymied in their recovery in the name of risk management, and does this in turn have the potential to actually increase their risk?

Whose risk is it anyway?

Another consequence of this attempt to control is that whilst the risk is located with the patient, it is rarely fully 'owned' by the patient. More often than not it seems the risk is held by the clinical team, nursing team, or service in which the person is held. Thus risk assessments are done on the patient, and care plans are devised to reduce 'challenging' behaviours. Holding professional responsibility for the patient's risky behaviour may well reduce anxiety about risk, as described above, but because it is driven by fear, it can often result in over-control. Moreover, this control is mostly illusory, because the service user still has a choice about how they act. Yet by removing the responsibility for the patient's risk, or at least controlling risk in this way, it can in turn invalidate the position of the service user, disempower them, and inhibit the possibility of them fully accepting responsibility for their behaviours. On the other hand, recovery is not an excuse for failing to protect patients, staff and the public, and some element of control is required, particularly when individuals experience distressing symptoms. Timing seems to be the issue: when do we relax control enough for individuals to start to take on responsibility for their risk? When do those conversations start? There is a danger that if the timing of this handover of responsibilities is not correct, then fledgling recovery goals become stymied and invalidated by the need to demonstrate a reduction in risk, when the risk remains held by the team or the service.

Mr. B noted this when his risk was discussed with him early on in our sessions:

Mr B – *I know I'm not going to do it again.*

RB – Okay, I believe you when you say that this is what you mean, but how can you prove that to others?

Mr B – Why should I have to? It was a stupid thing I did, it wasn't related to my mental illness, I should be in prison for it, and if I was in prison for it, I would have been out in six months without any of this crap. It's your problem, not mine, I know I won't do it again.

In this example, because the risk of a harmful act remains more located with the team than with Mr B at this point in his recovery, he takes the position that he would not do it again (because he perceives that he has no other way to prove it is so) and that he does not have to prove that to anybody, because his offence (a burglary) was not related to his mental illness in any direct way. Moreover, there is an element of denial and avoidance, perhaps because, at that time, it was not clear to him how he might go about reducing his risk, or he did not feel able to address it because of shame or guilt.

Offender recovery

Returning to first principles of the recovery process outlined at the beginning of this chapter, recovery is a process of change and adaptation in the face of aversive life events. Harmful behaviour is just that – behaviour usually prompted by a response to some stimulus or combination of stimuli. Thus, I would like to propose a different way of considering risk in relation to recovery. Instead of risk being seen as something separate to, or more important than an individual's recovery, formulating the risk behaviour as one important aspect of the individual's aversive life events shifts risk from being the core focus of secure service provision to being one of a number of recovery goals. Supporting recovery then becomes the overarching goal of the service, with offender recovery being the specialist and distinctive aspect of secure services. In taking this view a number of positive cultural changes can occur.

The role of collaboration and partnership

Offender recovery should have the goal of supporting the individual to understand the contribution that their experiences and life choices have made to their risk of acting harmfully, and the degree to which such choices are contrary to the living of a satisfying, meaningful and socially contributing life. If the aim of offender recovery is to facilitate the individual in owning and taking responsibility for their offending behaviour, then the approach to risk assessment and management itself needs to change to reflect that new goal. Thus risk assessments will need to be completed in a more overtly collaborative and empowering way. Rarely, in my experience, do clinicians pull back the curtain on the inner workings of the risk assessment process. Often clients may read about their risk in a document prepared for a tribunal or case conference, or passed onto them by their legal representative. Being asked to accept something about yourself written by another person is hardly likely to result in trust or cooperation, and may in most cases simply result in the person rejecting the view of the clinician (perpetuating denial and entrenchment in the currently held view or the development of cognitive distortions and justifications about the behaviour). This further encourages avoidance of the real issues about their risk, and further control by the clinician, justified by the battle cry that the patient is in denial or lacks insight.

Working collaboratively on risk involves a shift in mindset and a willingness to accept the hypothetical nature of the process of risk assessment. It also means supporting patients in realistic appraisals of their situations, including the pragmatic realities of dealing with the necessary limitations imposed by Mental Health Review tribunals and the Ministry of Justice. Yet, by sharing offender recovery tasks in this way, we would demonstrate a willingness on the part of clinicians to be transparent, and instead of avoiding the issues, to being open in discussions about how harmful acts or offending behaviour are less likely to result in the sort of satisfying life to which people often aspire. Moreover, there should be an emphasis on helping individuals understand what that satisfying life could be like. Many individuals entering secure service have had difficult backgrounds that they may not wish to return to if they have a positive alternative. Repper (2006) stresses the importance of 'discovery' as an important part of recovery, and discussions about living lives without crime or offending can help empower clients towards a direction of travel that is more likely to yield a pro-social and risk-reduced outcome. Moreover, this approach of being transparent and open about risks and having a shared formulation about risk with the client fits well with publications such as *No Health without Mental Health* (DoH, 2011); Challenge six of the Centre for Mental Health document *Implementing Recovery: A new framework for organisational change* (2009) and the development of the Shared Pathway by the National Commissioning Network for Specialist Services.

One example of this process at work is that demonstrated by Dr Amory Clarke and colleagues at South London and Maudsley NHS Trust. A group-based programme teaches patients about the process of risk assessment, and the

HCR-20 specifically. Observed outcomes have included appearing to enhance the patients' sense of self-efficacy and collaborative working, although as yet research findings from this approach have not been published. In a similar way, the National Commissioning Network for Specialist Services have developed a series of workbooks to aid in collaborative working. One of these, 'My Risk and Safety', explicitly examines the patients' risk to themselves and others and is aimed at empowering patients towards greater ownership of their risk.

Through individual work with Mr B, collaborative discussions on his risk assessment took over eight months to complete. The assessment itself became the intervention, and during that time his perspective on his background and his insight into how he came to that juncture in his life changed. The work required a trusting therapeutic relationship, as well as appropriate challenges to his thinking. His risk – as a set of choices he has made – began, and continues, to shift.

Mr B – I know it was a stupid act that I did, but at the time I had to have it (the purpose of his burglary). Looking back on it, I could have just waited. I don't know why I didn't.

RB – Well, you told me previously how you survived when you were younger.

Mr B – Yeah right, Mum was dealing with her own stuff, my brother and I just took money from her handbag. If she found out, she never said anything. We needed money to buy food, what else were we going to do?

RB – So you got used to taking things?

Mr B – 'Course, but it was stuff we needed.

RB – and the burglary?

Mr B – I could have waited a week to buy what I wanted, but I convinced myself I had to have it.

These collaborative approaches to risk assessment have yet to demonstrate more than anecdotal efficacy, but they are at least consistent with the principles of recovery. Yet, we know from wider research on therapy and therapeutic relationships (e.g. Lambert and Barley, 2001) that acknowledging problems and difficulties and taking responsibility for one's behaviours are the foundations upon which change can occur. Are risk behaviours intrinsically different from other behaviours?

As noted earlier, what is crucial, and perhaps as yet unanswered, is the timing of when to introduce collaborative risk assessments. This is something of a 'Goldilocks' question. Attempt to work collaboratively on risk too early and if the patient is not in a position to own the responsibility for their behaviours and actions at that time we run the risk of alienating or overwhelming them, leading to further avoidance and denial; too late and it becomes tokenistic and weakens the use of recovery values as applied to risk because the patient may not want to 'own' something that requires such changes late in their admission to in-patient services. When to do it becomes something that individual patients, clinicians and teams must decide, but it is a complex issue to which there are no easy answers.

Useful things to consider before undertaking a lengthy joint risk assessment might be to introduce the concept of risk early on, through introducing regular CPA risk forms, psycho-educational groups about risk assessment generally, encouraging patients to comment upon any risk care plans that are drawn up early in their care, and generally making risk assessment (in whatever guise it may be) a regular, familiar and predictable process. When disagreement or friction does occur ensure that both sides of the view are represented and use those disagreements as an opportunity for discussion, rather than avoidance and polarized perspectives.

Strengths-based approaches to risk assessment

Risk assessments can also be deficit-laden documents, perhaps again stemming from the focus that risk engenders in secure settings. However, if a risk assessment and management plan is to be collaboratively written and developed, then it needs to reflect both the realistic limitations of the individual and their circumstances, but also the strengths and abilities that they can draw on in the face of their often difficult realities. This is something that has been recognised as a fundamental principle of best practice (DoH, 2007), yet in my own limited experience is rarely done. Furthermore, if risk assessments are to be done truly collaboratively, an assessment that describes both strengths and deficits is one that is more likely to be accepted by the individual as a realistic appraisal of their circumstances, rather than one that is potentially stigmatising and only talks of problems, deficits, and 'bad' behaviour.

Integrating a strengths-based approach into common risk-assessment formats is something that is already being considered as part of the Shared Pathway process described by the National Commissioner teams. For instance the SAPROF (Structured Assessment of PROtective Factors for violence risk (de Vogel *et al.*, 2009) is under consideration as an outcome measure in respect of risk. This follows a format similar to the HCR-20, with 17 items that are coded as being either present, partially present or absent. When written side by side with the HCR-20, it provides a perspective on the individual that helps the professionals and the patient identify a more rounded view of the patient's position, skills, abilities and limitations. It uses the same structured professional judgement approach as that of the HCR-20, so is easily understood and integrated into existing practices. The items are derived from research evidence on factors that could compensate for violence risk, and unlike other attempts at strengths-based approaches (e.g. Short Term Assessment of Risk and Treatability, Webster *et al.*, 2004), focuses entirely upon strengths.

It remains to be seen if the SAPROF, or other assessments that incorporate strengths like the START, can influence the pathology-laden nature of risk assessments. As its authors conclude, it is 'a work in progress'. Again, anecdotal use of it with patients has proved useful in a number of ways. First, it has provided a fuller and richer description of the individual's circumstances, skills, deficits and limitations in a way that allows for greater collaborative formulation.

Moreover, it has the potential to be a less stigmatising approach to assessment. By identifying strengths in an individual, this can prompt further discussions about how these strengths might be further developed for added protection. The positive nature of a strengths-based approach also provides hope for change in ways that risk assessments based solely on negatives may not (Ullrich and Coid, 2011).

Risk reduction and recovery-supporting interventions

Once this assessment process has been completed, it usually leads to the question 'What can we do about it?' As noted in the earlier part of this chapter, the responsibility for managing harmful behaviours can often reside more with the clinicians than with the individual because: (a) it is easier to control the risk that way; (b) its gives (the clinicians, service management, Ministry of Justice, Tribunals) an illusory sense of reassurance; and (c) clear treatment approaches for harmful behaviours can be lacking in services that have historically focused on the experience of mental illness as the mediating factor for harmful behaviour.

Whilst risk assessments serve the obvious purpose of detailing an individual's perceived risk, the more important aspect, and one which sadly is sometimes neglected in my experience, is that they should also clearly outline a treatment strategy for the client. Again, using a collaborative approach this could be done in such a way as to support the individual in choosing treatment options and therapy goals that they believe they can engage in and benefit from. This may be about enhancing existing skills, or overcoming other difficulties or deficits. Mr B, for instance, recognised in discussions during sessions that he lacked skills in asserting himself in a pro-social way and quickly signed himself up to an assertiveness skills course. However, had he been told that he should do such a course it is unlikely that he would have done so, since his experience of authority may have led him to resist it, even if it would potentially have been of benefit to him.

In comparison, within the prison system patients like Mr B would have had much clearer access to prison-derived treatment programmes that are nationally accredited and evidenced. By completing these they are able to demonstrate to parole boards some change in their risk in a way that is measurable. Whilst such programmes do exist to an extent in secure mental health services (e.g. The Life Minus Violence programme, Ireland *et al.*, 2010), they are not widely available and have varying degrees of demonstrated efficacy. Yet with the development of payment by results, clustering and a homogenized shared care pathway, it is probably inevitable that nationally accredited treatment programmes will start to coalesce from the myriad of individually developed programmes that exist across the country, even if at the same time the prison system are abandoning some accredited programmes on the basis of cost. Certainly, work by the National Secure Services Quality, Innovation, Productivity and Prevention QIPP working group developing the Shared Pathway has been designed to make risk reduction as transparent a recovery outcome as other aspects of the pathway. Clearly, this then means that risk reduction-based programmes and interventions need to be available to meet this need.

Motivation to change, denial and avoidance

It also raises the question of motivation to change. Not all individuals are going to welcome the chance to undertake lengthy risk-reduction programmes. As noted earlier, denial, shame and lack of insight can often result in individuals struggling to acknowledge their risk. Within the context of recovery, how can offender recovery be construed to enable individuals to be motivated to undertake it, rather than to avoid it?

One useful conceptualisation of motivation, particularly in the context of recovery, comes from Self-determination Theory (Deci and Ryan, 2000; Ryan and Deci, 2000). This framework for understanding motivation, volition, initiation of action, performance and the consequential effects on wellbeing focuses on three particular conditions required for an individual to be motivated to act, and to maximally benefit from that action. Those three conditions are the experiences of *autonomy, competence* and *relatedness.* The authors argue that these three experiential factors stimulate engagement in activities, enhance performance, creativity and outcome. Crucially, these factors also need to be intrinsic to the individual's conception of self, rather than being extrinsically derived (e.g. 'I am competent' rather than 'others say I am competent').

The framework views individuals as active agents in their environments with an evolutionarily-derived prime towards mastering their environment, overcoming challenges and growth. This agency, however, requires 'fundamental nutriments – namely, ambient supports for experiencing competence, relatedness and autonomy' (Deci and Ryan, 2000) without which the individual is likely to have impaired motivation, struggle to develop skills and abilities and adapt to changing life circumstances. The authors remark that when these conditions are hindered – '…specifically when one's context is excessively controlling, over-challenging or rejecting – they will, to that degree, be supplanted by alternative, often defensive or self-protective processes, which no doubt also have functional utility under non-supportive circumstances' (p. 229). Compare this with many underlying principles of recovery and there are clear parallels between the ideas of autonomy (making choices), competence (strengths) and relatedness (relating to others, accepting the support of others) (Roychowdhury, 2011).

If, as proposed at the beginning of this chapter, recovery is a process of psychological human change, then a model of self-determination and motivation is also central to understanding how people move from a position of being stuck to motivating themselves towards recovery and growth. Treating risk as one aspect of this process (rather than a separate entity in and of itself) means that services might usefully integrate a theory of motivation into the ways in which they support recovery.

The reverse may also be true. Anxiety-derived over-control, custodial cultures and stigmatising inferences about risk are perhaps more likely to result in patients taking on a 'sealed-over' recovery style in which they deny or minimise their offending behaviour. Admitting to behaviours that are perceived negatively in terms of your progress along the care pathway is hardly likely to inspire patients to take on responsibility for those behaviours (or even admit them in the first place). Moreover, for many, admitting to the realities of their harmful behaviours can bring difficult feelings of shame and guilt, as well as anxiety that they may occur again. The need to formulate the purpose of an individual's denial is clearly crucial in understanding it, but at the same time we cannot ignore the potential for environmental and cultural influences, both at the micro and at the macro level, upon patients' willingness to accept responsibility for their harmful behaviours.

By treating harmful behaviour as one more behaviour amongst a complex interaction of behaviours, feelings and cognitions; by treating risk assessment and management in a collaborative, holistic way; and by agreeing clear treatment goals for security, this may help to create the conditions in which patients are less likely to deny or minimise their harmful behaviours, and more likely to embrace the possibility of change. Others have argued that a narrative approach will assist patients in making sense of their risky behaviour in the overall context of their lives, but still recognise that '...this can be painful when some aspects of the offender identity may be changed but others may not' (Dorkins and Adshead, 2011). It does remain to be seen, though, whether this approach to offender recovery will yield results, and it must be acknowledged that, for some patients, true acknowledgement of their harmful behaviours may be very difficult.

Living a 'good life'

One model of offender rehabilitation, pioneered in New Zealand and Australia by Tony Ward and colleagues, has proved useful in motivating individuals who commit crimes to work towards better, safer and more socially responsible lives. The 'Good Lives' model (GLM, Ward, 2002; Ward and Maruna, 2007), originally developed to work with sexual offenders, places a priority on the need for offenders to motivate themselves towards leading better, less risky lives. The GLM is based on the assumption that individuals have a set of intrinsic requirements in life that they actively seek. These requirements – or *goods* – include, amongst other things, healthy living and functioning, competence (excellence in work and play), agency or autonomy, friendship (relatedness), meaning and purpose, creativity and happiness. In this model, individuals are intrinsically drawn towards gaining these goods, but the mechanism (called a secondary good) by which they fulfil the need for the goods can be adaptive or maladaptive. For instance, in Mr B's case, his burglary was underpinned by a need derived of the good of creativity and relatedness, in the sense that he committed the burglary to acquire money to fund the printing of some personalized t-shirts. The strategy by which he met those goods was limited, anti-social and maladaptive and did not help him achieve either his goal (the t-shirts) or the underlying primary good (an expression of his creativity).

Applying the GLM to secure mental health settings, Barnao *et al.* (2010) suggest that the GLM has the potential to provide a richer understanding of patients' offending behaviour, and the ways in which the individual's experience of mental illness may have affected or motivated that behaviour, when compared to models based upon a relapse prevention model. Again, the model has the potential to be a more empowering way of understanding the roots of a particular offending behaviour, rather than simply telling patients that they should desist from a behaviour, without recognising that the behaviour was a means to an end. Helping offenders to identify the goals they have in life – and helping them to develop the skills to meet those goals in a socially constructive fashion – is perhaps also more likely to mean that they will (a) engage in that work and (b) result in a reduction in their risk because they no longer need to use criminogenic strategies to satisfy their need for primary goods. By comparison, previous models of offending-related work – such as the Risk-Needs-Responsivity model (Andrews, Bonta and Hodge, 1990) – focus more upon criminogenic needs than the wider human goals of the individual. This more traditional view echoes similar approaches to forensic mental health rehabilitation – the individual being focused on decreasing the frequency of maladaptive behaviours, and abstaining from distorted pro-offending beliefs. Ward and colleagues (Ward and Maruna, 2007) suggest that this earlier model does not motivate offenders towards more socially acceptable goals, such as helping them to understand the benefits of living a life with meaning and purpose.

The benefits of the Good Lives Model is that it would fit well with the wider social recovery goals of a recovery-orientated approach. As noted above, Barnao *et al.* (2010) have made suggestions about how a GLM approach could be used in a forensic mental health setting – and indeed at the time of writing it was hoped that Mr B would participate in a Good Lives Group developed for forensic mental health settings (Wilkes, Barker, Haddock and Wels, in prep).

Positive risk-taking and organizational support

If this approach to offender recovery holds, services also need to revise their approach to risk-taking. Returning to our discussion at the beginning of this chapter about the possibility of risk evoking considerable anxiety in the clinicians involved in their care, how do we challenge this anxiety sufficiently to provide patients with the necessary agency and autonomy to move forward in their recovery journeys?

Slade (2009) defines positive risk-taking as 'behaviors which involve the person taking on new challenges leading to personal growth and development' (p. 177). Slade rightly points out that the process of trying new activities, new skills and experiences is a fundamental part of human growth – in the act of trying, and sometimes failing, we construct a narrative of who we are and what is important to us. Moreover, such growth promotes (if sufficiently supported), exactly the sort of resilience and coping skills that are required by many patients in secure settings. Nor is positive risk-taking about a lax approach to security; rather, the approach to risk is one that is informed by the primary goal of supporting an individual's recovery – within the confines and limitations imposed by their situation, strengths and deficits.

Yet positive risk-taking can easily result in anxiety, and the vicious circle of reassurance-seeking and control that was described at the beginning of the chapter. If recovery as a set of values is ever to have parity with risk reduction in secure services then there has to be clarity at an organizational level about how the complexities that arise from the two are handled. An example of the difficulties inherent in managing this complexity can be seen in the Gonzales enquiry (Scott-Moncrieff, Briscoe and Daniels, 2009).

Daniel Gonzales murdered Marie Harding, Kevin Molloy, Derek and Jean Robinson and attempted to murder Peter King and Loumis Constantinou during a series of attacks in the south of England in September 2004. He had experienced symptoms of schizophrenia since the age of 17 and had been hospitalized and received treatment in the community. He was not a 'forensic' patient in the sense that he had been mainly provided with treatment by his Community Mental Health Team, until the murders. The enquiry noted various concerns with the application of the 'Recovery Model'. Specifically, they raised concerns that

> We see much value in mental health services following the philosophy behind the recovery model, particularly putting engagement at the centre of the therapeutic relationship. But failure to understand the rigour of the recovery model carries considerable risk. The emphasis on user acceptance may cause professionals to slide more easily into lack of action than is likely in the paternalistic, or even service, models. With these, providers are, at the least, aware that a person needs their services even if he does not want to accept them.
>
> (Scott-Moncrieff *et al.*, 2009, p. 144)

Recovery itself was not criticised, but the organization's support for it was, in so much as it was concluded that a truly recovery-orientated service would have made greater effort to engage Mr Gonzales. Had he been better known, it is possible that his greater need would have been recognised, and perhaps his risk recognised also. The authors conclude:

> A failure to understand the rigour of the recovery model carries considerable risks, as the emphasis on user acceptance may give rise to unacceptable inaction by professionals.
>
> (Scott-Moncrieff *et al.*, 2009, p. 146)

Clearly, there is comment in this that recovery – at least as it was applied in the Gonzales case – may well have contributed towards 'unacceptable inaction' in the guise of respecting a service user perspective. Balancing out the tensions between what is best for the individual patient versus the public's protection remains a complex challenge to bringing recovery values into secure settings. The importance of having recovery values embedded within guidelines and policies is important, as is learning and training on recovery, but even with that, recovery values need to be kept 'alive' in the day-to-day workings of an organization in order to thrive. Supervision, recovery workers (particularly those with lived experience) and recovery champions can all assist in making the values of recovery clear to all, both patients and staff.

Conclusions

I have argued in this chapter that offender recovery is a way of seeing recovery values through the lens of risk treatment. For a service to be truly recovery-orientated, recovery cannot be 'suspended' when it comes to dealing with issues of risk; rather, risk is understood as a behaviour that, like other aspects of behaviour and experience, can be changed, accepted or modified within a milieu that has at its core a set of recovery values. Offender recovery means supporting the individual to understand the contribution that their experiences, both good and bad, have had on their risk of acting harmfully, and the degree to which such choices are contrary to meaningful recovery and the living of a satisfying, meaningful and socially contributing life.

References

Andrews, D. A., Bonta, J. and Hodge, R. D. (1990) 'Classification for effective rehabilitation: Rediscovering psychology'. *Criminal Justice and Behavior*, 17: 19–52.

Anthony, W. A. (1993) Recovery from mental illness: the guiding vision of the mental health service system in the 1990s. *Psychosocial Rehabilitation Journal*, 16: 11–23.

Barnao, M., Robertson, P. and Ward, T. (2010) 'The Good Lives Model applied to a forensic population'. *Psychiatry, Psychology, & Law*, 17(2): 202–217.

Deci, E. L. and Ryan, R. M. (2000) 'The "What" and "Why" of goal pursuits: Human needs and the self-determination of behavior'. *Psychological Inquiry*, 11(4): 227–268.

Department of Health. (2007) *Best Practice in Managing Risk*. Department of Health.

—— (2010) *See Think Act: Your guide to Relational Security*. Department of Health.

—— (2011) *No Health Without Mental Health – A Cross-Government Mental Health Outcomes Strategy for People of All Ages*. H.M. Government.

Dorkins, E. and Adshead, G. (2011) 'Working with offenders: Challenges to the recovery agenda'. *Advanced in Psychiatric Treatment*, 17: 178–187.

Hare, R. D. (2003) *The Hare Psychopathy Checklist-Revised* (2nd edition). Toronto, ON: Multi-Health Systems.

Ireland, J. L., Turner, P., Money, C., Graham-Kevan, N., Ireland, C. A., Morris-King, S., Xuereb, S. and Power, C. (2010) *Developing and evaluating a long term aggression treatment programme: Life Minus Violence-Enhanced®™*. Division of Forensic Psychology Conference, Kent University, Canterbury.

Kübler-Ross, E. (2005) *On grief and grieving: Finding the meaning of grief through the five stages of loss*. Simon & Schuster Ltd.

Lambert, M. J. and Barley, D. E. (2001) 'Research summary on the therapeutic relationship and psychotherapy outcome'. *Psychotherapy: Theory, Research, Practice, Training*. 38(4): 357–361.

Moore, B. (1995) *Risk Assessment: A Practitioner's Guide to Predicting Harmful Behaviour*. London: Whiting and Birch.

Quinsey, V. L., Harris, G. T. Rice, M. E. and Cormier, C. (1998) *Violent Offenders: Appraising and Managing Risk.* Washington, DC: American Psychological Association.

Repper, J. (2006) 'Discovery is the new recovery'. *Mental Health Today*, Feb 37.

Roychowdhury, A. (2011) 'Bridging the gap between risk and recovery: A human needs approach'. *The Psychiatrist*, 35: 68–73.

Ryan, R. M. and Deci, E. L. (2000) 'Authors response: The darker and brighter sides of human existence: Basic psychological needs as a unifying concept'. *Psychological Inquiry*, 11(4): 319–338.

Sainsbury Centre for Mental Health. (2009) *Implementing Recovery; A new framework for organisational change.* London: SCMH.

Scott-Moncrieff, L., Briscoe, J. and Daniels. G. (2009) *An independent investigation into the care and treatment of Daniel Gonzales.* NHS South East Coast (formerly Surrey and Sussex SHA) and Surrey County Council.

Slade, M. (2009) *Personal recovery and mental illness: a guide for mental health professionals.* Cambridge: Cambridge University Press.

Ullrich, S. and Coid, J. (2011) 'Protective factors for violence among released prisoners – effects over time and interactions with static risk'. *Journal of Consulting and Clinical Psychology*, 79(3): 381–390.

Vogel, V. de, Ruiter, C. de, Bouman, Y. and de Vries Robbé, M. (2009) *SAPROF. Guidelines for the assessment of protective factors for violence risk.* English Version. Utrecht, The Netherlands: Forum Educatief.

Ward, T. (2002) 'Good lives and the rehabilitation of sexual offenders: Promises and problems'. *Aggression and Violent Behavior*, 7: 513–528.

Ward, T. and Maruna, S. (2007) *Rehabilitation: Beyond the risk-paradigm.* Key Ideas in Criminology Series (Tim Newburn, Series Ed.). London: Routledge.

Webster, C. D. Douglas, K. S. Eaves, D. and Hart, S. D. (1997) *HCR-20: Assessing the Risk for Violence* (Version 2). Vancouver: Mental Health, Law, and Policy Institute, Simon Fraser University.

Webster, C. D., Martin, M., Brink, J., Nicholls, T. L. and Middleton, C. (2004) *Short-Term Assessment of Risk and Treatability (START).* St. Josephs Healthcare, Hamilton and British Columbia Mental Health and Addiction Services.

3 'Nothing for us without us either' – forensic service user involvement

Anita Bowser

Introduction

The starting point of this chapter is a belief that service user involvement is an essential component of recovery-orientated services. This chapter will review some of the national drivers and literature around service user involvement. I will go on to describe our particular experience of implementing service user involvement at Ravenswood House, a medium secure unit within Hampshire Partnership NHS Foundation Trust. This is not a formula or prescription, but a description of how one service developed and implemented service user involvement, the benefits we gained from it and some of the barriers we encountered.

Over the last decade clinicians have become more aware of the value of service-user involvement and this has been reflected in Department of Health guidance. In 1999 the National Service Framework for Mental Health identified the importance of involving service users in all aspects of modernising services. This was followed by the NHS Plan (DoH, 2001), which placed the service user at the centre of the NHS and the Health and Social Care Act (2001), which identified that service users needed to be consulted about ongoing service provision and not just major changes. Then in 2003 the Government established the Commission for Patient and Public Involvement in Health to ensure public involvement in decision-making about health services. However, making a reality of service user involvement is a real challenge for clinicians and it requires a great deal more than simple inclusion of token representatives on committees or a signature on a care plan. If the involvement of service users is to be meaningful it requires a major cultural change for service providers at all levels (Perkins and Goddard, 2004). These levels are identified as:

Strategic: input from service users in the development, planning and organisation of services.
Operational: gathering feedback from service users about their experiences.
Individual: service users making decisions about their individual treatment and support and the ways in which this will be provided.

Getting service user involvement right can bring many benefits as service users bring their own experiences of not only their mental health problems, but also the mental health system itself. They are able to provide an alternative perspective on services, models and approaches which complement the current system. They are also able to share their knowledge and experience of self-help strategies and coping techniques, which can enable service users to develop new skills and increase their confidence and self-esteem (NIHME, 2003). Inextricably linked with service user involvement in mental health is the concept of 'empowerment', reflecting the belief that genuine, meaningful involvement would both, as a process and in its outcomes, bring about positive change and improvement for service users, individually and collectively, as well as for the mental health system itself (Williamson, 2004). However, there are also barriers to service user involvement. Some professionals are reluctant to develop service user involvement for a variety of reasons. Some feel that meaningful involvement is too time-consuming and costly; some question whether a service user can really represent other service users on projects/developments; and some do not see the value of service user involvement at all. Another barrier is that service users may perceive mental health services to be coercive and may therefore be reluctant to engage in them in terms of offering their views and opinions. To compound this, those groups that can offer support to service users to engage in these projects have a lack of resources to do so (NIHME, 2003). Nevertheless, service user involvement is a key component to ensuring the success of recovery-orientated services. 'Participative approaches enhance staff understanding and awareness of person-centred working and ensures recovery services are relevant to the people using them' (CSIP, RCPsych and SCIE, 2007, p. 14). However, service users are already involved in services and therefore the focus should be on working with them as equals in partnership to help them build their lives in the ways they wish to (Sainsbury Centre for Mental Health, 2009; Spiers *et al.*, 2005).

Service user involvement at a strategic level

If we are to successfully involve service users at a strategic level of the organisation then we need their input in the development, planning and organisation of services. This can be particularly challenging as finding service users with the appropriate skills, motivation and time to get involved can be difficult. Hampshire Partnership NHS Foundation Trust has a Consumer Experience and Engagement Committee which consists of the leaders for service user involvement from the various services across the Trust. This group looks at how the Trust can meaningfully involve service users in a range of projects and it keeps its members up to date with national drivers. Recently, in a move to make involvement more meaningful, the Trust board has invited service users and carers to tell their stories at its meetings and has encouraged its members to visit services to talk to service users to gain a better understanding of their needs.

Consumer advisor role

To support the Trust to involve service users at a strategic level, a consumer advisor post was developed. A prerequisite for this post was that the applicants had to have their own experience of using mental health services. They are then able to offer advice from a service user perspective at strategic meetings and in policy development. The role has proved to be so successful that several Associate Consumer Advisors have been appointed to take on some of the increasing workload.

The Quality Network for Forensic Mental Health Services

The Quality Network for Forensic Mental Health Services is organised by the Royal College of Psychiatrists' Centre for Quality Improvement and it examines the quality of the services provided by its members. This process includes a visit to the service by a peer review team, who talk to staff, senior managers and service users about the quality of the service and the level of care received. The views of these different groups are incorporated into a report, with recommendations for service improvements. Therefore, service users are able to directly contribute to suggestions for change. The Quality Network itself also recognised the need for service user involvement within its organisation and began by employing two service user experts (one from Ravenswood House) to sit on their advisory group. The role developed to include service user experts conducting telephone interviews with service users from member units and participating in some peer review site visits. The Quality Network also employed two female service users to ensure that the views of women are represented.

> Working for the Quality Network has given me a job with financial rewards and a sense of purpose. It also helps you understand the service in a wider context as you see people are trying to help you recover and you appreciate the efforts made in your own service.
>
> (Quality Network Service User Expert)

Service user involvement at an operational level

In order to involve service users at an operational level we need to consult them about their experiences of services and how they are delivered. Beginning this process can be particularly challenging in forensic services, where some staff see their role as providing 'detention' and not facilitating recovery. They can struggle to understand why service user involvement should be encouraged and question its value. At Ravenswood House we began the process of changing attitudes and developing service user involvement, firstly by developing a lead role for service user involvement and secondly by setting up a Patients Reference Group.

Lead for service user involvement

When I took on this role one of my first tasks was to develop and implement a strategy for service user involvement that identified ways in which service users could be meaningfully involved in service developments, such as recruitment and improving the Care Programme Approach (CPA) process. This strategy has been updated annually to ensure that it remains relevant. Perhaps more importantly, I saw my role as being a 'champion' for service user involvement and exploring creative ways of involving our service users, and challenging negative attitudes when they arose.

The Patients Reference Group

The aim of this group was to provide a forum where there could be communication between service users and senior management about service developments. This group met once a month and consisted of one service user representative from each of five wards (ward representatives), the service manager, the lead for service user involvement and the clinical director. Agenda items were put forward by any member of the group, and also by other staff wishing to consult service users about new policies, projects or developments. These were discussed and taken back to the ward community meetings by the ward representatives to get the views of the service users across the unit. The ward representatives were also able to raise their concerns about the service and any areas they felt needed to be changed. For example, service users expressed frustration at a lack of opportunity to meet socially with their friends from other wards in the evenings, and this led to the development of the patients' coffee shop, which opened three evenings a week with satellite television, board games, movies and quizzes. The group was initially chaired by staff as the ward representatives did not feel able to take on this role. However, it evolved to having a rotating chair between the ward representatives as their confidence and skills developed. This forum has been successful in ensuring that service users are listened to and their views acted upon. It also enabled them to be actively involved in the development of a recovery-focused service.

> At the Patients Reference Group you can meet senior professionals and give a patient's perspective on care. I feel like I am helping other people and it gives me a sense of respect.
>
> (Ward Representative)

'Having your Say' Consultation

One of the challenges we faced was increasing involvement from a greater number of service users. We enlisted the help of the Trust Consumer Advisor, who arranged meetings on each of the unit's wards to provide service users the opportunity to express their views. With plenty of tea, coffee, biscuits and staff encouragement the meetings were well attended and there were some lively discussions about the service. The findings of the consultation were compiled into a report, 'Having your Say' (2005, unpublished paper), with recommendations and an action plan that were supported by the Service Clinical Governance Group. The recommendations focused on improving service user involvement in ward rounds and CPA meetings and ensuring that each ward held regular community meetings.

Ward representatives

As the lead for service user involvement and as an occupational therapist committed to vocational rehabilitation, I was keen to develop a ward representative role. The aim was to have one service user on each ward who could lead community meetings and represent their peers at the Patients Reference Group. This was initially a voluntary role, however the work undertaken by the volunteers was so valuable that it was developed into a paid role. A job description and a person specification were developed and the posts were advertised. Service users who applied were interviewed and, if successful, appointed on a Band 1 (Agenda for Change NHS staffing structure) Trust contract. They have fixed-term contracts for one to two hours per week but have the flexibility to work excess hours if the job requires this. They are provided with regular supervision and training which covers all aspects of the role.

The ward representatives are an important link between the weekly ward community meetings and the monthly Patients Reference Group. As they have become more confident with training and support, they have been able to take on the role of chair for the community meetings. The meetings are attended by service users living on the ward and a member of staff, often the ward manager. The aim of these meetings is to discuss day-to-day issues and concerns, and issues which have been raised at the Patients Reference Group.

> This job has been life-changing for me. It has made me feel more important and has given me a sense of purpose. It's very interesting and I look forward to everything I do as a ward representative!
>
> (Ward Representative)

This current system of regular consultation has proven to be very effective and service users report that they feel their views are valued and listened to, and it has also received positive feedback from the Quality Network for Forensic Mental Health. This role also links well with the principles of recovery in that it supports the development of a meaningful and satisfying role for the ward representative. There have, however, been challenges, which have included the movement of the ward representatives to different wards or units; the appointment of service users who then struggle to carry out the role and, more recently, ward representatives engaging in inappropriate activities such as drug-taking which has led to their dismissal. The service also became almost too enthusiastic about requesting ward representative involvement at various meetings, some of which the ward representatives found too confusing. Therefore requests for involvement are now monitored carefully to ensure that they are meaningful and relevant.

> It's difficult for people with a criminal record and mental health issues to get employment. Any job a service user gets in the system helps; it is a stepping

stone to either continue work in service-related issues or a different job. You can prove to employers that you have done something.

(Ward Representative)

Involving service users in the recruitment process

The development of recovery-oriented services emphasises the personal qualities of staff as much as their formal qualifications. It seeks to cultivate their capacity for hope, creativity, care, compassion, realism and resilience (Sainsbury Centre for Mental Health, 2009). Therefore, engaging service users in the recruitment process ensures that they can contribute to the selection of staff with the right qualities. Since 2003 Hampshire Partnership NHS Foundation Trust has developed policies and procedures to ensure that service users are involved in the recruitment of its staff. Ensuring that this happened in secure mental health services proved more challenging. For example, there were difficulties in having current service users on an interview panel as they would have access to staff members' confidential information.

In order to get service users involved in the recruitment process at Ravenswood House several steps were taken. The first was to consult with the Patients Reference Group about the person specifications written for staff job descriptions. Service users were asked about what qualities they would like to see in staff employed to work in the service. Suggestions included staff having good communication skills and a warm, friendly approach. These were then incorporated in all person specifications irrespective of job title. Once this was in place the Patients Reference Group was then consulted about questions that prospective staff could be asked at interview. They drew up a list of questions and expected responses, which was made available to recruiting managers, with an expectation that a minimum of two questions would be used each time they interviewed.

The ward representatives were also involved in showing candidates around the unit with a member of staff prior to their interview. This proved very successful and was developed further through the ward representative completing a feedback form on the candidate, which was then made available to the interview panel. This process was well received by interview panels, ward representatives and the candidates themselves. The occupational therapy department introduced a requirement that candidates make a presentation to the interview panel and ward representatives on the topic of 'involving service users in developing an occupational therapy service'. The ward representatives were then able to ask the candidates questions relating to service user involvement. Interestingly, the ward representatives found this useful but commented that they preferred showing the candidates around the service. We are in the process of writing best practice guidelines for setting up a separate service user interview panel and involving current service users on the panel itself.

I enjoy showing people around the unit. It makes you feel better about yourself to know you are involved in recruiting staff, after all they will be working with us. It also gives the prospective employee a chance to meet a patient.

(Ward Representative)

Involving service users in training for staff

For some time, services within the NHS have explored ways of involving service users in training staff, therefore involving the real experts by sharing their knowledge and experience. A comprehensive service user-led education and training programme for professionals at all levels is important to ensure that their behaviours and attitudes are changed (Sainsbury Centre for Mental Health, 2009). Our progress was hindered by concerns about ensuring that service user involvement was meaningful to them and the staff. We also wanted to ensure that the service users had the appropriate skills to contribute. Our first step was to involve the ward representatives in the induction of new staff. The ward representatives were supported to provide a short presentation on the staff induction programme that included a description of their role as ward representatives and some insight into what it was like for service users to live in the unit. The ward representatives describe their journey towards recovery and what staff can do to facilitate this process. A survey carried out by ward representatives in 2008 on consistency in care highlighted service users' concerns about how staff are not always consistent in how they implement policies and procedures. Sharing the findings of this survey at the induction increased staff awareness of how inconsistencies can impact on service users.

Service user involvement at an individual level

Involving service users at an individual level of their care and treatment is underpinned by the principles of recovery. Two of the themes of recovery have been identified as:

a) Recovery involves a process of empowerment to regaining active control over one's life. This includes accessing useful information, developing confidence in negotiating choices and taking increasing personal responsibility through effective self-care, self-management and self-directed care.

(CSIP, RCPsych and SCIE, 2007, p. 5)

Also:

b) Treatment is important but its capacity to support recovery lies in the opportunity to arrive at treatment decisions through negotiation and collaboration and it being valued by the individual as one of many tools they choose to use.

(CSIP, RCPsych and SCIE, 2007, p. 6)

Two of the main forums in which individual levels of care are addressed are within the service user's ward round and CPA meetings.

Ward rounds

Within Ravenswood House each service user has a ward round, a meeting with the multi-disciplinary team, every fortnight in which their care is reviewed. When the 'Having your Say' consultation was carried out, service users were asked if they understood the purpose of ward rounds and if they felt listened to. The majority of service users did feel that they had a good understanding of the purpose and that their views were heard. However, some expressed concern over the ward round process, including the numbers of people present and not feeling involved in decision-making.

> I sometimes feel that all of the feedback given to patients in ward round is negative – I would like to hear positives too.
>
> (Service User)

A new ward-round feedback form was developed to be used by primary nurses, which feeds back on the service user's strengths, as well as needs. It also takes into account the service user's views about their care and treatment. Ideally, to work in a recovery-focused way the service user should attend the whole meeting. However, one of the challenges of working in a forensic unit is that the multi-disciplinary team often need to discuss sensitive issues, such as third-party information, without the service user present. Meetings that are too large can be overwhelming for the service user, particularly when they feel anxious. The service user therefore typically joins at the latter part of the meeting to discuss their care. The service then looked at other ways to further improve ward rounds. This included implementing the 'Code of Good Practice for Meetings with Service Users' produced by service users for use in mental health settings (Hyphen-21, registered charity). An 'Experience-Based Design' project examined the ward round process. This approach was developed by the Institute for Innovation and Improvement and is a method of designing better health-care services by using the experiences of service users, carers and staff. The four stages of the process are: capture the experience; understand the experience; improve the experience; and measure the improvement. Service users are involved from start to finish, including project planning, participating in interviews, developing questionnaires and organised group events to gather views and ideas for improvements. It was evident from this process that staff and service users wanted ward rounds to be more recovery-orientated. Consequently the ward rounds have been renamed 'progress reviews', service users are able to attend from the start if they choose to and the discussions focus more on care plans, strengths and goals rather than problems.

Care Programme Approach (CPA) meetings

The Care Programme Approach (CPA) was introduced in 1991 and places a greater emphasis on ensuring that individual service users are fully involved in the planning, delivery and review of the care and treatment they receive. It aims to promote recovery and integration and 'will involve the user and the carer, where appropriate, as central participants in the process' (DOH, 1999a, p. 24).

At Ravenswood House each service user has a CPA meeting approximately every four months. This meeting is attended by the multi-disciplinary team, other relevant professionals (e.g. locality social worker), the service user and their family. The CPA is an integral part of the care planning for the service user and each multi-disciplinary team member is required to provide a report on the service user's progress. Historically the service user was brought in at the end of the meeting to receive feedback about the discussions, which demonstrated how far we had to go before we developed a recovery approach which saw the service user as being at the centre of all the discussions. The 'Having your Say' consultation asked service users if they understood the purpose of CPA meetings and whether they felt involved. The majority of service users felt they did understand the purpose and that they were involved. However, a number of concerns were raised, which included the number of people present and not knowing who they were, and not fully understanding the reason for the decisions made.

I'm not always clear about what the long term goals are.

(Service User)

Following the consultation, an action plan was put together to try and address these issues and make CPA meetings more recovery-focused. A CPA report form for the service user to complete prior to the CPA was developed. The form had key questions written in plain English which asked them to describe their achievements, strengths and hopes for the future. This report is read in conjunction with all the other professional reports. The format of the CPA was also changed so that the service user and their family could attend the whole CPA meeting. In order to ensure confidentiality, any third-party issues would be discussed in a professionals meeting prior to the CPA. One of the benefits of involving the service user from the beginning of the meeting has been that they are involved in all the discussions, can air their views and hear any concerns. They are also involved in writing the CPA care plan, which places a greater emphasis on the service user's achievements and strengths.

Co-facilitating therapy groups

The College of Occupational Therapists, in their strategy *Recovering Ordinary Lives* (COT, 2006), recognised the importance of identifying and maintaining service users' strengths and skills as a vital part of the recovery process. The occupational therapy service at Ravenswood House explored different ways of involving service users in therapy sessions in order to use their individual skills. For example, one service user had previously worked as a golf professional and his goal for the future was to work again in this role. With the support of an occupational therapist they developed an 'indoor golf' group in which he

provided the golf expertise and knowledge. The group proved extremely successful and enabled the service user to maintain his skills and to develop his
confidence. He reported that he felt empowered by being the expert in this environment and by being an equal, contributing to the planning, development and
evaluation of the group (Harvey and Larkin, 2009). Some members of the multi-
disciplinary team were concerned that involving the service user in this way
would give him false hope as they viewed his goal as unrealistic. This highlighted
some of the tensions that can arise in a team when attempting to work in a
recovery-focused way.

> I enjoyed working for the O.T. Department teaching golf in the gym. It was
> rewarding to be able to use my professional skills.
>
> (Service User)

Opportunities for employment

> It's demoralising being locked up. We have lots of time on our hands.
> Having a job gives you hope.
>
> (Service User)

The Sainsbury Centre for Mental Health outlines the importance of work and
employment in recovery in their paper Making Recovery a Reality (2008). They
write that 'if recovery is to become a reality employment must become one of its
key priorities' (p. 5). They describe how many people connect with the community
and build their lives and self-esteem through work and employment. Research has
also shown that most service users of mental health services want to work but that
they need to be given the right support to do so (Seebohm and Secker, 2005). The
Department of Health Commissioning Guidance for Vocational Services for People
with Severe Mental Health Problems (2006) outlined the importance of monitoring
the service user's occupational status on admission; identifying leads for vocation
within care teams; strengthening links with partner organisations such as Job Centre
Plus and education; and monitoring vocational outcomes through the CPA process.
Ross (in press) identified four types of work: paid, unpaid (e.g. voluntary), hidden
(e.g. work for cash) and substitute (e.g. sheltered workshop). The College of
Occupational Therapists (2007) identified a range of barriers to employment:

- Social barriers such as stigma and prejudice from employers and workplace
  colleagues.
- Organisational barriers which include the overall demands of the job, inflex-
  ible working practices and financial restrictions.
- Personal barriers such as lack of skills, fatigue, illness and symptoms, and
  lack of confidence.

For service users of forensic mental health services there is the added barrier
that they have a forensic history, as well as a mental health problem, making

accessing work even more difficult. In Mental Health and Work (Royal College, Psychiatrists, 2008) it is reported that one of the most successful work schemes for people with severe mental illness is Individual Placement Support (IPS). This addresses the importance of getting the service user into open employment and supporting them in this role if they are not symptom-free, providing 'real' work, whilst being able to respond to the individual needs of the service users. The occupational therapy service at Ravenswood House tried to adopt this model within the confines of a forensic setting.

The appointment of a vocational technical instructor, who had knowledge and expertise in employment issues, proved invaluable in developing a vocational pathway. We took the decision to develop paid employment for service users via NHS Trust contracts which pay above the minimum wage. This payment was carried out under the Supported Permitted Employment Scheme and payments were monitored to ensure that service users were not paid over the legal amount as this would affect their benefits. We felt that by developing real work the service users would have the opportunity to develop the skills they would need when looking for work in the community. For example, part of the process included applying for the job using Trust application forms, attending an interview and then if appointed working within the remit of a contract with supervision and appraisal.

The posts which were initially developed were a librarian role, a clothes-shop assistant and five ward representatives, all of which required limited working hours of up to three hours per week. These posts have now been in place for several years and have proved to be highly successful. Service users are employed on a six-month fixed-term contract, which allows more service users to have the opportunity to apply for these posts. However, developing and sustaining these roles has not always been easy! Following the increase in service user benefits there was a significant drop in applications. It became apparent that the increased benefits had decreased motivation to work. In spite of this the posts are usually filled.

> Work was always my identity so continuing some work-related tasks was crucial to my recovery.
>
> (Service User, Librarian)

We also developed a 'woodwork cooperative' to make furniture or undertake restoration. Each member of the cooperative received an equal amount of the profits made. This in itself enabled its members to understand the direct benefits of working hard. The cooperative also developed a team leader role, with one member of the group taking responsibility for coordinating the work of the others. This project also had challenges in terms of service user skill base.

Feedback from service users about the paid roles enabled us to think creatively about further developing the vocational service. Some service users told us that they did not feel able to apply for the available posts due to a lack of skills or lack of confidence. Therefore, in collaboration with the League of Friends shop, a voluntary role was developed. The volunteer, along with a member of occupational therapy staff, runs the shop once a week, where they are able to develop their confidence in retail skills and dealing with customers. Service users also asked for more physical jobs so we have established a car wash, a workshop cleaner, and have successfully tendered for the unit courtyard maintenance contract, which now employs two service users.

> Having a job gives you something to do. It makes you feel like you are important even if it's only for one hour a week.
>
> (Service User, League of Friends Volunteer)

Links have been forged with voluntary projects in the community which enable service users to develop work skills alongside members of the public. In order to ensure these services have the information and support that they need to manage risk we developed a policy that outlined the communication process with the voluntary organisation. This communication proved vital to the success of placements.

> Having a job helped my recovery. To have not done anything would have left a big gap in my CV. Employers expect to see something positive. It's made it easier to get along with daily life.
>
> (Service User)

Conclusion

In our experience, having service user involvement embedded into the organisation at a strategic level has proved to be important in driving the concept forward. The development of policies that identify service user involvement as essential has ensured that services have put in place action plans to implement these.

Involving service users at an operational level of the organisation required gathering their feedback about services and how they were delivered. This required a cultural shift within Ravenswood House and we have worked hard to develop processes and procedures which ensure meaningful involvement. Key to the success of this has been the development of a lead for service user involvement, with responsibility to ensure that a local action plan was implemented. We have developed the involvement of service users in the recruitment process and we are beginning to involve service users in the training of our staff. Another significant development has been that of the ward representative role, which has evolved into a paid contracted job. The ward representatives, who receive regular supervision, support and training, are highly valued and respected members of the service. They have proved to be an invaluable link between service users and senior managers. Their views have influenced many of the service changes and improvements that have taken place to develop a recovery-focused service.

Involving service users at an individual level is probably most important in terms of ensuring that recovery takes place. Consultation with our service users identified the importance of involving them meaningfully in clinical meetings. Alongside this the importance of employment has been recognised, and how engaging service users in real, meaningful work roles contributes to their overall sense of self-esteem and value. All aspects of individual care need to recognise service users' strengths, skills and hopes for the future to ensure that they are recovery-focused.

We have experienced a variety of barriers to embedding service user involvement in the service. Key amongst these has been staff attitudes that result in them being quick to identify problems rather than solutions. There have been practical problems and progress has been slow and time-consuming. However, there have also been considerable benefits. These include improved systems for communication and consultation with service users; improved ward rounds and CPA meetings; more employment opportunities; and service users influencing change within the service. A clear and multi-faceted focus on service user involvement has helped Ravenswood House move towards becoming a more recovery-focused service.

References

Anthony, W. A. (1993) Recovery from mental illness: the guiding vision of the mental health service system in the 1990s. *Psychosocial Rehabilitation Journal*, 16: 11–23.

Care Services Improvement Partnership (CSIP), Royal College of Psychiatrists (RCPsych) and Social Care Institute for Excellence (SCIE). (2007) 'A Joint Position Paper – A Common Purpose: Recovery in Future Mental Health Services'. Available at http://www.scie.org.uk/publications/positionpapers/pp08.asp. Accessed 27 October 2009.

College of Occupational Therapists. (2006) 'Recovering Ordinary Lives: The Strategy for Occupational Therapy in Mental Health Services 2007–2017, a vision for the next 10 years (Core)'. London: COT. Available at http://www.cot.org.uk. Accessed 18 November 2009.

—— (2007) 'Work Matters: Vocational Navigation for Occupational Therapy Staff'. London: COT. Available at http://www.cot.co.uk/homepage/publications/?l=l&ListIte mID=444&ListGroupID=201. Accessed 27 October 2009.

Department of Health. (1999a) 'Effective Care Coordination in Mental Health Services – Modernising the Care Programme Approach'. London: DOH Publications. Available at http://www.dh.gov.uk/en/Publicationsandstatistics/Publications/PublicationsPolicy AndGuidance/DH_4009221. Accessed 27 October 2009.

—— (1999b) 'National Service Framework for Mental Health – Modern Standards and Service Models'. London: DOH Publications. Available at http://www.dh.gov.uk/en/ Publicationsandstatistics/Publications/PublicationsPolicyAndGuidance/DH_4009598. Accessed 27 October 2009.

—— (2000) 'The NHS Plan: A Plan for Investment, a Plan for Reform'. London: DOH Publications. Available at http://www.dh.gov.uk/en/Publicationsandstatistics/Publications/ PublicationsPolicyandGuidance/DH_4002960. Accessed 27 October 2009.

—— (2001) 'Health and Social Care Act'. London: DOH Publications. Available at http:// www.dh.gov.uk/en/Publicationsandstatistics/Publications/PublicationsLegislation/ DH_4117459. Accessed 27 October 2009.

—— (2006) 'Vocational Services for People with Severe Mental Health Problems: Commissioning Guidance'. London: DOH Publications. Available at http://www.dh. gov.uk/en/Publicationsandstatistics/Publications/PublicationsPolicyAndGuidance/ DH_4009598. Accessed 27 October 2009.

Harvey, H. and Larkin, E. (2009) 'Service User Leads the Fairway', *Occupational Therapy News*, 17(4): 23.

Herbert, L. (2005) 'Having your Say'. *Unpublished paper*. Ravenswood House, Hampshire Partnership NHS Foundation Trust.

National Institute for Mental Health in England. (2003) *Cases for Change – User Involvement*. London: NIMHE.

Perkins, R. and Goddard, K. (2004) 'Reality Out of Rhetoric: Increasing User Involvement in a Mental Health Trust', *Mental Health Review* 9(1): 21–24.

Pitt, L., Kilbride, M., Nothard, S., Welford, M and Morrison, A. (2007) 'Researching Recovery from Psychosis: A User-led Project', *Psychiatry Bulletin* 31: 55–60.

Roberts, G. Dorkins, E., Woolridge, J. and Hewis, E. (2008) Detained – what's my choice? Part 1: Discussion. *Advances in Psychiatric Treatment*, 14: 172–180.

Ross, J. (In press) *Occupational Therapy and Vocational Rehabilitation*. Chichester. Wiley & Sans.

Royal College of Psychiatrists. (2008) *'Mental Health and Work'*. Available at http:// www.workingforhealth.gov.uk/documents/mental-health-and-work.pdf. Accessed 27 October 2009.

Seebohm, P. and Secker, J. (2005) 'What Do Service Users Want?' in, B. Grove, J. Secker and P. Seebohm (eds) *New Thinking About Mental Health and Employment*. Radcliffe: Oxford.

Shepherd, G., Boardman, J. and Slade, M. (2008) *Making Recovery a Reality*. London: Sainsbury Centre for Mental Health.

—— (2009) *Implementing Recovery: A New Framework for Organisation Change*. London: Sainsbury Centre for Mental Health.

Spiers, S., Harvey, K. and Chilvers, C. (2005) 'Service User Involvement in Forensic Mental Health: Can it work?' *Journal of Forensic Psychiatry & Psychology*, 16: 211–220.

Williamson, T. (2004) 'User Involvement: A Contemporary Overview', *The Mental Health Review*, 9(1): 6–12.

Wolf, R. (1997) 'The Code of Professional Conduct for ward rounds and similar meet- ings'. Available at http://www.hyphen-21.org/publicsite/ward-round-code. Accessed 18 November 2009.

4 Recovery in the forensic organization

Gerard Drennan, Kate Law and Deborah Alred

We write at a time of great change and uncertainty in the NHS in England and Wales. Anyone who knows the NHS will no doubt ask 'but when is this not the case?' Of course it is true that there will always be changes to how services are commissioned, funded or staffed, in the NHS and elsewhere. What will not change however is that services will be tasked with meeting the needs of men and women with mental health difficulties and offending behaviour, the group we have in mind throughout this collection. Put another way, in any organizational change or restructuring process within forensic mental health services, it is crucial that we do not lose sight of *the forensic patient*. As our focus here is on recovery, we must hold in mind the needs of each individual service user's 'internal organization', their individual emotional and psychological inner worlds in which recovery will need to occur, as this is what must be facilitated when creating and sustaining a recovery-supporting organization. One of the themes running throughout this collection is the question of how forensic mental health service provision can take up recovery, and how this might be similar to or different from how mainstream adult mental health services undertake the same task. Our focus in this chapter is on the organizational strategies and structures necessary to support services to move towards becoming increasingly recovery-oriented. In the first half of the chapter we set the scene by considering the internal world of the forensic patient, before moving on to consider the growing expectations of services, and then reviewing some of the guidance on implementing recovery in organizations. In the second half of the chapter we share some of our experiences and learning from incorporating recovery principles within a forensic setting.

Planning for recovery and the internal world of 'the forensic patient'

Pat Deegan (1988) wrote that recovery cannot be forced. As service providers we cannot 'do recovery to' individuals. What we can do is create environments that may foster an individual person's recovery, day to day and month to month (Anthony, 1993). It is argued that this requires a new response from services, a response which is positive, respectful, facilitating and empowering (Allott *et al.*, 2002). However, when considering choice (Roberts *et al.*, 2008), empowerment and participation we need to hold in mind what we know of how things can go wrong in trying to create a broadly therapeutic environment for forensic patients. The difficulty of achieving the necessary balance between risk management and providing therapeutic opportunities to promote recovery can be seen from the public inquiries that have taken place in high secure settings (DoH, 1992, Fallon *et al.*, 1999; NHS London, 2009) and in the community (NHS London, 2006, 2009; NHS South East Coast, 2009) when things have gone tragically wrong. The DoH publication See, Think, Act (DoH, 2010) has used the learning from these incidents to provide structured guidance for clinical teams that encourages the maintenance of security and vigilance while promoting recovery. Questions of risk and risk management will be specifically addressed elsewhere (see Richard Barker, this volume).

The literature on forensic psychotherapy offers an understanding of the challenges we encounter when supporting recovery in the individual patient, and in the work of teams and services. An understanding of these dynamics is crucial in supporting staff teams trying to meet the needs of the forensic patient in institutional care (Adshead, 2004; Bartlett and McGauley, 2010; Bowers, 2002; Campling, Davies and Farquharson, 2004). While it is important for staff to promote hope and optimism in the face of cynicism and despair, it is just as important to approach this with an awareness of how hopefulness can also take pathological forms and why (Akhtar, 1996; Kanwal, 1997; Vorhaus, 1977). If a service user's recovery can sometimes require a member of staff to 'go the extra mile', then it is important that this is done with a sophisticated understanding of the role of boundaries and emotional involvement in the recovery of the 'the forensic patient' (Aiyegbusi, 2009). The concept of 'conditioning', the application of incremental pressure to loosen boundaries in order to commit a further offence or to escape detention, in work with 'the forensic patient', is important if safety and risk management are not to be compromised by choice and empowerment. Similarly, personal responsibility and optimising independence must be matched with recovery-stage-appropriate support and structure to the therapeutic day (Bose, 2009). The response of staff teams to patients who have been extremely violent and who continue to be so, or who display sexually deviant behaviour, can mirror the underlying psychopathology of the service user's disturbance. Re-enactments of abuse can occur and it can be confusing and disillusioning to staff teams when care itself is experienced as abuse by the service user (Blumenthal, 2010; Motz, 2008). Specialised supervision and reflective practice needs to form the foundation of recovery-based organizational structures and processes to allow staff teams to gain a shared understanding of the organization of the internal world of each forensic service user and how this impacts on their recovery needs (Davies, 1996). It is important that this understanding is carried forward into the organizational structures put in place to develop the recovery approach in a service.

Planning for recovery in a landscape of change

The imperative to implement recovery-based practice within mental health organizations in general has gained increasing momentum in England and Wales through published government guidance, strategy documents (DoH, 2001, 2010; NIMHE, 2005) and the recommendations of professional bodies (COT, 2007; CSIP, 2007).

However, when the project of this book began it was very uncertain that 'recovery' would be taken up by sceptical and change-fatigued forensic services in England and Wales. One of the objections to the adoption of recovery as an overarching approach to the provision of services is the argument that there is little or no evidence base. It has been difficult for clinicians to publish recovery-focused articles in mainstream forensic journals on the grounds of the lack of an evidence base for recovery.[1] As recently as April 2010, recovery implementation was not in the list of the top 10 priorities for the Royal College of Psychiatry Quality Network (QN) for Forensic Mental Health Services. In April 2011 the implementation of recovery plans for service users was highlighted as a key future challenge.[2] The QN coordinates peer reviews amongst its 67-member medium secure units, encompassing 293 wards (Tucker and Reeve-Hoyland, 2011). The peer reviews assess each unit against their achievement of Medium Secure Standards (Royal College of Psychiatry, 2007) summarized under the rubrics of Safety and Security (incorporating Physical Security, Procedural Security, Relational Security, Serious and Untoward Incidents, Safeguarding Children and Child Visiting Policies); Clinical and Cost Effectiveness; Governance; Patient Focus; Accessible and Responsive Care; Environment and Amenities; and Public Health.

It is clear from the detail of the standards that they audit many aspects of recovery-oriented care. For example, a key achievement to emerge from the fifth cycle of unit reviews was the overall expansion and development of service user involvement. Indeed, the QN practise in a recovery-informed way by employing service users to carry out peer interviews as part of the audit process.

A wide range of good practice, expected in the QN standards, could be seen as contributing towards the implementation of recovery-oriented care. Relational Security, defined as 'the knowledge and understanding staff have of a patient and of the environment; and the translation of that information into appropriate responses and care' (DoH, 2010, p. 5) is a key theme, and the QN has published a standards document and has a strategy to implement relational security. This is surely also a recovery-oriented initiative in the context of forensic mental health services. The implementation of recovery practices could also be tracked over time by reviewing the evolution of QN standards. The implementation of recovery plans for service users was an area highlighted in Cycle 5 because 48 per cent of the units reviewed had not yet put this into place.

However, the focus of the QN is arguably not on the implementation of recovery, but on the implementation of the standards. In this sense the standards provide a series of end points and not a philosophy of care. As so many of the standards are a quantifiable index of aspects of recovery-oriented care, it is possible that efforts to meet them serve as a road map to providing a recovery-oriented service, without a requirement that any particular service identifies itself as using a recovery approach or being based on recovery values. The absence of an explicit recovery ethos as a principle, however, could be reflected in the current standards for Learning Disability Services, which make no reference to recovery (Phillips, 2010). We will expand on the distinction between recovery-oriented care and a recovery approach below.

Changes in how services are commissioned and monitored provide further important drivers for developing recovery-oriented practice in forensic settings. In England and Wales the Care Quality Commission (CQC) is the body with statutory powers to inspect and audit each mental health service against its set of criteria. A great many of these requirements broadly promote recovery-oriented care through, for example, requiring a focus on the service user experience through patient reported outcome measures (PROMs), involvement and service-user consultation. In addition, the Commissioning for Quality and Innovation (CQuIN) payment framework brings a financial incentive to organizations in England and Wales to deliver on quality initiatives for the first time (DoH, 2008b). This links quality goals to a proportion of the value of the service contract. In order to ensure CQuIN schemes cover the dimensions of quality identified in high-quality care for all (DoH, 2008a) the DoH guidance recommends that they should monitor safety, effectiveness (including patient-reported outcomes), user experience and innovation. The user experience and the service-user voice has therefore become increasingly central to the way services are commissioned and monitored. In addition to user experience, CQuIN targets include individual recovery outcomes. This is achieved through the implementation of self-management tools such as the Recovery Star (MacKeith and Burns, 2011) and the mandated requirement to administer EssenCES, a brief measure of the therapeutic environment (Schalast *et al.*, 2008). While it is imperative that services comply with the requirements of these agencies, there is a risk that the implementation of measures to meet externally specified standards can create an exoskeleton around a service in which management or clinical teams may not have fundamentally taken on the values and principles of recovery. Ashcraft and Anthony (2006) identified this bluntly as 'pretend recovery' that can be little more than a rebranding exercise.

Service-specific standards will no doubt be part of the landscape in whichever level of security or country forensic mental health care is provided. Our focus here is on describing the systems and practices that may support a service to develop and support a recovery approach systematically and consistently across an organization. We will review a selection of the relevant literature before describing a range of practical strategies for embedding recovery within a secure service.

Guidance on implementing recovery in organizations

There is a growing body of literature that provides guidance to services trying to implement recovery within their organization. It is worth restating in this context the argument made in the introductory chapter to this volume, that there is a significant qualitative difference between the organizational tasks of implementing a psychiatric rehabilitation approach and a recovery approach. Harrison (2006), writing a mere few years ago on the organizational challenges of psychiatric rehabilitation to enable recovery in long-term mental illness, highlighted the role of leadership in contrast to management and the complexities of teamwork. The challenge of organizational change in the recovery approach goes far beyond this.

Ashcraft and Anthony (2006) identify eight factors that contribute to the development of a recovery in the mental health organization in such a way that it brings about a transformation in how services operate.

- Saturation factor: Integrating recovery principles and values in order to positively impact on all aspects of the organization.
- Relationship factor: Ensuring the organization supports and values the development of healthy relationships, among service users, between service users and staff, and between the different layers of the organization.
- Continuity factor: Supporting continuity of staff by minimising turnover, by providing opportunities to experience meaning and purpose in work roles.
- Flexibility factor: Building in a structure that can adapt and grow as understanding of recovery develops.
- Accountability factor: Ensuring progress is monitored and that there are ways to hold leaders and staff accountable.
- Alignment factor: Reviewing policies and procedures to be consistent with recovery principles, to modify the form and content of documentation, and to engage external agencies to support recovery outside of the organization.
- Momentum factor: Developing a system that responds at an appropriate pace and maintains the momentum of initiatives, rather than weighing them down with lengthy protocols and delays in implementation.
- Enticement factor: Embedding incentives that reward desired outcomes.

The Sainsbury Centre for Mental Health has consistently provided grounded and practical guidance to health services in the implementation of recovery. This has grown out of Geoff Shepherd's work on articulating the relationship between rehabilitation and recovery for NHS services (Shepherd, 2006). Their initial publication addressed the need for a 'bottom-up' approach of ten top tips to practitioners on how they could make each interaction with a service user more recovery-oriented in the context of wider system changes and 'top-down' approaches (Shepherd, Boardman and Slade, 2008). This was followed in 2009 by published guidance on the ten key organizational challenges that any organization faced in making recovery a reality in routine practice (Sainsbury Centre for Mental Health, 2009). These challenges included many of the problems that forensic services face in trying to embed recovery into the work of secure services, but the paper does not address itself to the specific challenges of forensic settings.

The Sainsbury Centre went on to develop a methodology that commissioners and providers could use for assessing how far services have implemented the ten organizational challenges. This paper highlighted an organizational commitment

Box 4.1 Ten organizational challenges (Shepherd *et al.*, 2008)

- Changing the nature of day-to-day interactions and the quality of experience
- Delivering comprehensive, service user-led education and training programmes
- Establishing a 'recovery education centre' to drive the programme forward
- Ensuring organizational commitment, creating the 'culture'
- Increasing 'personalisation' and 'choice'
- Changing the way we approach risk assessment and risk management
- Redefining service user involvement
- Transforming the workforce
- Supporting staff in their recovery journey
- Increasing opportunities for building a life 'beyond illness'

to recovery and to establishing a recovery education centre as the two priorities for services to move forward. Shepherd, Boardman and Burns (2010) suggest that each Trust or service should have an education centre to 'train and support people with lived experience of mental health problems to tell their stories and to promote awareness of recovery principles among staff and other service users' (p. 6). However, implicit in the implementation of all of the challenges is the requirement for leadership. The document sets out three stages in the development of recovery in organizations. It suggests that each service would move from initial engagement with the recovery agenda, to a development stage, where there was a clear commitment and active recovery initiatives, through to transformation.

The (renamed) Centre for Mental Health has taken this work forward through the Implementing Recovery Organizational Change (ImROC) Project, in partnership with the Mental Health Network of the NHS Confederation, and the National Mental Health Development Unit, with a cluster of six demonstration sites identified. As a branch of this work, the Centre for Mental Health project leaders have formed a partnership with an informal network of forensic services supporting each other to develop recovery-oriented practice with a view to publishing good-practice guidance in 2012. Other recovery implementation initiatives are also underway.

Similar themes to the Sainsbury Centre methodology are echoed by Mike Slade (2009) when discussing transformation into a recovery-orientated organization. He identifies the importance of leadership to facilitate the process, the need to identify clear organizational values and how these will fit with working practice, the need to maximize pro-recovery orientation amongst staff, the need to develop specific recovery skills in the workforce, and finally to ensure that there are clear and visible recovery role models (Slade, 2009). Maddock and Hallam (2010) describe the implementation of the recovery approach as 'an

Box 4.2 Three stages in the development of recovery in organizations (Sainsbury Centre for Mental Health, 2009)

Stage 1 – Engagement

The organization is clearly intent on implementing recovery, and has Trust/ Board 'buy in'. There are pockets of good practice and a commitment to improve. Plans to develop a recovery-orientated service are developed and a timetable is agreed for implementation.

Stage 2 – Development

The organization is committed to a recovery-orientated service and has made significant developments, but this is not consistent throughout the service.

Stage 3 – Transformation

The organization has fully achieved the features of a recovery-orientated service. Policies, procedures and practice linked to recovery are fully embedded in the organization.

innovation journey' for any service that is unpredictable, oblique and multi-faceted (p. 45). They describe the implementation experiences of the Devon Partnership NHS Trust and the South West London and St George's Mental Health NHS Trust and highlight the importance of Trust Board support, leadership, creativity and innovation strategies, the role of early implementers followed by mainstreaming. The recommendations of these authors are mirrored in similar guidance in the literature emerging from the United States (Ashcraft and Anthony, 2009, 2010; Davidson *et al.*, 2007; Spaniol, 2008).

Strategies for implementing recovery

'If adopted successfully and comprehensively the concept of recovery could transform mental health services and unlock the potential of thousands of people experiencing mental distress. Services should be designed to support this directly and professionals should be trained to help people to reach a better quality of life. This will mean substantial change for many organizations and individuals.'

(Future Vision Coalition, 2009, p. 23)

The position paper 'A Common Purpose' describes the background to a recovery approach to mental health care, but expressly not a recovery 'model'. The authors

make the point that offering a checklist or targets would also be somewhat disso-
nant with a 'recovery-based approach', which emphasises collaborative working
and the value of those involved taking responsibility for working out actions,
implications and consequences at a more local and personal level (CSIP, 2007,
p. 24). This feature of recovery makes it both liberating and an immense challenge
to services. Services often want clear models of implementation that explain what
to do, when, and how. At the core of recovery approaches are the service users
and how they want to be supported to progress. Any service model that is consistent with a recovery approach needs to derive from the views of service users and
the staff who work with them. These are likely to vary according to the location
and specific needs of the service user group and the staff complement.

The scale of organizational change anticipated by the Future Vision Coalition
statement, and others like it (Maddock and Hallam, 2010), is the difference between
piecemeal improvements to clinical practice and a service adopting recovery as a
whole systems approach. Of course, changing clinical practice is at the heart of the
recovery approach, and the reason why the Shepherd, Boardman and Slade (2008)
emphasizes the priority of education in organizational change. However, changing
the practice of each profession and clinical team in a service requires systemic
change in many facets of the organization. This is because instead of the process of
implementing a new model or set of instructions, services are charged with reviewing all aspects of service delivery through a recovery lens and from the perspective
of the receiver of the service. We will highlight a selection of themes, starting with
the entry of a new member of staff into the organization:

- Recruitment: service user inclusion on interview panels, service user and
  recovery considerations in the skills and competencies assessed, service user
  recruitment onto staff teams.
- Induction programmes and in-service training programmes: the wide inclusion of service users, developing a new knowledge base and associated
  material, new skills and competencies. Workforce training and continuing
  professional development built around recovery principles.
- Guidance on changing the ways in which clinical reports and care plans are
  written in terms of language and service user participation.
- Guidance on partnership working in risk assessment and risk management,
  and new staff guidance and competencies in managing this effectively.
- Clinical skills and competencies for recovery-oriented care in forensic settings.
- Service information documents that reflect the priorities and commitments of
  the recovery approach in the service.
- New roles for service users in the development, operation and evaluation of
  the service.
- New roles and posts: peer support worker posts, participation lead roles,
  recovery champions, service user consultant supervisor, peer support worker
  coordinator and peer support worker trainer or supervisor.
- New intervention programming: service user participation in scheduling and
  facilitating groupwork programmes, involvement in developing materials,

new types of interventions, new types of vocational and educational opportunities.

- Care/Recovery planning: service user-led care and recovery planning, enhanced partnership working with staff, involvement of carers.
- Appraisal: the integration of recovery skills and goals, recovery approach priorities and service user feedback into staff appraisal.
- Policy and protocol development in line with changing practice, including service user views.
- Outcome measurement (e.g. PROMs) and audit priorities and processes.
- Service evaluation and research: service user participation in choosing priorities and active engagement in undertaking projects.

The scope and multiple facets of organizational change that are possible from a thoroughgoing project to implement a recovery approach are vast. The Star Wards initiative (Janner, 2006) identified three levels of change that can be brought about though changing practice: tweaking, turning and, like the Centre for Mental Health, transforming. Working through each of these areas would be very likely to take a service beyond tweaking and turning in the direction of transformation. Leadership, direction and support for innovation are, however, imperative to initiate change (Maddock and Hallam, 2010).

Leadership and building the vision

Our experience has been that it is difficult to begin with formulating a 'mission statement' to implement recovery in any particular organization. There are two earlier steps that are necessary to build the capacity to formulate a vision. The first is that some form of identified leadership is necessary to begin the organizational work. Leadership needs to be of sufficient seniority, with sufficient access to managerial decision-making and resource utilisation, to be effective. While perhaps less imperative, but worth noting, two or more people in joint leadership roles may be more effective than one person. The scale of the task and the risk of marginalisation as a 'recovery zealot' are too great for a single person to be solely responsible, and partnership working at a leadership level is important to success. It is crucial that the leadership, however constituted, recognizes that the task of educating themselves about recovery and what it can mean for organizational transformation is substantial. The education has to start at the top before it can cascade. The development of a 'vision' needs to be held in some form by the leadership in order to begin to support the service to describe and embrace a shared vision. It may also be inadvisable to simply appoint an available member of staff to a key recovery leadership role. It may be important for the leadership to choose the role and not to be allocated to it as a task.

We are where we are

It is typical for a programmatic approach to implementing recovery to recommend an initial assessment or appraisal of the current stage of the service in relation to recovery. Many services that we have experience of have found that this is best achieved not through an external or 'expert' assessment, but through workshops and events that engage the staff who work at a 'grassroots', ward or practitioner level and with current and/or previous service users. Since recovery is mobilized through conversation, we should look for dialogue with people that promote recovery (Ashcraft and Anthony, 2009). It is important, first of all, that a vision or local interpretation of recovery is not imposed, but is seen to have been generated by the service itself, service users and staff. A vision needs to be grounded in a grasp of the complexities of what is involved, but also the continuities with good practice that already exists in the service. This promotes confidence and counters the fear that 'in the place of disempowered users we will end up with disempowered professionals' (Allott *et al.*, 2002). A number of services have used the approach of consulting with clients to look at what recovery means to them, what helps and hinders recovery as a way of examining the process of recovery, and looking at how the organization can change, for example Broadmoor Hospital (see Moore *et al.*, in this volume), Kent Forensic Services, South West London & St George's Forensic Services (Mezey *et al.*, 2010), South London & Maudsley Forensic Services, Farmfield Hospital in the Priory Group, and Sussex Forensic Service. Other services have held Recovery Awareness training events, often with external speakers or facilitators, as a starting point from promoting the understanding of recovery principles within the service as a whole.

An empirically based approach to the adoption of recovery in a service can involve undertaking a 'baseline' assessment of the current state of the service. This can also be undertaken after a period of work to get the service into a position to accept and support a baseline measure. This has been undertaken using the DREEM (Developing Recovery Enhancing Environments Measure) assessment (Ridgway and Press, 2001) (see Baker *et al.*, this volume; Corlett and Miles, 2010). This can be used to identify priority areas in which to target resources to bring about developments.

The second task of such an exercise would be to address the concerns of those within the service who are sceptical of the value of recovery, or who do not perceive a recovery orientation as any different to how services were structured and operated with a rehabilitation ethos. This is not only true of forensic services but has been noted in mainstream adult mental health as well (Reynolds and O'Hanlon, 2011). This requires the gradual untangling of misunderstandings amongst professionals and service users 'divided by a common language'. This will involve acknowledging the need for risk and security considerations to be clearly held in mind so that the balance of containment and support is maintained, even while possibly beginning to shift the means by which that balance is maintained. It is essential not to alienate the more security-focused staff in this process. The recovery focus on service user strengths can be taken to mean a neglect of vulnerability, and in our experience even the service users we consulted were concerned that their 'weaknesses' would not be recognized in a rush to emphasise strengths, and that this would retard their progress. They quite rightly recognized that it was their 'weaknesses' and not their 'strengths' that had brought them to hospital, and which held back their return to the community.

The third important task of having a process by which recovery is seeded in the organization, is that it can allow staff and service users to express their disillusionment and disappointments at how things have been. This is crucial to initiate the process of recovery in the organization as a whole. All forensic mental health services will carry the history of failed initiatives, hard lessons learnt through serious untoward incidents and occasionally the external scrutiny and criticism they bring. It is inevitable in a forensic service that there will be a degree of risk-averse attitudes and behaviours as 'best defensive practice' becomes the means of survival in the organization and in the face of the pressures created by the nature of the work. In our experience it has been important to recognize and accommodate processes in response to a shift towards the values and principles of recovery that parallel the service users in staff teams and the organization as a whole.

As a result of these initial exercises, services have developed their own versions of recovery principles (Law, 2008) or their own philosophy of care documents.

Building organizational structures

Out of the initial consultation process with the organization, a form of organizational framework to direct and oversee the implementation of recovery needs to be agreed. This will evolve over time as the project of implementing recovery develops, and can take the form of a steering group. Some services have explicitly subsumed a social inclusion dimension into this structure. Good multi-disciplinary representation and service user representation, preferably involving more than one service user at any one time, terms of reference and a strategy or action plan will be needed. External stakeholder representation can be considered. In the Sussex Forensic Services it suited our service not to restrict membership of the steering group, but rather to be as inclusive as possible in order to promote interest and ownership at all levels of the organization. As the Forensic Services in Sussex cover a large geographical area, meetings were held at different sites, with the host site giving presentations about progress. The meetings gave each unit of the service opportunities to swap ideas, share good practice and common approaches across each area, whilst still allowing each unit to maintain their own unique approach to recovery in line with their particular client group, resources and setting.

A steering group for recovery implementation can also include therapeutic activity coordination functions. This can assist with embedding recovery principles in daily practice, as well as with resource allocation and prioritisation. Large services may continue to operate separate groups for these functions but their links need to be clear and their activities well-coordinated. It is helpful for separate therapeutic activity coordination groups to report into the steering group. The steering group can then report upwards in the organization to an overall governance group or directorate management team, ideally through overlapping membership.

The work of a steering group is greatly enhanced by ward or team-level implementation groups, supported by identified recovery champions or 'culture carriers'. The Hampshire Forensic Service benefited from appointing a recovery nurse on each ward, for example.[3] The work of these smaller working groups can then be brought together and coordinated. Some services which have taken up recovery have chosen to start on a smaller scale with a particular ward, often a rehabilitation ward. The development experience of that ward or team can then be generalised to other wards or parts of the service. This form of 'bottom-up' approach has its limitations and can delay the recognition that a much larger scale of change throughout the organization may be possible. Service developments can also be led through what is sometimes referred to as clinical improvement groups that are ward- or unit-based.

It is imperative that role modelling of service user participation is integral to the operation of a steering group or other structures that implement recovery. Embedding service user participation in all aspects of the service will be a key task for a steering group. The many ways in which service users can take on involvement and participation roles in the forensic organization are expanded upon in Anita Bowser's chapter (this volume). Through the creation of service user consultant posts (with job descriptions, interview selection and formal one-to-one supervision in the role) the overall contribution of service users to the running of the service can be greatly enhanced. This can facilitate the development and sustaining of service user participation in the group treatment and activity programme, the development of new initiatives, audit and evaluation, and policy development.

The functions of a steering group

The task of leading the implementation of a recovery approach requires a great deal of focused activity outside of formal steering group meetings. There is also a need to integrate the implications of the changes across multiple domains of the organization, and broad-based support for this within the organization is essential. The steering group is, however, a hub to bring about change. Our experience of the functions of a steering group include many strands across a service.

We have found that the production of an annual report with an overview of recovery developments across the service, including a report on service user consultants, is an important way in which all staff and service users can see how their contribution fits within the whole, and how the whole can be more than the sum of its parts in the sense of momentum and direction in a service. (See the Appendix to this chapter – the contents page of the Sussex Forensic Service 'Secure Recovery Annual Report 2010' – as an illustration of the scope and breadth of the recovery implementation tasks in the third year of implementation.)

Keeping the momentum going

It is all too easy to lose initial momentum in developing a service model to implement recovery, particularly at times of increasing financial pressures and

Table 4.1 The functions of a steering group

- Identifying potential service innovations, scoping the possibilities for implementation, creating capacity and integration of service innovations;
- conceptual discussions regarding the meaning and interpretation of recovery in the service in order to develop a robust capacity to grasp the vision and support it into action;
- moral support when there are discouragements, inevitable frustrations and bureaucratic obstacles;
- supporting the maintenance of a dual awareness of recovery and the need to maintain security and manage risk;
- oversight of implementation and sustaining of service user participation across the service;
- forming and coordinating the work of local implementation groups;
- integration of recovery principles into the therapeutic groupwork and therapeutic activity programmes;
- the need to respond to and integrate into the programme of work external drivers from commissioners, peer networks and quality networks;
- leading the development of induction and training to provide recovery training and integrate recovery principles into all other training;
- introducing or supporting new educational and vocational initiatives;
- dissemination of relevant publications, literature relevant to service users;
- initiating, planning, directing and co-ordinating the organization of service-wide events and activities (such as an annual conference, a service-wide newsletter, resident induction materials);
- identifying and supporting attendance of recovery champions and other staff members or service users at national training or workshop events.

competing demands to implement regulatory and commissioning requirements. Taking on board and meaningfully engaging with a diverse and often critical range of service user views regarding the service is itself demanding and requires sustained commitment and time. It has often felt like the easy option would be to direct from the centre and not to consult or ask for the views of others. The rewards of the inclusive approach in terms of quality and ownership make the effort worthwhile.

Maintaining initial enthusiasm and commitment requires the leads to maintain the profile of the recovery agenda in the organization. This can be done through, for example, publicizing achievements and examples of good practice, informing residents and staff of what has been achieved through posting updates on notice boards and highlighting progress. Finding new ways to enthuse staff and residents, promoting hopefulness and optimism, and stimulating interest are key tasks. We have found that a programme of annual events, including an in-house conference, a summer activity week, an evaluation week with feedback to each unit in the subsequent week, external speakers and visits all contribute towards sustaining momentum.

A place to start

Forensic services tend to value stability above all else. This is for good reasons to do with the needs of their service users. For this reason it is to be expected that forensic services may wish to introduce recovery-oriented practice in an incremental way that maintains continuity with what went before. A service may support recovery-oriented practice at the level of the individual practitioner, through for example endorsing Sainsbury Centre tips for individuals. A service may also promote recovery-oriented practice more broadly through developing service user participation, using recovery plans, implementing a ward climate measure, perhaps even identifying recovery champions at ward level and so forth. This may not, however, mean that a service has adopted a recovery approach. Recovery as a service approach to providing forensic mental health care will require that the whole system changes, at all levels of an organization, in order to embrace the approach, and work through its implications.

Acknowledgements

We are grateful to the members of the Recovery in Forensic Settings Network for sharing their experiences of developing recovery with their services and for helping us to develop some of the ideas expressed in this chapter.

Appendix: Secure Recovery Annual Report 2010

Notes

1 Helen Miles, personal communication.
2 http://rcpsych.ac.uk/pdf/Key%20Findings.pdf. Accessed 21 May 2011.
3 Helen Eunson and Suzanne Sambrooke, personal communication.

References

Adshead, G. (2004) 'Three degrees of security: Attachment and forensic institutions'. In F. Pfafflin and G. Adshead (eds), *A matter of security: The application of Attachment Theory to forensic psychiatry and psychotherapy*. London: Jessica Kingsley Publishers.

Aiyegbusi, A. (2009) 'The nurse-patient relationship with offenders: Containing the unthinkable to promote recovery'. In A. Aiyegbusi and J. Clarke-Moore (eds), *Therapeutic relationships with offenders: An introduction to the psychodynamics of mental health nursing*. London: Jessica Kingsley Publishers.

Akhtar, S. (1996) '"Someday..." And "If Only..." Fantasies: Pathological optimism and inordinate nostalgia as related forms of idealization'. *Journal of the American Psychoanalytic Association*, 44: 723–753.

Allott, P., Loganathan, L. and Fulford, K. (2002) 'Discovering hope for recovery: a review of a selection of recovery literature'. *Canadian Journal of Community Mental Health*, 21(3): 1–22.

Ashcraft, L. and Anthony, W. A. (2006) 'Factoring in Structure'. *Behavioral Healthcare*, August, pp. 16–18.

Ashcraft, L. and Anthony, W. (2009) 'What a recovery organization looks like: targets you should aim for to promote people's healing'. *Behavioral Healthcare*, 29(6): 10–13.

—— (2010) 'Tools for Transforming Facilities: our columnists pinpoint exterior and interior design strategies that promote recovery'. *Behavioral Healthcare*, 30(5): 10–13.

Bartlett, A. and McGauley, G. (2010) *Forensic Mental Health: Concepts, systems, and practice*. Oxford University Press: Oxford.

Blumenthal, S. (2010) 'A psychodynamic approach to working with offenders: an alternative to moral orthopaedics'. In A. Bartlett and G. McGauley (eds), *Forensic Mental Health: Concepts, systems, and practice*. Oxford University Press: Oxford.

Bose, S. (2009) 'Containment and the structured day'. In A. Aiyegbusi and J. Clarke-Moore (eds), *Therapeutic relationships with offenders: An introduction to the psychodynamics of mental health nursing*. London: Jessica Kingsley Publishers.

Bowers, L. (2002) *Dangerous and Severe Personality Disorder: Reactions and Role of the Psychiatric Team*. London: Routledge.

Campling, P., Davies, S. and Farquharson, G. (eds) (2004) *From toxic institutions to therapeutic environments: residential settings in mental health services*. London: Gaskell.

Care Services Improvement Partnership, Royal College of Psychiatrists and Social Care Institute for Excellence. (2007) *A Common Purpose: Recovery in Future Mental Health Services*. CSIP, Royal College of Psychiatrists and SCIE.

College of Occupational Therapists. (2007) *Recovering Ordinary Lives: The Strategy for Occupational Therapy in Mental Health Services 2007–2017*. College of Occupational Therapists.

Corlett, H. and Miles, H. (2010) 'An evaluation of the implementation of the recovery philosophy in a secure forensic service'. *British Journal of Forensic Practice*, 12(4): 14–25.

Davidson, L., Tondora, J. and O'Connell, M. J. (2007) 'Creating a recovery-oriented system of behavioral healthcare: Moving from concept to reality'. *Psychiatric Rehabilitation Journal*, 31(1): 23–31.

Davies, R. (1996) 'The inter-disciplinary network and the internal world of the offender'. In C. Cordess and M. C. Cox, C. M (eds) *Forensic psychotherapy: psychodynamics and the offender patient*. London: Jessica Kingsley Publishers.

Deegan, P. E. (1988) 'Recovery: The lived experience of rehabilitation'. *Psychosocial Rehabilitation Journal*, 11(4): 11–19.

Department of Health (1992) *Report of the Committee of Inquiry into Complaints about Ashworth Hospital.* Volume I & II. London: HMSO.

—— (2001) *The journey to Recovery – The Government's vision for mental health care.* London: Department of Health.

—— (2008a) *High Quality Care For All.* London: HMSO.

—— (2008b) *Using the Commissioning for Quality and Innovation (CQuIN) payment framework for the NHS in England.* London: Department of Health.

—— (2009) *New Horizons: A shared vision for mental health.* London: Mental Health Division, Department of Health.

—— (2010) *See Think Act.* London: Department of Health.

Fallon, P., Bluglass, R., Edwards, B. and Daniels, G. (1999) *Report of the Committee of Inquiry into the Personality Disorder Unit, Ashworth Special Hospital.* London: Stationary Office.

Future Vision Coalition. (2009) *A future vision for mental health.* London: NHS Confederation.

Harrison, T. (2006) 'Rolling the stone uphill: Leadership, management and long-term mental health care'. In G. Roberts, S. Davenport and F. Holloway (eds) *Enabling Recovery: The Principles and Practice of Psychiatric Rehabilitation.* London: Gaskell Publications.

Janner, M. (2006) *Star Wards.* London: Bright. http://www.brightplace.org.uk/starwards.html

Kanwal, G. S. (1997) 'Hope, respect, and flexibility in the psychotherapy of Schizophrenia'. *Contemporary Psychoanalysis*, 33: 133–150.

Law, K. (2008) *Ten recovery principles.* Unpublished manuscript, Farmfield Hospital, Surrey.

MacKeith, J. and Burns, S. (2011) *The Recovery Star.* 2nd edition. London: Triangle Consulting & the Mental Health Providers Forum. http://www.mhpf.org.uk/recoveryStarResources.asp. Accessed 25 May 2011.

Maddock, S. and Hallam, S. (2010) *Recovery begins with hope.* London: Centre for Mental Health.

Mezey, G. C., Kavuma, M., Turton, P., Demetriou, A. and Wright, C. (2010) Perceptions, experiences and meanings of recovery in forensic psychiatric patients. *The Journal of Forensic Psychiatry & Psychology*, 21(5): 683–696.

Motz, A. (2008) The place of psychotherapy in forensic settings. *Psychiatry*, 7(5): 195–230.

National Institute For Mental Health in England. (2005) *NIHME Guiding Statement on Recovery.* London: DoH Publications.

NHS London. (2006) *Report of the independent inquiry into the care and treatment of John Barrett.* http://www.london.nhs.uk/publications/independent-publications/independent-inquiries

—— (2009) *Independent inquiry into the care and treatment of Peter Bryan.* http://www.london.nhs.uk/publications/independent-publications/independent-inquiries

NHS South East Coast. (2009) *An independent investigation into the care and treatment of Daniel Gonzales.* http://www.london.nhs.uk/publications/independent-publications/independent-inquiries

Phillips, N. (ed.) (2010) *Standards for People with Learning Disabilities in Medium Secure Care.* London: Royal College of Psychiatry Centre for Quality Improvement.

Reynolds, T. and O'Hanlon, L. (2011) 'Recovery-focused practice in mental health services'. *Mental Health Practice*, 14(7): 25–26.

Ridgway, P. and Press, A. (2001) *Assessing the Recovery-Commitment of your Mental Health Service: A user's guide for the Developing Recovery Enhancing Environments Measure (DREEM)*. UK pilot version 1. Sourced from http://www.recoverydevon.co.uk. Accessed November 2008.

Royal College of Psychiatry. (2007) *Standards for medium secure units*. London: RCPsych.

Sainsbury Centre for Mental Health. (2009) *Implementing Recovery: A new framework for organizational change*. Position paper. London: Sainsbury Centre for Mental Health.

Schalast, N., Redies, M. Collins, M. Stacey, J. and Howells, K. (2008) 'EssenCES, a short questionnaire for assessing the social climate of forensic psychiatric wards'. *Criminal Behaviour and Mental Health*, 18: 49–58.

Shepherd, G. (2006) 'Mapping and Classifying Rehabilitation Services'. In G. Roberts, S. Davenport and F. Holloway (eds) *Enabling Recovery: The Principles and Practice of Psychiatric Rehabilitation*. Royal College of Psychiatrists/Gaskell Publications, London.

Shepherd, G., Boardman, J. and Slade, M. (2008) *Making recovery a reality*. London: Sainsbury Centre for Mental Health.

Shepherd, G., Boardman, J. and Burns, M. (2010) *Implementing Recovery: A methodology for organizational change*. London: Sainsbury Centre for Mental Health.

Slade, M. (2009) *Personal Recovery and Mental Illness: A Guide for Mental Health Professionals*. Cambridge: Cambridge University Press.

Spaniol, L. (2008) 'What Would a Recovery-Oriented Program Look Like?' *International Journal of Psychosocial Rehabilitation*, 13(1): 57–66.

Tucker, S. and Reeve-Hoyland, M. (2011) *Preliminary Findings: 5th Annual Cycle*. Presentation to the 5th Annual Forum, London, 13 April.

Vorhaus, P. G. (1977) 'The Development of optimism during therapy'. *Psychoanalytic Review*, 64: 455–459.

5 Giving voice to recovery

Perspectives from within a high secure hospital

*Estelle Moore, Darren Lumbard,
John Carthy, Joe Ayres, 19 hospital
residents and one former patient*

Introduction

'Being detained in high security is the lowest point...'

There is one thing about high security hospital that probably unites the public, the staff *and* its residents: high security represents the end of the road, it is the 'last chance saloon' for people who have transgressed interpersonal, community and legal boundaries.

There are different wards/units within the external walls of a high security hospital, with various functions. Living on an intensive care ward could mean having to ask for soap to wash your hands, and being required to wait for every door to be opened before and closed after you. Whereas, with parole access from an 'assertive rehabilitation' ward, you could walk freely on a terrace at designated times. The hospital's purpose in protecting the public is also to ensure that risk is reduced to a minimum *within* the walls, and that action is taken to promote ongoing risk management when an individual leaves.

From the point of entry to such a place, significant aspects of personal responsibility are temporarily suspended and taken over by others (Roberts *et al.*, 2008). As a consequence, multiple layers of intervention are required to counteract forces of despair. We list here some of the key 'ingredients' of an admission to high security, alongside a comment on each from the reflections of a former high secure hospital patient.

Working alliances are a primary mechanism of change (Adshead, 1998; Repper *et al.*, 1994), wherein support and understanding can be communicated. It takes time and mutual respect for these to develop healthily (Moore *et al.*, 2002).

> 'Recovery, without the heart, is an intellectual exercise, another wall to run into for a patient. At all levels of the system, be the person working as a cleaner or a consultant, the heart is king, there is no faking it in its healing capacity. I have met professionals from all levels and this is exactly what I found. A cleaner could be more helpful than the most highly qualified consultant.

In fact, when professionals base their skills on intellect and status alone, they often end up as another brick in the wall, another dead end to run into in the search for healing.

When I was in hospital I was very fortunate or fated to find someone who provided that level of care. Through her close support over three years I was able to leave the hospital and come out of the devastation of my psyche that resulted from my childhood, the illness, and the violence I committed and from then being in an environment which I experienced as horrendous.

Caring is simple, it is not necessarily easy. The young woman who cared for me was made like that; she was very gifted where others are not. She understood what was needed and she could provide it. At the time, it seemed to me that she was the heart of the ward and that both the staff and patients responded to her very well indeed. She had universal traits of holding others in high esteem that are invaluable anywhere.'[1]

Medication can provide relief from distressing symptoms. Pharmaceutical management of symptoms, generally a primary role for doctors in the rehabilitation of offenders with mental disorder (Gunn and Taylor, 1993), often assumes primacy in the multi-disciplinary discourse about what works in forensic units (Davies *et al.*, 2007).

'Recovery is not medical although it might use western medicine as one of the tools of recovery. It is based on finding what heals you and that can be as diverse as fishing, psychotherapy, work, family, a spiritual practice or simply employment. Drugs only offer so much. This has been understood at well equipped secure hospitals for decades.'

Specific therapies in emotional (Cordess and Cox, 1996), cognitive (Wykes, 2006), physical, social, interpersonal (Repper and Perkins, 2003), 'criminogenic' (McGuire, 2002), supportive, spiritual, rehabilitative (Roberts *et al.*, 2006; Brown, 2001; Randal *et al.*, 2003), vocational and educational domains, all play a part in addressing complex needs (Glorney *et al.*, 2010).

'Meaningful diverse activities are essential for recovery...Football, cricket, summer fetes, drama, education, discos, church, gym, swimming, domestic work, gardening, cookery, shopping, and art all go on. These are really helpful, although I recall a friend who took part in very little of this abundance but gained insight into his life by studying the characters from EastEnders and Coronation Street and now lives a relatively successful life. One size does not fit all.'

This chapter is not seeking to make a display of all these contributions, despite their importance; our goal is to share the views of current service users about their experience of recovery in the context of detention. The term 'recovery' only comparatively recently infiltrated general parlance at Broadmoor, though elements of recovery are possibly implicit in much of the activity mentioned above. We took this opportunity to ask high security experts by experience for their reflections via a series of focus groups. Our invitation is presented below.

We invite you to:

- *Consider the meaning of the word recovery*
- *Reflect on your experiences in forensic settings in light of this word*
- *Comment on links if any between illness/mental disorder, offending and recovery*
- *Comment on what might hinder or assist your recovery*
- *Share thoughts on the ways in which you might measure your own success.*

In collaboration

Using the invitation above, staff in Broadmoor Hospital's Centralised Groupwork Service (CGS) ran three 90-minute focus groups. This method of data collection was selected for its flexibility and capacity to elicit people's understanding and views (Wilkinson, 2008). The groups were facilitated by an experienced team of 'moderators' who presented the same invitation on each occasion, piloted for relevance and style via individual interviews.

We listed all the residents in the hospital in 2009, and randomly generated sub-lists of the names of eight to approach as participants who were representative of the total population, including those new to the hospital, those in the middle of their admission and some further along their rehabilitation pathway. Five of the eight on two occasions, and six on another, attended on the day. Non-attenders reported that they had changed their minds about participating and/or were unwell. All (but one) gave their consent for the audio taping of the group for transcription purposes. One group session was therefore not recorded; we took notes instead.

Because we work within the setting, it is inevitable that we have not accessed the fullest range of possible views: those of the more disenfranchised are likely to be under-represented. We appreciate that service users are not completely free to fully express their views about a system which is inclined to interpret opposition as a symptom of illness or criminality. In order to take this into account, we ensured that the facilitators were as independent as possible of teams responsible for ongoing care and that we actively sought out the views of three 'reluctant' service recipients (who had declined to attend groups) and met them individually.

We submitted each transcript to a content review, using thematic analysis steps described by Braun and Clarke (2006). Data codings were interpreted into (five) overarching themes by coherence of pattern and content. The themes were rechecked against the data to ensure their accurate representation and support via quotation evidence.

We further acknowledge that in the process of drawing this chapter together, we have selected some elements over others from the discussions we have had. In order to counteract any bias in this filtering process, we have re-presented the material to a sample of the focus group participants, and their opinions have further shaped the information in the following text. The quotations in speech marks throughout are the contributions of patients as recorded verbatim.

Group members spoke about: the impact of their environment; key elements in their recovery journeys from the point of admission; what works to support recovery; their experience of living with an offence history; barriers to recovery; and finally their observations on risk.

Living behind two 30-feet-high perimeter fences

'You can't underestimate how much the system can penetrate you'

Life behind bars is about loss: of freedom, family, companionship, company, self-esteem, status, options, and choices (Zamble and Porporino, 1990). On reading this chapter after the group, one contributor commented:

> 'You've got to realise, happiness is something you can't buy, they don't sell it in the supermarket...this place is sad. Sad for yourself, sad for victims, their family and your own family.'

Detention for those held under restriction (the majority in high security) is overseen by the Ministry of Justice, whose primary responsibility is to victims past and future. Living with mental illness, and/or other disorders that describe perpetrators of offences as 'abnormal', inevitably demands adjustment to changes and can be redefining of personhood and possibility:

> 'It's hard to relax or be yourself when you are always being watched, analysed.'

Physical security measures in 'maximally secure' forensic settings (cameras, room searches, Level 1 security checks) are present as reinforcers of these identities and associated segregations in all internal buildings, even though the height and monitoring of the perimeter fences was intended to empower some freedom of movement within the walls (Tilt *et al.*, 2000). There are restrictions on families and friends who visit, particularly with regard to what they are allowed to bring with them. There are restrictions on patients leaving the hospital, even for planned rehabilitative contact with relatives. Access to IT and the number of possessions/purchases each person is allowed are all governed by security policy and procedure. Staff are no more trusted than patients (Taylor and Dunn, 2006). Despite the comparative freedoms conferred by their badges, keys and pouches, they too are routinely searched on their way in and out. All this, designed to enhance and maintain safety, can equally present barriers. If there is a well-guarded recovery-oriented system of care, supported at each level of the organisation (Ashcroft and Anthony, 2006), necessary institutional practices and procedures should not derail efforts to rehabilitate (Stowers *et al.*, 2009).

In the main, security was accepted as a 'given': 'after a couple of years you get used to it'. The service users' focus was more on distinguishing individual identities (preferred and otherwise) for themselves within the internal society of the hospital, and in the communities that they had been excluded from. Comment was passed on the intensity of the experience of 'living in a gold-fish bowl':

> 'Every move you make, everything you say, the way you walk, the way you talk, you see them analysing things all the time.'
> 'It can be like an environmental game of snakes and ladders – those snakes will be yourself, the environment, socials, medication…the closer you get to the end without having a snake that is going to put your ass at square one, the better.'

Hence we became aware of the acute tension for service users in high security between their experience of 'treatment', and 'clinical' recovery, and their personal experience of changes in their relationship to their problems.

Settling in: 'You tend to lose self-respect in a place like this…'

Recalling the time of their arrival, patients described the experience of having to 'get [their] heads round' being in high security: how it is different from prison and other hospitals, and in what ways it is similar, 'how people treat you, what the expectations of the place are'.

The importance of the provision of information was highlighted:

> 'I really wanted information about my diagnosis.…but I don't think I would have been able to remember it if I had been given it on admission.'

'…and anyway your diagnosis can change,' agreed several in the group. Also common is the experience that fears about the hospital are worse than the reality of the day-to-day existence:

> 'I really didn't want to come here.…but it's not so bad as I feared.'

For this reason:

> 'it helps to see people further along the recovery conveyor belt'. 'Seeing people get out is an inspiration. People doing well here are role models.'

What is recovery? A 'journey – it's about learning to walk again'

Several focus group participants observed the many differences between themselves and others similarly diagnosed, and yet it was a common feeling that living in hospital requires each patient to identify with his diagnoses and act accordingly. This is not surprising, given that the 'clinical' model of mental illness is the dominant explanatory framework for making sense of unusual mental experiences (Slade, 2009), heavily drawn upon in forensic services. There are, however, individual costs associated with non-conformity: 'In this system, there is no room to disagree. It seems like you either agree with the doctors or you are in a very bad situation where you can't win.'

The definitions of 'recovery' shared by those in the focus groups who described themselves as mentally ill tended to impart a 'getting back to normal' theme, consonant with a 'clinical' interpretation of what recovery is (for patients with mental disorder). For at least one person, recovery is about 'becoming like your average Joe'. For another, it is: 'not going back to a previous state, it's about growth'. One of the most thought-provoking definitions came from a patient with a history of residence in high security hospitals of over twenty years. He said:

> 'recovery is not the same as discharge and release...it means being healthy in yourself, not being a prisoner in your own mind.'

The role and impact of taking prescribed medication was an experience in common for the majority. Some focus group participants reported finding it very difficult to accept the unwanted effects: 'medication actually hinders my engagement'. 'But it can also help', another added.

Therefore, illness/diagnosis has a profound, all-encompassing and defining impact on every aspect of life in the hospital. For most, it also distinguishes the nature of the recovery journey.

For those living with symptoms of psychosis, recovery can be about 'alleviating or diluting symptoms', whereas for those with a diagnosis of personality disorder 'it's about discovery'. One discussion about this ran as follows:

Contributor A, a man with a diagnosis of Dissocial Personality Disorder and a history of offending that included rape and murder:

> 'Recovery depends on the individual...at the end of the day, going back [to re-cover your wellbeing] is not curing anything...recovery means two different things for personality disorder and mental illness...'

Contributor B, a man with a diagnosis of Paranoid Schizophrenia and a history of offending that included manslaughter:

> 'If you got something wrong with your personality, you can't really recover from that...'

Contributor A:

> 'No, but you can change it...if it's a personality disorder which has an effect on yourself and others, then you need to change that...so it is about discovery.'

Ingredients of (high secure) recovery: readiness and honesty – 'You have to be in a state of readiness to be able to consider explanations'

Patients in the focus groups were clear that recovery implies personal growth:

> 'You automatically change when you come into a situation like this, you change your views...to say you were going back to how you were before would be ignoring such an important experience because you don't come here for no reason.'

Different understandings of recovery, with the most contrasting being clinical versus personal recovery, have been articulated by Slade (2009). The patients who spoke with us most richly and spontaneously described *personal* recovery: 'your inner journey, physical freedom, mental and spiritual world, you never fulfil... your own individual path where your judgement is best.' Several mentioned a need for self-acceptance: 'you need to forgive yourself and move on'; 'you have to be honest with yourself and open with doctors'; 'honesty can set you back, but you need it to move forwards'. This may be a dimension of particular relevance to offenders with mental health needs who have to trust others with information not only about mental illness, but also about their offending, and often very detailed and personal aspects of their lives: 'your offence never leaves you'.

The role of hope: 'the only way is up'

The stage for aggression is set when losses, fears and threats activate feelings of anger and a retaliatory attack (on the self in suicide, or against others) is mobilised as a solution (Hillbrand and Young, 2008). This process was related by focus group participants via their description of hope, defined as 'having something to live for':

> 'I've seen people fight staff over small things...but there are people that have been in the system so long and have been told they are not getting out, so they've got nothing to lose.'
>
> 'If you can look to the future without saying I am not even going to bother going there because I am going to fall on my ass, when you have got past certain issues you can be optimistic about your future.'

Despair is a familiar companion for many in high security. It can be experienced as 'contagious' for patients, but also for the staff who work with them if they identify with it (Hillbrand and Young, 2008):

> 'When you are put at the bottom you start to care less, do careless acts. If people are told they are not getting out, the hospital can't really do anything for them, they've got nothing to lose.'

One focus group member described his struggle with depression and his inclination when depressed to withdraw from treatment into social isolation:

> 'I do not want to lower the mood of the room, but I am unable to shed the skin of my past, and make my own destiny. I can cope with the dice that has been thrown for me, but I will always be held with chains from the past. My inner self is in tangles…and I have done bad things…I live in an existence within an existence.'

Listening, a peer added:

> 'You know you are at the bottom of the pile here, you can't get much further down, so you know going up is the only step.'

What works? 'Whose job is it to recover my life?'

Some focus group members took the opportunity to comment on the interventions that had assisted them in making changes (such as particular therapies), but the majority described how they had scripted this aspect of the recovery journey *themselves*:

> 'There is only so much that staff can do – you have to change your outlook.'
> 'Medication only does so much, the rest of it is acceptance.'
> 'I loved 23-hour bang up – it's therapeutic to be with your own time, you get the chance, whether you like it or not, to recover.'

Such comments seem to illuminate the 'innate healing mechanisms of the mind' described in personal accounts of recovery in the context of mental illness (Turner, 2009).

The idea that you get out what you put in to psychological work also emerged as a discussion point. Participants seemed to relate to the experience of 'jumping through hoops':

> 'You got a certificate to say you've done it, but it doesn't actually mean you've taken anything on board and accepted anything.'
> 'You got to be honest with yourself before you can go to the doctor anyhow.'
> 'Yes,' added another, 'for a time you have to surrender your autonomy, and trust that the system will give it back to you in better shape.'

Thus treatment that is enabling and self-change processes were seen to work together.

Several patients alluded to the value of the relationships they were forming with key people: 'it's important to share problems and to have someone to go to'; 'I was shocked by people wanting to help me – it turned out to be a blessing in disguise.'

Conversely, the absence of key alliances constitutes a missed opportunity:

> 'There are people on my ward, nursing staff even at team leader level, you don't see them interact, there is not time, and you are expecting someone to know you and you are also expected to have trust in somebody when you have problems and difficulties...I've barely had a conversation with these people in the five months that I have been there.'

Focus group participants appeared tolerant of this reality:

> 'That happens, you have to accept it...they have a lot of paperwork to do nowadays.'

But it is not without consequences:

> 'High case loads for [staff] impact on the time allocated to understanding patient needs. As a result they prescribe everything in their arsenal to the problems but miss the underlying issues.'

Barriers to recovery

Loss of individuality

The experience of being treated the same as others who you experience as *dissimilar* was raised in all three focus groups:

> 'We are all different, we all have different ideas about who we are', but in hospital: 'the foot has to fit the shoe, otherwise it is made to fit.'

The loss of individuality in the tension to conform had presented a barrier to recovery for several participants over the duration of their illness:

> 'Mental health institutions, especially high security, usually label somebody...well, unless you actually break the label down, say how this is how that person got to that stage, all you are doing is treating the label...'
>
> 'People should be treated as individual, and I think that's the problem...in the prison system, everyone is treated exactly the same, you get a number and you know that's it.'
>
> 'Each person's recovery is different, yet patients can be painted with the same diagnosis and treatment brush.'

The impact of stigma: 'it's all about exclusion here'

Internalised stigma (viewing the self as dangerous or incompetent), common among people with severe mental illness (Yanos *et al.*, 2008), is negatively related to hopefulness, self-esteem and social functioning (Lysaker *et al.*, 2007).

Occupying a position in/outside a community as a 'mentally disordered offender' carries enormous impact and this was keenly felt by several participants:

> 'There's a whole level of rejection about being here. You say, I've been in Broadmoor and people back up, leave you alone, don't talk to you, like it's a dirty word, an X on your back or something. You just have to wise up to how people are going to accept you – if they do accept you – you have to do a lot of work on accepting yourself.'

Treatment resistance: 'You can't recover from something you don't think you have'

Non-compliance in any health-related service is not celebrated, as it renders staff and patients impotent in relation to their respective responsibilities. Non-agreement is a stark and impasse-creating position for those who say they are not ill, and for those who claim innocence despite convictions for serious offending. This view was expressed in an individual interview:

> 'Recovery means nothing to me – recovery from what? I don't need groups, I don't need anything from anyone here, just a light so that I can see my books. Recovery for me would be being allowed to get on with my life.'

On reading this, a participant who had engaged in a focus group was moved to comment:

> 'I had that mentality for a long while on a previous ward...that was me for the first eight years. This is where a mentor scheme would be helpful, to help see the place from another perspective.'

There is a role for fellow patients (Faulkner and Morris, 2003; Spiers *et al.*, 2005), and also staff here: collusion with passivity and opting out is ironically tantamount to perpetuating detention (Roberts *et al.*, 2008). Breaking through denial, engagement and active coping are dimensions of recovery as identified by users of other psychiatric services (Ridgway, 2001; Ramon *et al.*, 2007):

> 'I would like to have more insight, by which I mean taking responsibility for my state of mind. It's easy to blame others for your problems, you do feel better if you take responsibility, other things you want fall in place if you take responsibility for your situation.'

Recovery-focused responses to dangerousness

'When recovery is taken away or told that it is hopeless, the risks increase'

It is well known that the events which precede admission to high security are typically chronically traumatic and/or acutely toxic, such that the patient has become irrevocably separated from the kinds of skills he needed to cope safely outside. Relationships (e.g. with extended family members) that survive a major trauma and the impact of rare and horrifying events (such as an offence) can take on a special significance and role in recovery (Stanton and Simpson, 2006). Sometimes virtually all contacts are severed. This creates a 'vacuum' which is high-risk due to the absence of potential stabilisers:

'Putting someone in a place like this makes them more dangerous in some ways because they have got less to care about. Their social integrity is in tatters so they might flip at any time.'

Can recovery as a guiding principle incorporate risk issues without committing 'doublethink' (that is, the simultaneous acceptance of contradictory beliefs)? (Mezey and Eastman, 2009). One participant put it like this:

'Trust in others to help you recover....trust should be based on an individual basis, so [you] can grow and find inner peace...it's hard to build up trust, more difficult to trust people as you are not trusted yourself.'

Others suggested valuing the dignity of risk and their being able to contribute to decisions about their future. The importance of emphasising the centrality of lived experience, and its role in the expression of distress, is underscored in the Tidal Model of care outlined by Barker (2003). The Tidal Model prompts staff to facilitate a high level of engagement with patients via individual and group processes, with the patient's story placed at centre stage, guiding care planning. In this way, the disempowerment engendered in the absence of a 'proper hearing' of the person's narrative of events preceding their admission, which is likely to be vital in engaging them in future work, can be avoided. Transparent practice emerges as having the potential to moderate risk within an institution. The co-authoring of risk strategies may support improved outcomes (Roberts *et al.*, 2008). Provided a risk-management plan is firmly in place, and the strategies proposed are not naïve, rigorous risk assessment can generate a platform *for* hope, as opposed to annihilating it.

There was acknowledgement in the focus groups that useful risk management would take some time:

'Rushing recovery in terms of moving on is not safe...wanting to recover too much can be a bad thing.'

Particularly given the uncertainties about risk prediction and staff confidence in this, which inevitably influences length of stay:

'It feels like the goal posts are always changing here...your life in high security is not your life.'

Society determines the offender as one who must walk with some shame thereafter. Often, the less comprehensible the offending act, the greater and more enduring the associated rejection: 'You can feel as if you are the victim when shame is forced upon you.' This may lead to a fear of, or reluctance to address, offending: 'opening up chapters like your index offence can slow down recovery.'

In summary, what have we learnt? Pointers for assertive action

It must be acknowledged that detained patients will have different levels of curiosity about themselves and their situation, which will impact on their interest in 'treatments' and on their recovery style (Startup *et al.*, 2006). Personal growth is likely to be associated with some hope, a sense of control and getting problems into perspective (Higginson and Mansell, 2008), and these processes will take longer for those who resent everything about their placement in a secure setting.

Overall, the patients contributing to the focus group work underscored the value of working together; the importance of a 'human face' component to their experience of high security (see Cook *et al.*, 2005). This resonates well with the 'academic' literature and practice-based recommendations. A focus on day-to-day interactions and the quality of experience is the number-one tip for the implementation of recovery (Sainsbury Centre for Mental Health, 2009). Given the need for balance and professionalism in alliances, forensic services place a significant extra demand on their staff to hold a therapeutic line at all times, compassionate yet not yielding to manipulation, clear and firm without resort to punishment during conflict.

Skilled and collaborative assessments, the promotion of opportunities for taking personal responsibility, therapies that promote insight and understanding, and valued social roles (which buffer against taking action without thought) are recovery promoters, if conducted with care. Intervening with only minimum compulsion, and where necessary, applies just as much in secure services as elsewhere (Slade, 2009). Expectations must be hopeful yet realistic. In the words of an experienced recipient of high security hospitals:

> 'Recovery means being healthy in yourself. Your heart can recover. Feeling good in a place like this is recovery, having a healthy heart.'

High security embodies the reality that compulsion can be necessary, but as a step in the direction of recovery, and possibly never as an end in itself.

We asked group participants: How might we take our recovery discussion forwards?

'We should make this information available to all new patients on the admission ward,' said a focus group member. 'Yeah, and give it to all the trainee staff,' others chuckled.

A range of 'recovery' interventions are in progress that should create a culture within which recovery will continue to thrive:

- Recovery is 'one of the principles of care that underpins the hospital's service model'.
- The Recovery and Social Inclusion Group supports the work of the hospital senior management team.
- Staff receive training on recovery and in generating recovery-focused care plans.
- The range of available treatments remains diverse and accessible, (such as groups on stigma and discrimination groups; recovery groups on high-dependency wards; reflective groups on offending).
- Increased time is allocated for reflection on wards.
- Forums for disseminating patient views to clinical staff have been created.
- Focus groups for staff have been organised.

Ensuring that service users are fully informed about interventions (including advantages and limitations) demands an acknowledgement from professionals that all is not known, and holding such uncertainty in mind can be unsettling. It is nevertheless probably the only sound basis for designing mental health services that people in need – and, we could add, for those 'at the end of the line', with *greatest* need – will want (Bentall, 2009).

Acknowledgements

We would like to thank James Tapp and Derya Ratip for the part they played in organising and analysing the focus group material.

Note

1 Excerpts taken from a speech entitled: 'Recovery Comes From Within', written by a former high secure hospital resident, delivered via audio-tape at a symposium on Assertive Rehabilitation in 2007.

References

Adshead, G. (1998) 'Psychiatric staff as attachment figures'. *British Journal of Psychiatry*, 172: 64–9.
Ashcraft, L. and Anthony, W. A. (2006) 'Factoring in structure: Recovery needs a solid foundation to take root'. *Behavioral Healthcare*, August, 16–18. http://www.behavioral.net
Barker, P. (2003) 'The Tidal Model: Psychiatric colonization, recovery and the paradigm shift in mental health care'. *International Journal of Mental Health Nursing*, 12: 96–102.
Bentall, R. (2009) *Doctoring the Mind: Why Psychiatric Treatments Fail.* London: Allan Lane.
Braun, V. and Clarke, V. (2006) 'Using thematic analysis in psychology'. *Qualitative Research in Psychology*, 3: 77–101.

Brown, C. (2001) (ed.) *Recovery and Wellness: Models of Hope and Empowerment for People with Mental Illness.* London: The Haworth Press.

Cook, N. R., Phillips, B. N. and Sadler, D. (2005) 'The Tidal Model as experienced by patients and nurses in a regional forensic unit'. *Journal of Psychiatric & Mental Health Nursing*, 12: 536–540.

Cordess, C. and Cox, C. M. (1996) *Forensic psychotherapy: psychodynamics and the offender patient.* London: Jessica Kingsley.

Davies, J., Howells, K. and Jones, L. (2007) 'Evaluating innovative treatments in forensic mental health. A role for single-case methodology?' *Journal of Forensic Psychiatry and Psychology*, 18(3): 353–367.

Faulkner, A. and Morris, B. (2003) *Expert Paper: User Involvement in Forensic Mental Health Research & Development.* Liverpool, UK: National Forensic Mental Health R&D Programme.

Glorney, E., Perkins, D. Adshead, G. McGauley, G. Murray, K. Noak, J. and Sichau, G. (2010) 'Domains of Need in a High Secure Hospital Setting: A Model for Streamlining Care and Reducing Length of Stay'. *International Journal of Forensic Mental Health*, 9(2): 138–148.

Gunn, J. and Taylor, P. J. (eds) (1993) *Forensic Psychiatry.* Oxford: Butterworh-Heinemann.

Higginson, S. and Mansell, W. (2008) 'What is the mechanism of psychological change? A qualitative analysis of 6 individuals who experienced personal change and recovery'. *Psychology & Psychotherapy, Theory, Research & Practice*, 81: 309–328.

Hillbrand, M. and Young, J. L. (2008) 'Instilling hope into forensic treatment: the antidote to despair and desperation'. *The Journal of the American Academy of Psychiatry and the Law,* 36: 90–4.

Lysaker, P. H., Davis, L. W. Waman, D. M. *et al.* (2007) 'Stigma, social function and symptoms in schizophrenia and schizo-affective disorder: Association across 6 months'. *Psychiatry Research*, 149: 89–95.

McGuire, J. (2002) (ed.) 'Offender *Rehabilitation and Treatment: Effective Programmes to Reduce Re-Offending'.* Chichester: Wiley.

Mezey, G. and Eastman, N. (2009) 'Choice and social inclusion in forensic psychiatry: acknowledging mixed messages and double think'. *Journal of Forensic Psychology & Psychiatry,* 20: 503–7.

Moore, E. Yates, M. Mallindine, C. *et al.* (2002) 'Expressed emotion between staff and patients in forensic services: changes in relationship status at 12 month follow up'. *Legal & Criminological Psychology,* 7: 203–218.

Ramon, S., Healy, B. and Renouf, N. (2007) 'Recovery from mental illness as an emergent concept and practice in Australia and the UK'. *International Journal of Social Psychiatry,* 53: 108–22.

Randal, P., Simpson, A. I. F. Laidlaw, T. (2003) 'Can recovery-focused multimodal psychotherapy facilitate symptom and function improvement in people with treatment-resistant psychotic illness? A comparison study'. *Australian and New Zealand Journal of Psychiatry,* 37: 720–727.

Repper, J., Ford, R. and Crooke, A. (1994) 'How can nurses build trusting relationships with people who have severe and long-term mental health problems? Experiences of case managers and their clients'. *Journal of Advanced Nursing*, 19: 1096–1104.

Repper, J. and Perkins, R. (2003) *Social Inclusion and Recovery: A Model for Mental Health Practice.* London: Balliere Tindall.

Ridgway, M. (2001) 'Re-storying psychiatric disability: learning from first person narrative accounts of recovery'. *Psychiatric Rehabilitation Journal,* 24: 335–343.

Roberts, G., Davenport, S., Holloway, F. and Tattan, T. (2006) *Enabling Recovery: The Principles and Practice of Rehabilitation Psychiatry.* London: Royal College of Psychiatrists.

Roberts, G., Dorkins, E., Wooldridge, J. and Hewis, E. (2008) 'Detained – what's my choice? Part 1' Discussion. *Advances in Psychiatric Treatment,* 14: 172–180.

Sainsbury Centre for Mental Health (2009) *Implementing Recovery. A new framework for organisational change.* London: Sainsbury Centre. http://www.scentre.org.uk

Slade, M. (2009) *Personal Recovery and Mental Illness: A Guide for Mental Health Professionals.* Cambridge: Cambridge University Press.

Spiers, S., Harvey, K. and Chilvers, C. (2005) 'Service user involvement in forensic mental health: Can it work?' *Journal of Forensic Psychiatry & Psychology,* 16: 211–220.

Stanton, J. and Simpson, A. F. (2006) 'The after-math: Aspects of recovery described by perpetrators of maternal filicide committed in the context of serious mental illness'. *Behavioural Sciences & the Law,* 24: 103–112.

Startup, M., Wilding, N. and Startup, S. (2006) 'Patient adherence in CBT for acute psychosis: the role of recovery style and working alliance'. *Behavioural & Cognitive Psychotherapy,* 34: 191–199.

Stowers, C., Blacker, R., Elliott, S. and Hayward, L. (2009) 'Recovery of what by whom?' *Clinical Psychology Forum,* 196: 50–53.

Taylor, P. J. and Dunn, E. (2006) 'Secure hospitals and hospital units in the UK and mainland Europe. Provisions for safe psychiatric assessment and treatment for people with major mental disorder who have committed serious offences and/or are considered to pose a risk of harm to others'. In D. Bertrand and G. Niveau (eds) *Medicine, Sante et Prison.* Medicine et Hygiene: Chene-Bourg, Switzerland.

Tilt, R., Perry, B., Martin, C. *et al.* (2000) *Report of the Review of Security at the High Security Hospitals.* London: Department of Health.

Turner, J. (2009) 'On recovery'. *Openmind,* 155: 10–11.

Wilkinson, S. (2008) 'Focus groups'. Chapter 9, pp. 186–206 in J. A. Smith (ed.) *Qualitative Psychology: A Practical Guide to Research Methods* II Edition. Sage: London.

Wykes, T. (2006) 'Cognitive rehabilitation'. In G. Roberts, S. Davenport, F. Holloway, and T. Tattan (eds) *Enabling Recovery: The Principles and Practice of Rehabilitation Psychiatry,* pp. 200–210. London: Royal College of Psychiatrists.

Yanos, P. T., Roe, D., Markus, K. and Lysaker, P. (2008) 'Pathways between internalised stigma and outcomes related to recovery in schizophrenia spectrum disorders'. *Psychiatric Services,* 59: 1437–1442.

Zamble, E. and Porporino, F. (1990) 'Coping, imprisonment and rehabilitation: some data and their implications'. *Criminal Justice & Behaviour,* 17: 53–70.

6 Recovery for men with cognitive difficulties and impulsive challenging behaviour in a high secure hospital

What does it mean and how do we promote it?

Patricia Abbott, Anthony Hague and Andre Jedrzejcyk

Introduction

Hope is always necessary but often insufficient. The hopeful stance must be combined with ever-expanding psychiatric rehabilitation technology. Hope and advance in technology are intimately related. Hope begets new technology and new technology begets hope.

(Anthony *et al.*, 2004)

The Cognitive Rehabilitation Service (CRS) at Ashworth High Secure Hospital provides an example of a new technology (or rather an older technology adapted for a new population) developed to offer hope to a client group previously considered to have limited prospects for recovery. The population in question has cognitive difficulties, caused by a range of conditions, with severe impulsive challenging behaviour. The CRS was developed to address a need for an effective intervention for this group of patients, who often found themselves 'stuck' within high dependency wards in high security, seemingly trapped within an endless cycle of aggressive incidents and other challenging behaviours. CRS team members have described our client group and the work we do with them to a wide range of audiences within mental health and criminal justice settings. It is clear that there are people with similar difficulties throughout the system, sometimes falling outside the admission criteria of existing services or presenting considerable challenges and making limited progress within those that are prepared to accept them.

The CRS is committed to promoting recovery amongst its client group and sees its role as not just enabling recovery amongst its own in-patients, but also supporting other services in meeting the needs of this population and advocating for this client group throughout the mental health and criminal justice systems. The first step is to engender hope that they can progress, not just within services with which they may come into contact, but also within these individuals themselves.

Philosophy and values of the Cognitive Rehabilitation Service

The CRS operates within a recovery-oriented philosophy and a person-centred tradition, with every effort being made to enable patients to be firmly at the centre of their own care. The recovery paradigm places a strong emphasis on maintaining hope and focusing on real life beyond illness and disability, particularly relationships, education, work and recreation (Roberts and Wolfson, 2004, for review). Maintaining hope is essential to achieving a good outcome for patients with severe disabling mental health problems, including serious cognitive difficulties. For many patients of the CRS, who have lived through repeated negative experiences over many years, regaining a sense of hope and optimism for the future is an essential first step towards recovery. In the early stages of engagement, staff may need to be the carriers of hope, whilst patients regain hope for themselves by increasing positive experiences.

Recovery is not about 'cure', it is about living well in spite of illness and disability. This is particularly relevant for our client group, many of whom have permanent cognitive difficulties, as well as psychoses which are relatively poorly responsive to standard treatments. Central to the cognitive rehabilitation approach is the provision of support to enable the person to experience positive achievements in the 'real life' sphere, whether this is successful self-care, education, engaging in social events or creative pursuits. The person's own interests and preferences will determine the type of positive experience which will be pursued.

Cognitive rehabilitation techniques, based on knowledge of the impact of the individual person's cognitive difficulties on his ability to function in any given situation, provide the 'technology' to create an environment which enables the person to function at his best and support him in achieving his goals. This is analogous to the recovery concept in relation to physical disability. It is accepted that people with physical disabilities may need additional supports (including physical aids, environmental adaptations and input from other people) in order to lead the lives they want to lead. It is enshrined in legislation that they should receive these supports and be viewed appropriately in terms of basic civil rights. For people with cognitive difficulties who may need compensatory aids, environmental adaptations and support from other people, recovery can be perceived in the same way, as a fundamental right to self-determination and social inclusion. 'Recovery' in this context, and its analogy with physical disability, is referred to by Davidson *et al.* (2006) as 'recovery in', as opposed to 'recovery from', serious mental illness.

Achieving a functional lifestyle of the person's choosing is not the end point in itself. A person-centred philosophy is based on the principle that the individual should be supported in a process of self-acceptance and provided with the supports he needs to enable him to develop towards achieving his full potential (Rogers, 1961). This involves using every means possible to determine his wishes and preferences with a view to assisting him in making his own decisions. This approach is particularly important when working with a client group with cognitive difficulties, who may need active support in decision-making and communicating preferences and goals, which may be at risk of being overlooked.

Person-centred therapeutic approaches emphasize the importance of listening to the person, accepting where he is and creating a climate in which he can grow (Mearns and Thorne, 1999). Cognitive rehabilitation fits in well with this approach as it is geared towards acceptance of the individual person's difficulties, providing him with an environment which enables him to function at his best and engaging him in activities which will increase his skills, self-efficacy and self-esteem.

Both person-centred therapeutic approaches and the recovery paradigm emphasise the importance of the relationships between patients and those who support them. These must be based on respect for the person's autonomy and genuine concern. In keeping with the central principle of psychiatric rehabilitation, that environment is of paramount importance in enabling patients to function at their best (Anthony *et al.*, 2004), the CRS team places a great deal of emphasis on the physical and social environment in which patients live and engage in activities.

How did the Cognitive Rehabilitation Service develop within Ashworth Hospital?

Cognitive Rehabilitation, based on a neurobehavioural rehabilitation model (Wood and Worthington, 2001, for review), was first used in Ashworth Hospital over ten years ago to meet the needs of patients with cognitive difficulties, initially due to acquired brain injury, who exhibited severe impulsive challenging behaviour. The Ashworth Hospital CRS team has adapted and refined the techniques of cognitive neurobehavioural rehabilitation used in some mainstream brain injury services to take account of the needs of a forensic population with a range of mental disorders, including high levels of co-morbidity, severe behavioural problems and serious risk issues. This group often exhibits high numbers of incidents of challenging behaviour, including physical violence, self-injury, sexual disinhibition and property damage.

The Service initially provided programmes on an outreach basis to individuals with acquired brain injury throughout the hospital. Since 2005 the service has developed a dedicated in-patient unit and has extended its remit to accept individuals with similar cognitive deficits and impulsive challenging behaviour due to other conditions, such as treatment resistant schizophrenia. Some have shown limited improvement with pharmacological treatment and other therapeutic approaches and have spent years in high security. Their level of persistent challenging behaviour has prevented progress to lesser security and some have required restrictive management methods, such as seclusion and highly staffed special observations, because of their level of risk and unpredictability. Cognitive rehabilitation has proved a useful paradigm by which to understand the clinical presentation and needs of this population, and has provided a basis for successful intervention.

What difficulties do this population experience and how do they impact on recovery prospects?

Individuals with acquired brain injury and impulsive challenging behaviour may show evidence of fronto-temporal cognitive difficulties on neuropsychological testing, as well as clinical features of these difficulties and consistent abnormalities on physical investigation (Wood 1987; Lezak, 1989; Silver *et al.*, 2005). Aggression and irritability are increasingly recognised as valid symptoms of acquired brain injury (Mitchell, 2004). In contrast to the physical sequelae, the psychosocial and behavioural consequences of acquired brain injury are persistent and may even worsen in impact and severity with time (Alderman, 2001). It is not surprising, therefore, that studies have indicated that acquired brain injury is common in criminal justice and forensic psychiatric populations. Prison studies (Mottram, 2007; William et al., 2010) found 48–60 per cent of the population had histories of brain injury, with 10 per cent categorised as severe (Williams et al., 2010). The brain injury organisation Headway (2011) has described acquired brain injury as 'a hidden disability within the criminal justice system'. Similarly, in forensic mental health services, high rates of central nervous system trauma have been found. Lumsden *et al.* (1998) found a 59 per cent prevalence of neuropsychological impairment within a high secure hospital population, whilst a Canadian study (Colantonio *et al.*, 2007) found 23 per cent prevalence of acquired brain injury, concluding that the evidence supports routine screening in forensic populations.

Frontal and temporal areas of the brain are particularly vulnerable to damage resulting from traumatic brain injury. Frontal lobe damage in the orbital region may be associated with disinhibited, impulsive behaviour, poor judgement and reduced empathy, the so-called 'pseudopsychopathic' syndrome (Mitchell, 2004). Damage to the medial frontal area is associated with reduced motivation and drive. The 'dysexecutive' syndrome is associated with dorsolateral damage, and this presents with poor attention and distractibility, poor planning and self-monitoring (Salloway *et al.*, 2001). These consequences, which are shown in Box 6.1, can seriously impact upon the ability of individuals to function effectively in terms of community living and sometimes neuropsychological testing results do not reflect the level of disability evident in 'real life' conditions (Allin and Fleminger, 2006).

Temporal lobe damage may have profound effects on personality and mood, as well as potentially giving rise to complex psychopathology and seizure activity. It is clear that the combination of irritability and disinhibition, impaired judgement and self-monitoring may have a serious impact on social function, predispose to challenging behaviours and reduce response to standard rehabilitation interventions. Individuals with fronto-temporal impairments may have difficulty learning from experiences and be sensitive to environmental stimulation.

Box 6.1 Consequences arising from fronto-temporal cognitive difficulties

- Impaired attention, concentration and working memory
- Impaired planning and organizational skills
- Problems with understanding social situations and appropriate social behaviour
- Reduced problem-solving and reasoning abilities
- Problems with emotional responses and empathy
- Difficulty coping with environmental stimulation
- Impulsive disinhibited behaviour (including physical aggression, sexual disinhibition, self-harm)

(*adapted* from Mitchell, 2004)

The total rehabilitation setting needs to be geared towards minimising the impact of their impairments, creating what has been referred to as a 'prosthetic' environment (Wood, 2001). At the same time, all professionals working with this population need to share a common understanding of the nature of these individuals' disabilities and apply a consistent model of care in keeping with cognitive neurorehabilitation principles (Wood and Worthington, 2001). In contrast to cognitive remediation approaches, cognitive rehabilitation does not aim to reduce cognitive deficits but to reduce the disability associated with them.

Some individuals with severe treatment-resistant psychosis also have fronto-temporal neuropsychological difficulties and behavioural manifestations related to poor functional outcome (Green, 2000; Pantelis *et al.*, 2003), similar to those recognised in acquired brain injury. Dysexecutive impairments and impulsive challenging behaviour may be seen across both groups, with positive psychotic symptoms sometimes operating as trigger factors for incidents (see Figure 6.1).

There appeared to be a rationale for employing cognitive rehabilitation approaches used within acquired brain injury services to support these individuals with schizophrenia and cognitive deficits. The service has also provided programmes for individuals with other complex neuropsychiatric conditions giving rise to fronto-temporal impairments and impulsive challenging behaviour such as Huntington's Disease and other early onset degenerative conditions, as well as conditions which share some similar cognitive and behavioural manifestations such as attention deficit hyperactivity disorder (ADHD), Asperger's Syndrome and other neuropsychiatric disorders.

It is clear that dysexecutive deficits and motivational difficulties experienced by this client group may seriously impact on their ability to function on a day-to-day basis and achieve their chosen lifestyle in the community. However, it is the behavioural manifestations, including sensitivity to environmental stimuli and impulsive aggressive and other problematic behaviours, which hinder their progress through the secure mental health system. These impulsive behaviours

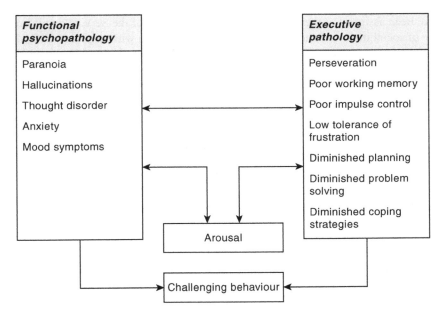

Figure 6.1 Interaction between illness symptoms and cognitive difficulties

may have the characteristics of 'organic impulsive aggression' (Yudofsky *et al.*, 1990, see Box 6.2) and may be preceded by few warning signs, which makes risk more difficult to assess and manage safely without restrictive conditions being employed. It is this characteristic which tends to militate against the therapeutic risk-taking process which is central to recovery-oriented practice. A structured cognitive rehabilitation programme will increase the confidence of the patient and staff in taking risks in a graduated way which increases the chances of a successful outcome without setbacks.

Box 6.2 Organic impulsive aggression – characteristics

- Reactive (only small triggers necessary)
- Non-reflective (unplanned)
- Non-purposeful (not goal-directed)
- Explosive (sudden onset)
- Periodic (brief episodes)
- Ego-dystonic (no explanation, individual may feel uncomfortable)
        (*adapted* from Yudofsky *et al.*, 1990, cited in Mitchell, 2004)

The CRS does not exclude individuals based on diagnostic categories which may have been assigned to them. This is a fundamental part of the Service's philosophy of social inclusion and advocacy for the client group with cognitive difficulties, who are often unrecognized, excluded from or otherwise poorly served by mental health services, precisely because they fall outside of the admission criteria of many services. Instead, the CRS selects individuals based on their clinical need and the likelihood that they may benefit from a model of care based on an adapted neurobehavioural rehabilitation model.

Cognitive rehabilitation: characteristics of the programme

The programme delivered in Ashworth Hospital is based on neurobehavioural rehabilitation, developed for a population with acquired brain injury, with a theoretical basis in behavioural and cognitive psychology and learning theory (Wood and Worthington, 2001). The core features of the programme are outlined in Box 6.3.

The principles behind the CR programme are simple and have a high level of face validity in relation to the nature of the cognitive difficulties and their effects on function and behaviour for this population. The need for programme adherence

---

Box 6.3 Core features of the programme

- Emphasises the importance of a positive therapeutic alliance, which has been found to predict good outcomes in brain injury rehabilitation (Klonoff *et al.*, 1998)
- Is a learning process (based on 'errorless' principles) geared towards the acquisition of functional and social skills (Wilson and Evans, 1996)
- Uses operant conditioning principles and procedural learning methods to support the development of pro-social and functional behaviours, within a 'coaching' model
- Adopts a non-aversive approach to reduce potential negative responses to the programme (Giles *et al.*, 2005)
- Uses cognitive behavioural approaches to increase awareness, motivation and to increase response options including verbal mediation (Christensen, 1996)
- Uses a 'whole system' approach, with the environment acting as a 'prosthetic' to optimise social learning (Wood, 2001) and minimise triggers for challenging behaviour ('antecedent control', Zencius *et al.*, 1989)
- Utilises compensatory systems (such as planners, notebooks, charts) to reduce the risk of information overload

and consistency necessitates high levels of commitment and motivation in care delivery. A simple, non-confrontational style of communication, with a great deal of attention to day-to-day interactions, is necessary, as minor triggers may lead to impulsive challenging behaviour.

The effectiveness of programmes is dependent on the quality of assessments and the detailed understanding of potential environmental triggers (such as a noisy environment, cancellation of sessions) or internal triggers (such as fatigue, symptoms of psychosis, anxiety). The development of a trusting relationship and positive therapeutic alliance is the essential first step towards achieving a good collaborative assessment and programme and has been found to predict good outcomes in acquired brain injury rehabilitation (Klonoff *et al.*, 1998). Programmes are highly individual in terms of their activities, time schedules and compensatory aids used, and are geared towards enhancing skills and self-efficacy and reducing challenging behaviour. They include work and occupation, self-care and leisure – and educational as well as therapeutic activities are designed around the individual's own interests in order to harness intrinsic motivation and a sense of self-determination. Self-determination theory (Ryan and Deci, 2000), with its emphasis on social competence and environmental support, is a potentially useful framework in which to conceptualise recovery in individuals with high levels of disability (Mancini, 2008; Abbott, 2008).

Programmes need to be graduated at a pace at which patients will achieve success without setbacks in a process of 'errorless' learning (Wilson and Evans, 1996) and the environment is geared towards controlling antecedents for challenging behaviour (Zencius *et al.*, 1989). A cautious approach is necessary, when considering the individual's potential for impulsive acts, learning ability and self-esteem issues, particularly in the early stages of programme implementation. The programme needs to include support for the individual in planning his day, a balance of activities and rest and relaxation. Rest periods are formally timetabled into cognitive rehabilitation programmes, as individuals with cognitive difficulties tire easily and fatigue may be a trigger for challenging behaviour.

In addition to the need for high-quality assessment and programme development, there is also a need for close monitoring of programme integrity. The ward routine must be established in such a way as to reduce stress and prevent potential triggers as far as possible. This is achieved by predicting stressful events and putting safeguards in place as part of the programme of the patient concerned. All members of the multi-disciplinary team need to be actively involved in this process at a day-to-day level.

Medication: a tool for recovery?

The complex nature of the mental health problems of the population in the CRS, including high levels of psychosis and other co-morbidities, means that a proactive approach to medication management needs to be taken. The CRS team aim to use the best available evidence in medication management in order to gain optimal levels of mental state stability with minimum negative impact on cognitive

---

Case Example 6.1 Jim

Jim has a history of schizophrenia and acquired brain injury, with cognitive deficits giving rise to poor working memory and impaired self-regulation. He experienced distressing, auditory hallucinations instructing him to self-harm and assault others on a daily basis. When taking a combination of clozapine, low-dose risperidone and valproate, auditory hallucinations were decreased in frequency and strength. He was able to engage more with others and develop therapeutic relationships. He was able to identify specific times of the day when he experienced increased arousal and at these times auditory hallucinations would be more prominent. Jim's preferred coping strategy was to have periods of rest in his room timetabled for these occasions. Assaultative behaviour and self-harm decreased significantly in frequency but persisting incidents usually occurred following interactions with others which resulted in negative cognitions and increased arousal. Addition of propranolol to his medication was associated with decreased internal arousal and, although the negative cognitions persisted, there were no further assaults or episodes of self-harm. Jim engaged in addressing these cognitions with a modified cognitive behavioural approach.

---

functioning, in order to enhance rehabilitation prospects. In practice, this often means that medication regimes are complex, using combinations of antipsychotics, mood stabilizers and anti-convulsants, with slow and careful dosage increases. It may take many trials of alternative regimes to obtain the optimal medication regime for each individual, and it is important the team is systematic in evaluating the benefits of each individual medication and dosage change (see Case Example 6.1). The team aims to gain the best possible engagement and motivation of patients in relation to their use of medication as a support for their recovery, by using adapted mental health psycho-education and simplified, pictorial drug information.

Positive experiences promoting recovery: even in a high secure hospital?

Work, education and recreation are crucial aspects of this model as the aim is to enhance the functional and creative strengths of the individual, increase self-efficacy and self-esteem. Attending off-ward settings enables patients to experience a wider range of social interactions, practise skills they have learnt on the ward and acquire new and more complex skills, including educational and vocational expertise. This is very important for generalization of skills. In our experience, success in the areas of education, work and creativity are an essential component of recovery, enabling the person to develop an alternative identity to that of a 'sick' or 'disordered' person. Patients within the CRS frequently have

---

Case Example 6.2 Bill

Bill was very keen to maintain contact with his mother, who also had severe mental health problems. He would telephone her regularly, but these telephone calls appeared to increase his level of stress and would often be followed by violence towards others. He worked with staff in coaching sessions to plan the timing and duration of his calls, and work on conversations which were simple, straightforward and unlikely to be stressful for himself or his mother. He would write these conversation questions in his notebook for use during the call. This programme was maintained on a long-term basis and since it was commenced there have been no incidents of challenging behaviour following telephone calls.

---

had major difficulties with behaviour and positive social functioning from early life and this may have led to problems within family relationships. Supporting these individuals to build and maintain positive, sustaining relationships with family members and friends is a priority for the service in terms of promoting recovery. In our experience the relationships developed with team members (particularly key nurses and coaching staff) provide important experiences of positive, trusting relationships on which to model relationships with others. Team members also assist patients to manage their relationships at a practical level through specific programmes around visits, telephone calls and letter-writing, for example (see Case Example 6.2).

Family and carers are likely to need help in understanding the person's difficulties and how best to provide the support needed to enable the person to 'live a satisfying and hopeful life in spite of the presence of illness' (Anthony, 1993).

Moving forward: high security and beyond

The narrative recovery literature describes examples of 'turning points' in individuals' lives in which they may move from being trapped in a spiral of mental distress and its negative consequences, towards moving forward on their recovery journey. It is our view that for some patients, their admission to high secure hospital may offer them an opportunity to experience such a turning point. Some have had multiple experiences in a range of mental health and criminal justice services, in which their behaviour has been highly challenging, and they may have felt 'out of control' and unsafe in themselves. The opportunity to feel safe and psychologically 'contained', to develop supportive relationships and enjoy positive experiences of work, education and creativity, sometimes for the first time, may help them to change their view of themselves and their futures.

The usual 'next move' for people in high security is to a medium secure mental health setting (MSU). This transition may be difficult for this population, due to the disabling effects of dysexecutive disorder. Frontal neuronal systems appear to be minimally activated in routine tasks but are heavily employed in non-routine activities (Norman and Shallice, 1986). A number of components of cognitive functioning described in Mateer's (1999) model of executive function are of paramount importance in coping with non-routine or new situations. These include: initiation (starting behaviour), response inhibition (ability to stop automatic responses), task persistence (ability to focus attention for a sufficiently long time to complete a task) and generative thinking (ability to come up with solutions to problems in a flexible way).

Adapting to a new living or working environment also requires a level of self-awareness, monitoring and modification of the person's own behaviour and this is impaired in dysexecutive disorders. Hence a person with dysexecutive disorder may show no signs of obvious impairment in a familiar setting, but may be unable to cope with even basic functional activities in a new environment. The familiar environment may also be compensating for deficits in ways which are not immediately obvious, but which may be critical to effective basic functioning. There is also evidence that environmental stress has a potentially detrimental effect on people with psychosis (Wing and Brown, 1970; Zubin and Spring, 1977), so for those with psychosis and dysexecutive cognitive difficulties, transitions may be particularly difficult (see Case Example 6.3).

Case Example 6.3 James

James is a 34-year-old man with a history of two serious brain injuries who developed symptoms of psychosis, including persecutory delusions and command auditory hallucinations, in his late teens. He had a history of serious impulsive violent behaviour which had proven unmanageable in medium security, and was subsequently admitted to a high-security hospital. James was diagnosed as suffering from treatment-resistant schizoaffective disorder and on neuropsychological testing he performed very poorly on tests of executive function and working memory. He improved considerably in terms of mental state and behaviour when treated with clozapine and a mood stabiliser (semi-sodium valproate), with a programme based upon cognitive rehabilitation principles. James's daily routine was highly structured and predictable, with the use of daily planners and wall charts to assist in this process. He was felt by the multi-disciplinary team to be sufficiently behaviourally improved to move from a 'high dependency' CRS ward to a pre-discharge ward within the hospital. On transfer there was an immediate deterioration in his mental state and behaviour, culminating in an apparently unprovoked assault upon a peer in the dining room whilst queuing for a meal. He was transferred back to the CRS high dependency ward and his mental state and behaviour immediately improved, with no change in his medication being necessary. It was felt by the team that the level of ambient environmental stimulation in the twenty-bedded pre-discharge ward, plus the absence of the structured programme which had been compensating for his difficulties, were the reasons for this deterioration. His structured pro- gramme was recommenced and he rapidly improved. He subsequently made a very carefully planned and graduated move to the CRS Recovery ward and has now been accepted for transfer to medium security.

The experience of 'failure' in a new environment may have a detrimental impact on the person's confidence and self-esteem. It is the responsibility of the 'environment', specifically the team who create it, to ensure that the person makes a successful transition.

A detailed examination of the person's needs, in terms of skills and supports required to cope in the new setting, is required in accordance with a psychiatric rehabilitation model (Anthony *et al.*, 2002, for review). Careful consideration must also be given to the demands of the new environment, and the development of key supportive relationships in advance of any move is essential. Compensatory aids can help with this process. It is often helpful for pictures to be used (such as photographs of the new setting), for information to be written down in a simple format (such as the routine in a new setting, key professionals' names) and for other compensatory aids (such as planners, notebooks, wall charts) to be taken to the new setting to support familiarity and continuity.

A fundamental principle underlying the psychiatric rehabilitation model is that the goals of the patient and of the team are shared, and that the process is recovery- oriented, with maximum emphasis on personal choice, self-management and peer support. On the face of it, these may be difficult principles to work from with a client group in secure settings, due to issues related to risk to others, with severe cognitive difficulties giving rise to impaired problem-solving, planning and self- management. However, risk issues too may be viewed in terms of the skills and environmental supports required to manage them. In our experience it is both necessary and possible to collaborate with patients, even with serious cognitive difficulties, in self-management of their risk behaviours (see Case Example 6.4).

Conclusion

Cognitive rehabilitation has been found to be an effective technology to support people with severe cognitive difficulties giving rise to impulsive challenging behaviour within a high secure hospital. It has given them an opportunity to commence a recovery journey leading to transfer to lesser security and, for some, even beyond. The approach has provided the support to enable them to develop new positive lifestyles, relationships and self-esteem. The recovery-orientation and person-centred approach of all of the team are essential factors in engaging,

---

Case Example 6.4 Wilfred

Wilfred suffered from treatment-resistant schizophrenia and was admitted to high security from a medium secure unit (MSU) due to repeated serious and unpredictable assaults on staff. These appeared to be triggered by command hallucinations (voices telling him to 'kill' and 'urges' to be violent which he felt he could not resist). He also experienced marked persecutory delusions in relation to staff, believing that they were trying to poison him or would rape him. There was little warning of these assaults and he spent considerable periods of time in seclusion due to the unpredictable nature of his risk to others. Through the development of a trusting relationship with key staff, particularly his key nurse, he gradually began to self-report his symptoms rather than acting out aggressively as an immediate response to them. This enabled him to spend time safely in social contact with others and he gradually became more confident and able to go to workshops and trips into the community. He has now been accepted by the MSU from which he was admitted, and staff there have been trained in Cognitive Rehabilitation in order to be able to continue his programme.

---

harnessing hope and delivering the support these patients need to achieve their potential.

Acknowledgements

The CRS Team are very grateful to Drs Kathy Chapman, Ivan Pitman, Jonathan Rogers and Ryan Aguiar for the work they have done in developing the service from the late 1990s to the present. We would also like to thank Drs Barbara Speake and John Holland, Ms Julie Bradley and the Ashworth Hospital Management Team for their support for the service, as well as Mrs Mary Flight for her outstanding administrative support over many years. Finally, they would like to acknowledge the continuing hard work of all patients and staff within the service, which makes positive outcomes possible.

References

Abbott, P. (2008) 'Another step towards understanding recovery? Invited commentary on....Self-determination theory'. *Advances in Psychiatric Treatment*, 14: 366–368.
Alderman, N. (2001) 'Management of challenging behaviour'. In R. Ll. Wood and T. M. McMillan (Eds), *Neurobehavioural Disability and Social Handicap Following Traumatic Brain Injury, Brain Damage, Behaviour and Cognition: Developments in Clinical Neuropsychology Series*. Hove, U.K.: Psychology Press.

Allin, M. and Fleminger, S. (2006) 'Acquired Brain Injury'. In G. Roberts, S. Davenport, F. Holloway and T. Tattan (eds) *Enabling Recovery: the principles and Practice of Rehabilitation Psychiatry*. London: Gaskell.

Anthony, W. A. (1993) 'Recovery from mental illness: the guiding vision of the mental health service for the 1990s'. *Psychosocial Rehabilitation Journal*, 16(4): 11–23.

Anthony, W. A., Cohen, M., Farkas, M. and Gagne, C. (2004) *Psychiatric Rehabilitation* (2nd edition). Boston: Centre for Psychiatric Rehabilitation, Sargent College of Health & Rehabilitation Sciences.

Christensen, A. L. (1996) 'Alexandi Romanovisch Luria (1902–1977) Contributions to Neuropsychological Rehabilitation'. *Neuropsychological Rehabilitation*, 6: 279–303.

Colantonio, A., Stamenova, C., Abramowitz, C., Clark, D., Christensen, B. (2007) 'Brain Injury in the forensic psychiatry population'. *Brain Injury*, 21: 13: 1353–1360.

Davidson, L. O'Connell, M. Tondora, J. Styron, T. and Kangas, K. (2006) The top ten concerns about recovery encountered in mental health systems transformation. *Psychiatric Services,* 57(5): 640–645.

Fluharty, G. and Glassman, N. (2001) 'Use of antecedent control to improve the outcome of rehabilitation for a client with frontal lobe injury and intolerance for auditory and tactile stimuli'. *Brain injury*, 15(11): 995–1002.

Giles, G. M., Wager. J., Fong, L. and Waraich, B. S. (2005) 'Twenty month effectiveness of a non-aversive, long term, low cost programme for persons with persisting neurobehavioural disability'. *Brain Injury*, 19(10): 753–764.

Green, J. (2000) *Neuropsychological Evaluation of the Older Adult: A Clinician's Guidebook*. San Diego: Academic Press.

Green, M. F. (2006), 'Cognitive impairment and functional outcome in schizophrenia and bipolar disorder'. *Journal of Clinical Psychiatry*, 67, suppl 9: 3–8.

Headway. (2011) *Managing anger after brain injury*. Nottingham U.K.: Headway.

Kielhofner, G. (2008) *Model of Human Occupation: theory and application* (4th edition). Baltimore: Lippincott Williams and Wilkins.

Klonoff, P. S., Lamb, D. G., Henderson, S. W. and Shepherd, J. (1998) 'Outcome assessment after milieu-oriented rehabilitation: new considerations'. *Archives of Physical Medicine & Rehabilitation*, 79: 684–690.

Lezak, M. D. (1989) 'Assessment of psychosocial dysfunctions resulting from head trauma'. In M. D. Lezak (Ed) *Assessment of the Behavioral Consequences of Head Trauma, Vol 7: Frontiers of Neuroscience*. New York: Alan R. Liss (p. 113–144).

Lumsden, J., Chesterman, L. P. and Hill, G. M. (1998) 'Neuropsychiatric indices in a high security admission sample I: estimating the prevalence'. *Criminal Behaviour and Mental Health*, 8(4): 285–310.

Mancini, A. D. (2008) 'Self-determination theory: a framework for the recovery paradigm', *Advances in Psychiatric Treatment*, 14, 358–365.

Mateer, C. A. (1999) 'The Rehabilitation of Executive Disorders'. In D. T. Stuss, G. Winocur and I. Robertson (eds) *Cognitive Neurorehabilitation*. Cambridge: Cambridge University Press.

Mearns, D. and Thorne, B. (1999) *Person-Centred Counselling in Action* (2nd edition). London: Sage.

Mitchell, A. J. (2004) *Neuropsychiatry and Behavioural Neurology Explained*. London: Saunders.

Mottram, P. G. (2007) *HMP Liverpool, Styal and Hindley Study Report*. Liverpool: University of Liverpool.

Norman, D. A. and Shallice, T. (1986) 'Attention to Action: willed and automatic control of behaviour'. In R. J. Davidson, G. E. Schwartz, and D. Shapiro (eds), *Consciousness and Self-regulation: Vol 4 Advances in Research and Therapy.* New York: Plenum Press.

Pantelis, C., Velakoulis, D., McGorry, P. D., Wood, S. J., Suckling, J., Phillips, L. J., Yung, A. R., Bullmore, E. T., Warrick, B., Souldby, B., Desmond, P., and McGuire, P. K. (2003) 'Neuroanatomical abnormalities before and after onset of psychosis: a cross-sectional and longitudinal MRI comparison'. *Lancet*, 361: 281–288.

Roberts, G. and Wolfson, P. (2004) 'The rediscovery of recovery: open to all'. *Advances in Psychiatric Treatment*, 10: 37–48.

Rogers, C. (1961) *On becoming a Person: A therapist's view.* London: Constable.

Ryan, R. M. and Deci, E. L. (2000) 'Self determination theory and the facilitation of intrinsic motivation, social development and well-being'. *American Psychologist*, 55: 68–78.

Reid, D. (2008) 'Exploring the relationship between occupational presence, occupational engagement, and people's well-being'. *Journal of Occupational Science,* 15(1): 43–47.

Salloway, S. P., Malloy, P. F., Duffy, J. D. (Eds) (2001) *The Frontal Lobes and Neuropsychiatric Illness.* Washington, D. C.: American Psychiatric Press.

Schofield, P. W., Butler, T. G., Hollis, S. J., Smith, N. E., Lee, S. J. and Kelso, W. M. (2006) 'Traumatic brain injury amongst Australian prisoners: rates, recurrence and sequelae'. *Brain Injury*, 20(5): 499–506.

Silver, J. M., Mc Allister, T. M. and Yudofsky, S. C. (Eds) (2005) *Textbook of Traumatic Brain Injury.* Washington D.C.: American Psychiatric Publishing.

Wilson, B. A. and Evans, J. J. (1996) 'Error-free learning in the rehabilitation of people with memory impairments'. *Journal of Head Trauma Rehabilitation*, 11: 54–64.

Williams, W. H., Mewse, A. J., Tonks, J., Mills, S., Burgess, C. N. W. and Cordan, G. (2010) 'Traumatic brain injury in a prison population: Prevalence and risk for re-offending'. *Brain Injury*, 24(10): 1184–1188.

Wing, J. K. and Brown, G. W. (1970) *Institutionalism and Schizophrenia.* London: Cambridge University Press.

Wood, R. Ll. (1990) 'Neurobehavioural paradigm for brain injury rehabilitation'. In: R. Ll. Wood (ed.), *Neurobehavioural Sequelae of Traumatic Brain Injury*, pp 153–174. London: Taylor and Francis.

Wood, R. Ll. (2001) 'Understanding neurobehavioural disability'. In: R. Ll. Wood and T. McMillan (eds) *Neurobehavioural Disability and Social Handicap following Traumatic Brain Injury.* West Sussex: Psychology Press.

Wood, R. Ll. and Worthington, A. D. (2001) 'Neurobehavioural Rehabilitation: a conceptual paradigm'. In: R. Ll. Wood and T. McMillan (eds) *Neurobehavioural Disability and Social Handicap following Traumatic Brain Injury.* West Sussex: Psychology Press.

Yudofsky, S. C., Silver, J. M. and Hales, R. E. (1990) 'Pharmacological management of aggression in the elderly'. *Journal of Clinical Psychiatry* 51, (Suppl 10): 22–28.

Zencius, A. H., Wesolowski, M. D., Burke, W. H. and McQuade, P. (1989) 'Antecedent control in the treatment of brain injured clients'. *Brain Injury*, 3: 199–205.

Zubin, J. and Spring, B. (1977) 'Vulnerability – a new view of schizophrenia', *Journal of Abnormal Psychology,* 86(2): 103–124.

7 Recovering personhood

Using recovery principles on a long-stay medium secure ward

Jay Smith and Veronica Garcia

Introduction

In late 2003 we opened a 15-bedded ward in the Forensic Directorate of the East London NHS Foundation Trust. Our long-term rehabilitation ward was established for the treatment of male service users who had spent many years in secure psychiatric settings. In psychiatric language, they demonstrated a combination of ongoing psychotic symptoms, behavioural problems, personality disorder and risk. As people, our service users shared a common background of neglectful, abusive or chaotic parenting, which greatly compromised their ability to trust themselves, other people or their environment. These adverse life experiences contributed to an inability to receive help and work collaboratively with others, which at least partly explained how they had found themselves spending a large part of their adult lives in institutions.

In this chapter we seek to describe how the application of recovery principles within the ward setting helped our users to take the first step on the road to recovery: namely, the rediscovery of their personhood. As Anthony (2004) states, 'people want to self-determine their own goals, be involved in their own lives, believe in their capacity to grow and have hope'. Although this statement is simple and self-evident, as with so many simple principles difficulties arise when translating it into practice. Without careful attention, secure psychiatric hospitals readily become dehumanizing environments, riven by fear, persecutory anxiety and ruthless struggles over power and control. Such environments often iterate the service user's difficulties (Cordess, 2006) by, for example, emphasizing power at the expense of relatedness or by dismissing the importance of attachments. All who have worked in secure psychiatric institutions will have experienced the shockingly abrupt transfers of staff and patients or witnessed the almost 'knee-jerk' repressive response to an infraction of one of the many rules. As Hyatt-Williams (1998; p. 217) rightly points out, such environments can promote stasis, but not change.

In designing the ward, we thus had to meet a number of potentially conflicting aims. We had to maintain safety and adhere to the structures of the institution while offering our users a different experience, one that would allow them to rediscover their personhood. For some of our users, we were offering long term care or a 'home' as some patients have come to describe it – but we had to make room for the possibility that things might change in a way that would allow some individuals to leave the ward to start a new life elsewhere. We had to have hope for our users, but also acknowledge that such hopes may not be fulfilled.

(Frey-Wehrlin *et al.*, 1989)

This chapter describes aspects of the recovery approach used in our particular community. We describe the structures and approaches we use, all of which has been informed by what our service users have taught us about being a person with mental illness. Several of our service users have contributed aspects of their stories, for which we thank them. We have removed any identifying information to preserve their privacy.

Being involved in life

Being involved in one's life and making decisions as to the path one wants to follow is at the heart of recovery-based practice, as it empowers people by providing a sense of choice; the choice of what we want to see happening, when and how. Although this could be seen as a straightforward initial step to recovery, for our users it can be an unexpected and at times seemingly unwanted task. After years of loss and failures, the prospect of taking control can seem alien and frightening. Thus, when people move to our ward they are often in the moratorium phase of recovery (Andresen *et al.*, 2006), gripped by powerful (if sometimes hidden) feelings of loneliness and despair. For some, this phase may persist for years. One of our first tasks, then, is to address apathy, detachment and indifference – often the outward manifestations of despair – and to encourage our service users to join our community and begin to share with us what they want and what is important to them. This process can be seen as having an external and an internal component. The external process is the way individuals project themselves into the outside world, define their identities and roles, and engage in life. The internal component can be thought of as an exploration of their own mind, a search for meaning and reconnection within themselves. For most of our service users, their first experience of the ward community and our recovery ethos is via the community meeting. This takes place on a Monday and is a completely unstructured group lasting forty-five minutes. It can be a powerful experience, often very different from anything users have encountered before. All are encouraged to attend, although attendance is not compulsory and individuals can leave during the meeting. We keep in mind that even individuals who do not attend are made aware by their peers of what is discussed in the meeting. When a new member (user or staff) joins, all who are present introduce themselves and someone gives a brief explanation of the purpose of the meeting – along the lines of, 'We all get together to talk about what is happening on the ward.' Over the years, we have fostered a welcoming atmosphere, with a culture of free and open expression. Thus, users are allowed to express anger and frustration, to be critical of staff, or to work on their problems living with each other. When the group is working well, staff have little to do but listen; at other times, the group may be angry, fragmented or depressed, requiring more active interventions to understand and work with what is being expressed. The community meeting is popular, with usually half the service users attending. Over time, participants become more confident at expressing their views and using their life experience and personal strengths to deal with the day-to-day problems they all face. A major ongoing theme of the meeting is acknowledging relationships and their losses; thus we attempt to give as much notice as we can when staff or users are leaving, and to discuss the reasons as openly as we can. For staff who are unfamiliar with a recovery style of working, it can be a powerful experience for them to have users thank them for their work and express how much they will be missed. In this way we honour the importance of relationships but also deal with the inevitability of change and loss – all moderated by the sense of support we gain by sharing the experience. For our particular user group, sudden, shocking, unexplained separations and losses are part of the fabric of their lives from their earliest years, so it is difficult to underestimate the importance of acknowledging such experiences in the here-and-now. For many, it helps to build a secure and supportive base from which they can begin to contemplate change. If the community meeting deals with the external element of getting involved, the support group tends to deal with the internal processes of individual meaning and reconnecting with their own life stories. The weekly support group has played an important role in our milieu since the ward opened. It takes place in the quiet room on the ward every Tuesday afternoon with three facilitators: the consultant psychiatrist (JS), the ward manager and the ward doctor (VG). Although the group offers supportive therapy, the work is heavily influenced by the analytic background and group experience of the consultant.

The seniority and expertise of the facilitators has probably contributed to the popularity of the group. Seniority is important as users of forensic services (and indeed the organizations themselves) are particularly concerned with power and hierarchy. The presence of two doctors and a ward manager helps to signal the importance of this space, as the users recognize us as important figures on the ward who will undoubtedly have a great influence on their care. By making ourselves available to be known and tested out by patients, we modelled an open way of communication where observing and being observed can be experienced as a benign form of communication and a way of being with one another. Facilitating groups for people with severe mental illness is not easy, but it is the personal qualities and attitudes of the facilitators which are more important than knowledge or skills (Smith, 1999). Characteristics that have been identified in the literature include sincerity of therapeutic attitude, patience and flexibility, an ability to contain destructive behaviour, a sensitivity to obscure and oblique communications and a tolerance for failure or minimal success (Betcher *et al.*, 1982; Leopold, 1976; Takahashi and Washington, 1991; Milders, 1994).

Choosing to have three facilitators was a response to an awareness of the negative impact that breaks may have for our particular user group. We can and often do facilitate sessions with only two facilitators, but make every effort to ensure the group takes place every week without fail.

As with the community meeting, the support group is unstructured. Users are invited to talk about anything but we do not engage in discussions about treatment or care plans such as medication, leave, legal matters and so on, to avoid the group being turned into either a continuation of the ward round or a business meeting where users can continue discussing concrete aspects of their care. By setting these boundaries, we managed to create a private and separate space where service users can discuss things with us in a more open way, as nothing said in the group is held against them or discussed elsewhere. This has allowed service users to trust that they can be more honest and open about their feelings and states of mind. As with the community meeting, every service user on the ward is invited to attend, although attendance is by no means compulsory and is not linked with changes to their management plan. Most of the work of the facilitators has been to provide a friendly and tolerant environment where users could begin to form links with each other and to create an identity as part of the group. The facilitators' non-intrusive curiosity about the users' lives and feelings helped to model a way of being curious and open-minded about their own minds and the minds of others. By providing this regular, free and predictable space over the course of several years, we have been privileged to learn a lot about our users and about life with mental illness. We have seen how the attempt to make shared meaning helps our users to feel understood; for some, particularly those in a prolonged moratorium phase, being understood may not progress to awareness but nevertheless remains valuable (Hinshelwood, 2008). One of the most surprising and rewarding aspects of the group has been the way that a number of individuals have used the space to construct a narrative of their lives. Sometimes this process has taken years. Stories often begin with tales of the different institutions they have been in, medication they have taken, recollections of times of drug use and disclosures about entanglements with the law. Over time the story deepens, and we hear of abandonments as children, violence in the family, disastrous marriages and unfulfilled dreams. This process of narrative building happens at the user's pace; we have come to learn that these deeper disclosures indicate that the individual is moving into the awareness phase of recovery (Andresen *et al.*, 2006), having the courage to share their failures and disappointments because somewhere there is a sense that all is not lost. Sometimes the move into the preparation phase is associated with the group hearing and understanding a vitally important experience; once this has happened, the user may loosen his ties to the group as he becomes more involved in focused recovery work with others in the team. Examples are given below.

Jerome is a middle-aged man with diagnosis of paranoid schizophrenia. He had been continuously detained in hospital for over 20 years following being convicted of three counts of theft, robbery and use of an imitation firearm.

During his long admission he presented as acutely psychotic, paranoid and violent, requiring treatment in High Security for many years. He took up a defiant and contemptuous stance towards authorities and was often belligerent, abusive and dominating. After several years on the ward, he began to 'flirt' with the support group, sometimes dropping in to deposit a long, grumbling complaint before leaving. He then began to attend for longer periods, listening and offering advice to others. He took the opportunity to tell us stories from his past, and this seemed important one day when we put his stories together to see that they were connected by a sense that he had always felt alone and unsupported against a hostile and arbitrary world. After this, he began to engage more confidently with the outside world, and was able to work with us to achieve his goal of moving on from the ward.

Peter is a man in his mid-forties with a diagnosis of paranoid schizophrenia and a personality coloured by antisocial and narcissistic elements. He was admitted to hospital at the age of 27 after committing a serious assault on a stranger. He did not agree with us that he suffered from a mental illness. However, he did agree that he could lose his temper, sometimes with disastrous results. His primary nurse and psychologist worked with him on how frightening he could be; this allowed him to confide that he had been frightened himself during several potentially violent encounters with staff. Then, over two sessions in the support group, he recounted witnessing life-threatening violence in his family as a child. After this disclosure, he stopped attending the group regularly but began to make good progress in formulating and meeting his goals.

In a secure psychiatric setting, the service user's sense of despair and demoralization may be compounded by the many restrictions and rules that, while necessary to ensure safety, enhance feelings of powerlessness We have found that by providing unstructured group spaces we can allow our users the psychological freedom to rediscover their individuality and a sense of agency. Our users value and respect these groups, perhaps because they have the freedom to use them as they wish. It has been a humbling experience at times to see how many of our users have used these groups to begin and support their own recovery processes.

For a recovery approach to work, we found that staff need to be as involved as patients in the life of the ward and the ethos we promote. In order to involve staff we have a number of forums where we discuss the work we do and the rationale behind it. Staff need to adjust to a completely different way of working and this can at times be anxiety-provoking, as staff may feel de-skilled and worried at what could be perceived as giving control and expertise away. On a long-stay ward respecting that change can only happen at the speed patients can manage can also cause considerable frustration.

Just as we have the weekly support group for patients, we have a fortnightly staff support group for members of the team. Here we discuss team dynamics as well as have supervised clinical discussions of patients. These meetings can often be important venues where resistance to take up a recovery-oriented approach can be discussed. The pull to move to what is known and to regain control can be a powerful one and come from users as well as staff. The role of senior figures in the unit is important in retaining a recovery focus and resisting the ever-present pull towards a more institutionalized and less user-focused approach.

Every six months we have a team discussion where we discuss the work we do, paying special attention to educating new members of the team. In this meeting we aim to have an overview of where we are with each patient, the work ahead of them and the distribution of resources to maximize our input. Team away days are also important venues where team dynamics can be discussed and where we can take stock of resources as well as discuss limitations to the work we do. The weekly support meeting and weekly ward round are also important forums used to introduce staff to our way of working and to show through direct clinical input the way we empower patients to take responsibility for their lives and to self-determine their goals.

Being involved in relationships

Being accepted and valued in one's community is perhaps one of the most important aspects of social recovery. In the ward, we stress the value of relationships and the need to be involved in the life of the ward. We aim for this connection to be not just with the physical environment but the emotional life of the ward as well. We do this by celebrating special occasions on the ward such as ward anniversaries, festive holidays and service user's birthdays. With time these celebrations have become part of the collective memory of the journey we have shared. Special attention is paid to the relationships patients have built with staff, and with fellow patients, over time. With this in mind we aim to provide spaces where users can celebrate as well as mourn the loss when staff or service users leave, or on the two occasions when fellow service users have died from natural causes. At these times of change and emotional turmoil the community meeting and the staff support group become important venues where service users can explore the difficult feelings they are left with at such times.

Violent incidents or episodes of acting out behaviour tend to affect all the service users on the ward. In the community meeting, we make a point of discussing any incidents (sometimes for weeks), whether those involved attend the meeting or not. Often service users express feelings of fear, or disapprove of violence directed towards staff. They may offer advice to the individual or individuals involved as to how to manage such situations better in the future. These discussions, while performing a function of containing anger and aggression on the ward, also allow users to experience and reflect on the effects of violence in the 'here-and-now.' Vivid examples of the community coming together have been the times when we have faced the proximity of death on the ward. At these times of profound pain and sadness we have seen the most genuine expressions of care and empathy among service users. These demanding times have also required the community to come together to decide aspects of the care that will be provided to their terminally ill peer, from discussions about transfer to a hospice to ideas about funeral arrangements and ways to pay our respects to the deceased and his or her family. Having a forum where these discussions are facilitated has helped our service users to feel respected and valued, and their relationships validated. Encouraging healthy friendships on the ward is not always an easy task. Staff in secure hospital settings traditionally view such relationships with suspicion and anxiety, and it is certainly true that there may be a strong pull for peer relationships to become exploitative and deviant. Irritability and arguments may erupt when users are bored or frustrated, and envy and rivalry can arise when individuals progress in their recovery. At such times we tend to intervene by bringing the issues to group meetings where these dynamics can be openly discussed and users can benefit from receiving direct feedback from staff and peers. Although some confrontation takes place in more public settings, it is in the more private setting of the support group or in one-to-one work with their nurses that users have been able to work through difficulties among themselves and to repair damaged relationships.

> Raymond was a middle-aged man with a diagnosis of schizoaffective disorder. He had been detained in hospital for years following allegations of indecent assault. Although his index offence was not particularly serious, it was the nature of his challenging behaviour which meant he remained in hospital until his last days. He engaged in a range of provocative interpersonal behaviours and was often mischievous and destructive with his peers. He was a regular attender of both the support group and the community meeting. Over time, the patients were able to confront him about the anger or distress his behaviour evoked. At times, this conflict was very intense, and patients would implore the staff to move Raymond to another ward, or to deal with him in a more punitive way. This conflict was difficult to stay with at times, but we were able to explore the dynamic of scapegoating and to maintain a space for Raymond within the group. He was eventually able to establish a place in our community where his humour and warmth were appreciated and his provocations, for the most part, tolerated.

The participation in recovery services of those who have recovered, as mentors and coaches for other service users, is often described in recovery programmes (Spaniol, 2008). Although we do not have a formal mentoring programme, our group programme and attention to interpersonal relationships allows and encourages all our service users to be involved in the process of their peers' recoveries. It can be a powerful experience to hear from a user in a group meeting how they thought there was no hope for them but now they have found a new home outside hospital. Service users learn from others about the range of residential and occupational facilities in the community, and about the benefits of a life outside hospital. On occasion, users who have moved on return to the ward for parties and share with their peers aspects of their new lives. In our community, we have found it helpful to separate the day-to-day business of the ward from the community meeting. This protects the community meeting as a space for examining feelings and relationships while allowing our service users to have a say in the practical ways the ward is run. The security restrictions inevitable in medium security do at times limit how much users (or even clinical staff) can influence things; however, it is important to encourage our users to use the influence they do have. Both the business meeting and the community meeting are attended by our representative on the User Involvement Group, and their role is to take the concerns or suggestions of our users to the official meeting. We have found over time that some service users will spontaneously take up doing chores on the ward, such as collecting breakfasts or tidying the communal areas. Others have used the cooking sessions on the ward to prepare meals for friends or relatives. In these simple ways, users begin to express their own autonomy and to function in a more independent manner.

Believing in the capacity to grow

The psychoanalyst Harold Searles (1998, p. 462) made the following interesting observation many years ago: '…as regards the total group of patients in any chronic hospital ward, it sometimes comes through to me that here is a place permeated by deeply submerged but explosively powerful growth-strivings, and the more static in appearance the patients are, the more anxiety-provokingly true this is.' Our experience bears this out. In our setting, we have concentrated on providing a place for 'moratorium' while welcoming and encouraging any small signs of growth. Even while in a stagnant state, service users are exposed to the growth and development of other service users, nursing students, medical students and staff. We have learnt that it is important for growth to happen under the control of the service user, and at their pace. Waiting unobtrusively in hope can be one of the most difficult tasks for staff in our setting, especially when service users may be withdrawn and inaccessible for years. As a team, we try to be alert for early signs of change and to nurture the process in an individual way. Often the social therapists (unqualified nursing staff) are the first to observe the early signs of growth in a patient, and sometimes we support them to follow the service user's lead in trying new experiences. Often it is at around this stage of recovery that the psychologist or occupational therapist comes to the fore, offering one-to-one support or encouraging engagement with the ward programme or the outside world. The story of Lee illustrates this process.

> Lee is a 52-year-old man with a diagnosis of paranoid schizophrenia. He was convicted of manslaughter at the age of 23 and almost 20 years later he was admitted to hospital after an incident where he terrorized public-sector employees using a weapon while in a psychotic state. He had been in hospital for four years when he came to the ward. Ever since his admission to hospital he had fiercely defended his personal space and maintained a stubborn independence from staff and service users. Much of his time was spent in his room shouting at voices; during his brief forays into the communal space his demeanour was tense and forbidding. He never attended ward groups, ward

rounds or care-planning meetings. Over time, he began to talk to selected staff members about his many delusional ideas and seemed less tense when out of his room. We allowed Lee to remain a recluse, gently inviting him to the community meeting and the ward round every week, even though we knew he would decline. Nursing staff sometimes became anxious about him and we had to try to understand and contain these anxieties in our reflective practice meetings. In his third year on the ward, Lee unexpectedly attended a party on the ward which was being held to mark the departure of a much-loved social therapist. We were all astonished when he made a warm and grateful speech, thanking her for her efforts over the years, and stayed to talk at the party. This marked a turning point for Lee; he gradually formed a close bond with another social therapist, who was able to persuade him to venture outside the hospital for the first time in years. Soon he was taking short trips outside the hospital alone, and began to work with the occupational therapist to venture further into the community. He began to attend ward rounds, became more communicative and has begun to talk to us about the cata-strophic loss that precipitated his index offence and admission to hospital.

Growth often involves a change in identity, a move from the known to the new which can raise anxieties and resistance. For our service users, the beginning of the move from mentally disordered offender to person might be quite simple: becoming seen as a friend to other service users, a football fan, a music lover, a good cook, a brother. Service users need to be allowed to express these aspects of their identities and to have them valued. Over time, as their recovery progresses, work opportunities may help to build confidence and to define a social identity. This process is well demonstrated in the account given by one of our service users, Peter (introduced earlier in this chapter).

> The training that I did in prison when I was young, the way it affected me, you could call that an illness. I went to a party, and at the party, I thought, what's going on, I can hardly dance. One of the guys on the sound system started singing, 'We don't want no weirdos', he called me a weirdo. It got to me. When I came outside I was crying. I used to dance a lot, when that was taken away from me, it was a big thing. I always used to like partying. I always used to make music from an early age. I was a musician, I was good at playing the saxophone, the organ, the piano. I didn't make money out of it, but I gave mixes to four of five friends of mine, I gave them lyrics and they made a lot of money out of it. These days I enjoy the Music Project [outside the hospital]. I'm making my music. When you make your own music you feel good that you're making your own things. I'm one of the best at making music and I get on well with the people there. Making music is like who I am, I get satisfaction from it.

Hope

Hope could be said to be the lynchpin of the recovery ethos (Spaniol, 2008; Allott *et al.*, 2002). However, it is important to recognise that some variants of hope are unhelpful, or even pathological. Both staff and users may harbour unrealistic hopes, which may function as a defence against despair (Hinshelwood, 2008). The laudable urge of the staff to cure their clients may be experienced by both parties as an intolerable burden (Searles, 1998, p. 456) which may, in fact, interfere with the authentic process of recovery. Initially, many of our service users will cling stubbornly to unrealistic hopes (for example that they can manage to live alone in the community with no support). These hopes may hinder the process of adapting to the reality of their situation, and a large part of the work of recovery may be embodied in the processes by which both service users and staff negotiate more realistic goals. Our service users may also demonstrate a form of hope that has been described as a pathological (Akhtar, 2003, p. 93). This type of hope is based on an omnipotent fantasy that all the pain and suffering of the past will someday be magically healed; a stoic endurance of all kinds of deprivation may accompany this wait. For example, one of our service users has been in hospital for many years after a serious offence; when asked what his wishes for the future were, he replied, 'I'm waiting for it to all work out.' When asked how long he had been waiting, he replied calmly, 'Twenty years.' Another service user refuses to contemplate future plans as he waits for what he views as the injustice of his conviction to be righted. We have found that for these individuals, active work to help improve the quality of their daily lives is the first step in promoting recovery, as such an attitude may indicate a 'pre-moratorium' phase in an individual who is not ready or able to tolerate the grief and mourning which might kick-start the recovery process.

Once our service users are in the awareness or preparation phases of recovery, they may begin to participate in focused groups directed toward goal planning and problem solving. We use the CPA meetings to negotiate and agree clear goals, which may extend a year into the future. In order to be genuinely committed to allowing the user to formulate their own goals, the team must be willing to accept that goals may sometimes be different from what they (or the organization) may wish. One of the luxuries of a long-stay environment is that we can allow both service users and staff to accept openly that a realistic and desirable goal may be to make a home in the hospital. It is our experience that service users may secretly harbour this goal but be prevented from verbalizing it as a result of the prevailing ethos that everyone must not only leave the hospital, but want to leave it as well. Realizing the hope to have their destructive impulses understood may be a great relief for some service users.

The account given by Jonathon, one of our service users, gives a clear account of the recovery process he has achieved without moving from the ward:

> I'm 35, going on 36 in ten weeks. I'm a little bit overweight but I'm quite fit and healthy. I sometimes say things and then change my mind but that's

basically me! My good points are I'm helpful, I go and collect the breakfasts, if they're short of staff I can understand that. I can be impatient as well, when I'm waiting for the post and that. But not as bad as what I used to be. Before, when my post didn't turn up, I'd kick off, but now I say, 'Well, maybe tomorrow.' So I've calmed down in that sense. When I first came to this ward, I think I was totally different to what I am now. I was younger, I was moodier, I was not very well at the time. At the time, I wasn't really thinking about the future, it was just settling into a new ward and getting to know the new team. I think the best thing that I've done – and I don't mean to be cruel here – is to dump my family. Maybe dump isn't the right word. Yes, it is the right word. Since then, I've started to live life. I've had problems but I've worked through them. I've had one-to-one sessions for eighteen months. That helped me talk about my feelings and my fears.

One of the biggest things that's helped me is the shop job. I think that's really helped me get my confidence up. Before I started, three years ago, I was very, very low in confidence. Now I'm more outgoing because I interact with people down there.

My future plan is to use my reception leave, then move outside to the bench. My next stage will be to go to the shop you can see from the hospital, before going around to the High Street. Just to get used to going to a shop again, outside of the hospital environment. I'd like to think I'll get to the shop in the next eighteen months. Longer term, this is my home for however long. The plan would be to stay here and go out on trips and travel on my favourite form of transport.

I want to take things slowly, I want to do things in steps. Not rushing like I did before. If I rush, I start panicking and I feel the hospital will kick me out and then I start getting worried and then I start having thoughts of running off. If I do it properly there's no need to run off – which I've done before. The first time was when I was in another hospital and they started talking about me coming back here. Then I absconded again when they were talking about moving me to a hostel. I didn't think I was ready. If I'm not ready I'll panic and I'll go. As I've said in ward round, I want to do it at my pace, so I'm in control. Being on the same ward and having the same doctor has helped. This is the longest I've spent with one doctor in my hospital treatment in the last fifteen years. People know my strengths and my weaknesses, rather than having to get to know a whole new team all the time.

Conclusion

We have tried to demonstrate how, even in a long-stay medium secure ward, recovery principles may be used to maintain hope and to underpin good quality care. We often have to stay with individuals for a long time in a place of stagnation and despair. However, we have learnt that individuals with severe mental illness who have faced disasters in their personal lives may still retain the capacity to grow and develop. Patience, genuine involvement and thoughtfulness are important qualities in this setting; but perhaps most important is an ethos that promotes respect for the unique human being who may be hidden beneath the persona of the long-term patient.

References

Akhtar, S. (2003) 'Psychological Dimensions of Terrorism'. In C. Covington (ed.) *Terror and War*. Karnac Books, London.

Allott, P., Loganathan, L. and Fulford, K. (2002) 'Discovering hope for recovery: a review of a selection of recovery literature'. *Canadian Journal of Community Mental Health*, 21(3): 1–22.

Andresen, R., Caputi, P. and Oades, L. (2006) 'Stages of recovery instrument: development of a measure of recovery from serious mental illness'. *Australian and New Zealand Journal of Psychiatry*, 40: 972–980.

Anthony, W. A. (2004) 'The Principal of Personhood: The Field's Transcendent Principle'. *Psychiatric Rehabilitation Journal*, 27(3): 205.

Betcher, R., Rice, C. and Weir, D. (1982) 'The regressed inpatient group in a graded group treatment programme'. *American Journal of Psychotherapy*, 36(2): 229–39.

Cordess, C. (2006) 'The Application of High-Security Models of Care to Other Less Secure Settings'. In C. Newrith, C. Meux, and P. Taylor (eds) *Personality Disorder and Serious Offending: Hospital Treatment Models* pp. 258–274. London: Hodder Arnold.

Frey-Wehrlin, C., Bosnak, R., Langegger, T. *et al.* (1989) 'The treatment of Chronic Psychoses'. In A. Samula (ed.) *Psychopathology: Contemporary Jungian Perspectives* pp. 205–212. London: Karnac,.

Hinshelwood, R. (2008) 'Introduction'. In J. Gordon and G. Kirtchuk (eds) *Psychic Assaults and Frightened Clinicians: Countertransference in Forensic Settings*. London: Karnac Books.

Hyatt-Williams, A. (1998) *Cruelty, Violence and Murder*. London: Karnac Books.

Leopold, H. (1976) 'Selective group approaches with psychotic patients in hospital settings'. *American Journal of Psychotherapy*, 30: 95–102.

Milders, C. (1994) 'Kernberg's object relations theory and the group psychotherapy of psychosis'. *Group Analysis*, 27(4): 419–32.

Searles, H. (1986) *Collected Papers on Schizophrenia and Related Subjects*. London: Karnac Books.

Spaniol, L. (2008) 'What would a recovery-oriented program look like?' *International Journal of Psychosocial Rehabilitation*, 13(1): 57–66.

Smith, J. (1999) 'Five questions about group therapy in chronic schizophrenia'. *Group Analysis*, 30: 515–524.

Takahashi, T. and Washington, P. (1991) 'A group-centred object relations approach to group psychotherapy with severely disturbed patients'. *International Journal of Group Psychotherapy*, 41(1): 79–96.

8 Harnessing hearts and minds for change

Sally Carr and Sue Havers

Introduction

Forensic services face significant challenges when attempting to introduce a recovery approach. The secure environment, legal context and traditional culture conflict with some of the core principles of recovery. People are detained against their will and experience significant limitation of their autonomy and rights. As a result they can become passive recipients of services rather than taking control of their own lives and making decisions for themselves. Further, the legal basis for detention requires a diagnostic label, thereby ingraining a medical model in the care of the 'patient'. This is in direct conflict with a recovery approach that seeks to reject the 'sick role' and reclaim the role of a healthy person. Paternalistic views about service users' ability to make informed decisions are reinforced by a belief that they cannot be trusted to make decisions around risk issues. The combination of a label of severe mental illness, a history of substance misuse and criminal convictions or risk to others lead to stigmatisation and mistrust of the individual. Hope and a focus on strengths and assets rather than pathology can be in short supply. Most forensic services lean towards Slade's (2009) description of traditional services, which highlights discrepancies with a recovery approach in: values and power arrangements, working practices, basic concepts and knowledge, and the goals of the service.

It has been our experience that the power imbalances and use of diagnostic labels associated with legal detention make implementation of a recovery approach in its purest form very difficult. Security and risk issues can, however, be addressed to create a culture that supports the principles of recovery. This allows the possibility of developing a 'recovery-orientated service', as described by Slade (2009), with the goals of enabling choice, self-control, transformation and positive health.

Secure units carry many of the features of the 'closed institution' described by Goffman (1968). As a result, the culture of the service is likely to be fixed and resistant to change. Therefore to achieve meaningful and sustained change requires particular attention to the culture of the unit, the attitudes and beliefs of staff and the associated policies and procedures of the system. These must all be addressed to ensure successful introduction of a recovery approach. Issues of service user motivation, security, confidentiality, public protection, risk and trust can be presented as barriers to the implementation of a recovery approach. In fact, we believe the barriers lie in the culture of the organisation and the attitudes and beliefs of staff. This is recognised and discussed in a position statement issued by the Sainsbury Centre for Mental Health (2009). This identifies key organisational challenges to recovery, which include 'Ensuring organisational commitment', 'Creating the 'culture'', 'Transforming the workforce' and 'Supporting staff in their recovery journey'.

At our medium secure unit, some staff understood and were already committed to a recovery approach, while others did not really understand or believe in the concept. Others, explicitly or indirectly, communicated a resistance to the very notion of recovery. We took the view that our service's progress towards implementing recovery must start with harnessing the hearts and minds of staff and changing the culture of the service so that it would support recovery principles and practice. Our journey so far has therefore been more about the service and the staff than the users of the service. In this chapter we will describe how we set about developing the people, processes, paperwork and practices to support the implementation of a recovery approach within our secure service. This is a 'work in progress'. There are many areas still to develop, but we will describe here what has been achieved and what we have learned along the way.

The service

The Hatherton Centre is a 47-bed medium secure unit serving Staffordshire and Shropshire. It admits adult men detained under the Mental Health Act with a primary diagnosis of mental illness. Service users are admitted from courts, prisons, local hospitals and other secure units. The average length of stay is approximately two years, but ten beds are commissioned as 'long stay'.

Developing the Hatherton Centre Rehabilitation Framework

In 2003 we began to develop a framework to formally describe the holistic, person-centred care and rehabilitation we aspired to provide to service users. At that time the academic and research literature on psychiatric rehabilitation did not readily, in our view, translate into a coherent, comprehensive, integrated recovery-based service model. Those models that did exist tended to be specific to a particular service (Roberts, Davenport, Holloway and Tattan, 2006). Models of in-patient psychiatric rehabilitation derived from the 1980s (e.g. Wing and Morris, 1981) and 1990s (e.g. Anthony, Cohen and Farkas, 1990). They were important in helping service users overcome the effects of institutionalisation and acquire skills for community living during the closure of the large psychiatric 'asylums'. However, after the move to 'community care' little was published about psychiatric rehabilitation until 2005 when Holloway declared 'The forgotten need for rehabilitation in mental health services' (Holloway, 2005).

Our view was that the psychiatric rehabilitation model was still applicable to forensic service users classed as requiring long-term medium secure care, particularly those transferred from high secure hospitals after many years of institutional care (Davies and Abbott, 2006). However, the models are couched in terms of disability, dysfunction, impairment and disadvantage, rather than the strengths and responsibilities emphasised in a recovery approach. Some models refer to service user involvement, empowerment and hope. Some even use the term recovery but, as highlighted by Drennan and Alred (this volume), the notion of recovery from psychotic experiences did not embrace today's expanded meaning of recovery, a distinction that is masked by the common language used by psychiatric rehabilitation and recovery paradigms.

In 2003, writings from the service user movement (e.g. Deegan, 1988; Allott *et al.*, 2002) were available in the UK, but the recovery approach was only beginning to take hold in a few general mental health services. It had not reached most forensic mental health services. Other models of care such as the Tidal Model (Barker, 1998) offered a valuable contribution but were uni-disciplinary. We wanted a framework that reflected the strong multi-disciplinary working which is a hallmark of our service. We recognised the value of healthy tension between medical, social, psychological, occupational and nursing models but wanted a framework that could integrate these to support holistic care planning. This was consistent with the guiding principles for the delivery of recovery-oriented mental health services subsequently published by the National Institute for Mental Health in England, which noted that recovery is most effective when a holistic approach is applied (NIMHE, 2005). We also required the framework to support and facilitate service user involvement in care planning. Finally, the service recognised that rehabilitation should commence on the day of admission (Holloway, 2005) and could provide the model of care throughout the service users' stay.

As we could not find a model that met these specifications, we decided to create one locally that was owned by the staff and service users who would use it. This began with a series of project days involving as many disciplines and ward-based staff as possible, looking at how to improve the quality of care and rehabilitation we provided. The framework was presented and developed at these meetings. Staff at all levels made significant contributions in shaping the framework as it evolved to the current version. For example, the pillars for sexuality and spirituality were added as a result of suggestions from nursing staff. Service users' views were sought at two points in the development process and changes were made in light of their comments. The final version of the Hatherton Centre Rehabilitation Framework (HCRF) is shown in Figure 8.1. This framework has not been published before. It continues to be developed and modified to reflect the position of the service in its journey towards delivering recovery-oriented care.

The HCRF comprises eight vertical pillars, representing components of care, and two themes, which underpin the forensic mental health rehabilitation process (represented as wavy lines across the page). The themes are recovery and

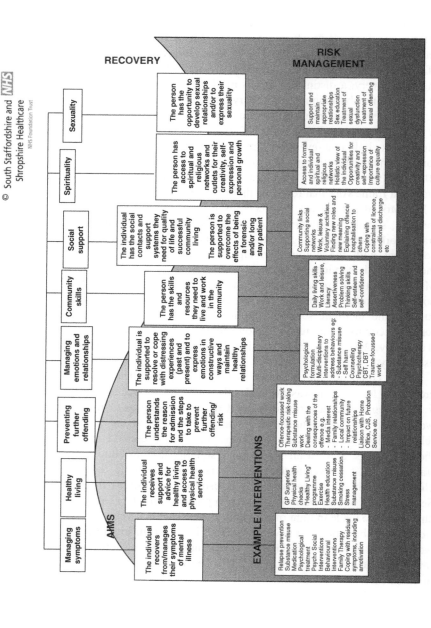

Figure 8.1 Forensic Mental Health Service Hatherton Centre Rehabilitation Framework

risk management. One of the ward staff initially proposed that recovery should be included as a theme, and its importance for us has grown over the years. This was endorsed in 2006 when the Chief Nursing Officer's review of mental health nursing stated that 'the key principles and values of the recovery approach will inform mental health nursing practice in all areas of care' (Department of Health, 2006). For a considerable time, 'Service User Empowerment and Choice', 'Quality of Life', and 'Social Inclusion' were additional themes. This was because staff recognised and valued those concepts before they had a full understanding of the recovery approach. At that time the themes also had particular prominence in the national guidance and were therefore useful in drawing the service's attention to the work required in these areas (Department of Health, 2005; Social Exclusion Unit, 2004). At the time of writing, 'Promoting Equality and Diversity' would be a useful sub-theme because the Equality Act (2010) requires particular attention to be paid to this area at present. We see these sub-themes as opportunities to further strengthen and drive forward the recovery approach in practice, harnessing the energy required for transformational change.

Risk management was the final theme to be added to the HCRF, in recognition that this is a core element of the rehabilitation process within forensic settings. The document 'Best Practice in Managing Risk' (Department of Health, 2007) clearly states that service users should be involved in assessing and managing their own risk. Yet for the reasons outlined at the start of this chapter, this often poses a significant challenge to forensic services and staff. Including risk management at the heart of the framework, on an equal footing with recovery, acknowledges these challenges, but also the opportunities it presents. It encourages honest discussion between staff and service users about the work that has to be done and the context in which risk decisions are made, including involvement of authorities outside the service user's care team such as the courts, Mental Health Review tribunals and the Ministry of Justice.

The eight pillars (represented as vertical columns in the diagram) are intended to cover all key elements of holistic care. Inevitably, there is some crossover between pillars. Substance Misuse, for example, could be relevant to managing mental illness, offending, physical health and social networks, so the most relevant pillar is designated to cover this area for each service user. Listed under each pillar are the types of tasks that would be relevant and some of the interventions used to implement care and rehabilitation under that pillar. This can be seen in the HCRF in Figure 8.1. The list is for illustrative purposes and is certainly not exhaustive. Linked to each pillar, we have created modules which describe the evidence base behind particular interventions or approaches. It has to be said that this is the least developed part of the entire project, partly due to competing demands on our time, but also because the current evidence base was relatively limited.

As the framework is used across the patient pathway, from admission to discharge, greater emphasis will be placed on different pillars at different points in the service user's stay. Thus whilst greater attention may be paid to

'Managing Symptoms' and 'Preventing Further Offending' on admission, the pillars for 'Community Skills' and 'Social Support' are likely to have more emphasis as the individual prepares for discharge.

Some pillars will more naturally fall to certain professional groups. Managing Symptoms is often the pillar with the greatest number of care plans, reflecting the multi-disciplinary teams' continued use of the medical model. It was put as the first pillar to facilitate staff use of the HCRF, despite service user feedback that they would prefer it was not first. This reflects the compromises that have to be reached to overcome resistance to change. However this pillar also embraces psychological and psychosocial models of mental 'illness' and 'symptom' management. Similarly, the Healthy Living pillar is placed second to facilitate efficient discussions and recording in multi-disciplinary team meetings.

Specialist psychological assessments and interventions are often recorded under the Managing Emotions and Relationships and the Preventing Further Offending pillars. The Community Skills and Social Support pillars are most closely linked to traditional rehabilitation and occupational therapy models, such as the Model of Human Occupation (Kielhofner, 1985). As such, they have the closest fit with traditional professional practice of nurses, social workers and occupational therapists. However the emphasis is on integrating the multi-disciplinary input to provide seamless, holistic, patient-centred care driven by service user need, not by professional discipline.

Spirituality and Sexuality tend to be addressed least by mental health services, despite being important from the service user's perspective (Perkins, 2003). Staff often lack confidence to discuss these areas with service users. There is clearly a need for more focussed staff training, but simply highlighting them as pillars in the HCRF has allowed more discussion about these topics. We found that the Sexuality pillar supported some staff to recognise the need to carefully monitor the effect of medication on sexual functioning and the impact of this on the individual. We also began to think about how the organisation could create an environment in which appropriate expressions of sexuality could be accepted, normalised and positive models of sexual relationships better communicated. At the time of the HCRF development the service was mixed-sex and had supported two marriages between service users.

There are various definitions of spirituality in the literature (Nolan and Crawford, 1997; Koslander *et al.*, 2009; Kissman and Maurer, 2002). The Spirituality pillar takes spirituality in its broadest sense. It addresses the needs of individuals who wish to practice a particular religion, but also considers cultural needs, personal development, fulfilment and self-expression. Colleagues within the service have developed an assessment and training pack for staff to help them discuss this area with service users (Vaggers *et al.*, 2008).

Care planning

The HCRF has proved valuable in structuring our thinking about the care we provide. This is reflected in multi-disciplinary discussions and record-keeping.

The HCRF is used as the structure for multi-disciplinary treatment plans, which are discussed at weekly multi-disciplinary meetings and at formal reviews held under the Care Programme Approach (CPA). Identified service user needs and planned interventions, as well as who is responsible for the implementation of this, are recorded under the eight pillars. For a while, the HCRF was also used for nursing care plans. This ensured that the framework was embedded within the day-to-day paperwork of the service. Training was provided to staff when the HCRF structure was introduced.

The impact of the HCRF on multi-disciplinary treatment plans was evaluated in spring 2009. The results inevitably varied to some extent between clinical teams, but overall a significant difference was found before and after implementation of the HCRF in the number of care plans listed under the pillars for Spirituality and Sexuality, suggesting that these areas were being considered for every patient (McAdam *et al.*, 2009). At the same time as the work to develop the HCRF and embed this in the paperwork and systems of our service, a number of other initiatives were underway to ensure organisational commitment, create the culture, transform the workforce and support staff in their recovery journey (Sainsbury Centre, 2009).

Harnessing hearts and minds in staff teams

Specialist Practitioner post

During the early development of the HCRF we recognised that we would need to dedicate considerable time and energy to promoting recovery in order to achieve culture change. We needed to send a message that we were serious about implementing a recovery approach. The service created the post of Specialist Practitioner in Recovery using money from a vacancy in the Psychology Department and some directorate underspend. This was one of three innovative posts developed using the principles of 'New Ways of Working' (NIMHE, 2007). The post was advertised externally and filled by a nurse with extensive ward-based experience (first author SC). The initiative was welcomed and supported by the service, which has always had strong multi-disciplinary working and service user focus. The post was based within the Psychology Department, but a multi-disciplinary steering group was set up to monitor and support this new role, ensuring whole-service ownership of the venture.

The Specialist Practitioner was first tasked with writing a 'Recovery Workbook' and also with raising staff awareness of the recovery approach. We felt that for the Recovery Workbook to be used consistently with service users in a meaningful way, staff must have not just an understanding but a commitment to the principles underlying recovery; we needed to address the hearts as well as the minds of staff. Further, to provide the best chance of any new approach being successfully introduced and sustained within a traditional institutional setting such as a secure hospital, it would be essential to achieve a critical mass of staff who were committed in 'heart and mind' to recovery. We knew that we also needed to get it ingrained into the paperwork and daily practices of the service in order to sustain it.

Staff Recovery Champions

In addition to the new Specialist Practitioner post, a structure was created whereby two nurses from each ward and an occupational therapist were appointed to act as 'Recovery Champions'. They meet monthly with the Specialist Practitioner and generate lively discussions and ideas for continuing to change the culture for the service users. These roles provide day-to-day support and advice to staff and service users on the principles of recovery.

Staff training

Every member of staff in the directorate attended Recovery Awareness sessions early in the process of organisational implementation. This was to give everyone a basic understanding of the principles and an awareness of the culture changes that faced the service. These sessions were embedded in the induction for all new staff joining the directorate, and were available as a refresher course for existing staff who required support. We also bought in a three-day training workshop (Working to Recovery, 2007). Eighty clinical staff attended this training, which encouraged participants to explore the philosophy of recovery and the underlying principles on which it rests. The training considered recovery as a process, while also introducing creative ways of helping people within mental health services to dream, plan and move on to a more fulfilled life. It also included an experiential element, in this way helping staff to think about recovery in their own lives. The training was evaluated and very well received, making a positive impact on the way staff understood recovery. In addition, all ward-based qualified staff had brief training on how to support the clients to use their workbooks.

Staff Recovery Workbook

Sticking to the principle that we should not encourage others to do something that we are not willing to try ourselves, we developed a recovery workbook especially for staff. We recognised that we needed to ensure that staff felt supported in their recovery journeys, making it 'safe' for them to prioritise the needs of service users and to raise their expectations and hopes. Staff will remain the key 'carriers of hope' (Sainsbury Centre, 2009). We wrote, piloted and printed a Staff Recovery Workbook. This was to encourage staff to think about all their experiences at work using the principles of a recovery approach, and enable them to support clients in working towards their own recovery. Loosely based on the eight pillars of the HCRF, the workbook encourages staff to reflect on their experiences at work, to look at what they would like to change, and to explore how to achieve this. Some staff chose to take some of these issues to their supervision and appraisal meetings.

Harnessing Hope: The Service User's Recovery Workbook

Following the successful introduction of the staff recovery workbooks, we continued to think about how to design a workbook for service users. We decided that the workbook should ask questions that are linked to the eight pillars of the HCRF, with sections as follows:

- Recovering from or managing my symptoms
- How can I live more healthily?
- What do I need to do, or learn about myself, to make sure I don't reoffend?
- What different feelings do I experience each day? What helps to change these feelings?
- What skills do I need to learn to help me look after myself and become more independent? Where and how can I learn these skills?
- Who are the most important people in my life? How would I like them to support me?
- What do spirituality and/or religion mean to me?
- Do I feel comfortable with my sexuality?

All the above sections also have subsections to support change as required. The workbook was developed and then piloted with clients and their key workers from each of our four wards. We interviewed all of the participants and some of the key questions and responses are shown in Box 8.1 below. The comments were taken up and changes made, particularly to the format of the workbook, as recommended by the service users.

All of the above comments were extremely useful in adapting the wording, and developing a service workbook with our own recovery logo, which was in full use across the Hatherton Centre from June 2008.

Box 8.1 Perspectives on the Workbook

Service user perspective

How did completing the workbook, with the support of your key worker, have an effect on your relationship with them?

'We've got a much better relationship now. I can talk about more personal stuff.'
'I didn't work with my key worker to do it. I wanted to do it on my own. I'm planning to discuss what I've learnt with him soon.'
'I could talk to him better and it improved my trust in him. Man bonding.'

***Were the subjects covered helpful/unhelpful? Which ones did you find
most useful? What did you find the least useful? Would you like to see
anything changed in the workbook, and if so what?***

'Helpful. The questions about living healthily and feelings that I experience were the most helpful. Spirituality and Sexuality were the most
difficult to do.'

'Very helpful. Health and reoffending were most relevant to me.
Spirituality and Sexuality were the least relevant. It is worded really
clearly and is easy to understand.'

'Helpful. Relationships and Skills were the most helpful. Spirituality
was the least helpful.'

'It's helpful. I've got closer to the staff. It'll be helpful for all
patients when they first arrive at the Hatherton.'

'This workbook will help people to discover every little thing about
themselves. Could we have a loose-leaf file?'

Staff perspective

***What effect did working through the workbook have on your
relationship with the service user?***

'Really positive, built up more of a rapport. I've got a better insight
into him. He's given me little snippets of information that I probably
wouldn't have been given if he wasn't using the workbook. A very
positive experience.'

'Improved, because he was able to talk to me more often and more
in depth and he didn't avoid me afterwards. I had to strongly encourage
him to write it himself because he wasn't keen to do so, and wanted
me to do it for him, but as it's his workbook I felt it was important for
him to own it.'

***Did the workbook help you to ask any difficult questions?
If so what?***

'Mainly questions about his Sexuality. It helped us to have a frank,
honest and open discussion. I also asked some difficult questions about
his relationships and he was able to talk about his dad and the index
offence, both of which he normally avoids.'

'Due to some of the prompting questions we were able to look more
deeply into the index offence and his previous drug use. His lack of
social networks became very apparent. He only has his mum and

dad and other drug users. He is now looking at what he wants to do about that.'

How has the workbook impacted on your one-to-one sessions?

Staff reported that the workbook helped them to structure and plan for their sessions with service users.

Every service user is given a workbook on admission and it is their property to keep. A number of service users are choosing to take them to their individual structured therapeutic sessions with their key workers and are working in depth on the areas relevant to them. They use them to inform the multi-disciplinary teams of their hopes, plans and goals, and to integrate their wishes into the care planning process. Recovery Awareness groups have been set up, as well as additional support sessions for service users. We established supervision sessions to support staff using the workbook in individual sessions with service users.

Evaluation of the workbook

The support the workbook provided to staff to have more recovery-orientated discussions with service users was formally audited (Carr and McGowan, 2009). The audit also aimed to identify areas for further training and development with respect to staff knowledge and skills. A self-report questionnaire was developed which consisted of a combination of rating scales and open-ended questions. All ward-based qualified nurses were invited to complete the questionnaire and all responses remained confidential. We had a 78 per cent response rate. Twenty-two clients were using the Recovery Workbook in individual sessions, with the majority of sessions taking place once a week. Other service users were choosing to use the workbooks on their own. Staff were asked to identify what they thought was most and least useful about the Workbook, and the responses were grouped into themes. Staff highlighted it as helping to structure individual sessions with service users. They also felt that it helped to support a holistic approach to care, to encourage active symptom management using methods other than medication, and to promote engagement and a sense of hope for service users. The sections on Sexuality and Spirituality were identified most often as being least useful, and the most difficult subjects to discuss. One hypothesis regarding this was that staff may lack knowledge, experience and confidence in discussing these areas with clients. Overall, the audit suggested that, in general, nursing staff found the workbooks to be a useful tool and that some of the objectives for introducing the workbooks were being met, such as helping to provide structure in individual sessions, engagement with service users and promoting an holistic approach to care. However, some staff still lacked confidence in their ability to use the Recovery Workbook as a tool for promoting a service user's recovery, and a number of institutional barriers were raised that need to be addressed, such as the balance between therapeutic interventions and security. This audit focussed on the experience of staff members. A further audit of the views of service users who have used the Recovery Workbook was planned at the time of writing.

The way forward

The Specialist Practitioner will continue to regularly attend multi-disciplinary meetings and team away days to promote a recovery approach. This role will continue to challenge and encourage other staff until the changes are absorbed and become self-governing. As the service continues to become more recovery-orientated, the service paperwork and training must continue to adapt and evolve accordingly. We have introduced staff-facilitated Recovery Groups on the wards and it is our intention to ensure that these become service user-led as soon as possible. We have altered our staff recruitment processes to include the assessment of values and beliefs which support the provision of a recovery-orientated service. We have also begun to work with staff and service users at our low secure service in Shrewsbury to introduce the Recovery Workbook there.

Harnessing hearts and minds – summary and conclusions

In this chapter we have described our journey so far in implementing a recovery approach within a medium secure setting. This has been a step-by-step process of staff training, developing tools such as the HCRF and the Recovery Workbook and ensuring that these became embedded in the day-to-day paperwork and practices of the service. As a result we have made steady progress towards the service becoming more thoroughly recovery-orientated. We been able to mobilise a groundswell of staff, from a range of disciplines, who are committed 'heart and mind' to the principles of the recovery approach. The Recovery Workbook and the Hatherton Centre Rehabilitation Framework have been embedded within the service and help to support holistic care planning. However, there remains much more to do, including developing more collaborative care planning, focussing on strengths/assets rather than pathology, more positive risk-taking and generating more opportunities for service users to make decisions and learn from mistakes.

What have we learned from our journey so far? We have confirmed the crucial importance of addressing the culture of the service and underlying staff attitudes in order to achieve sustainable change. Creating a post dedicated to developing a recovery orientation has provided the leadership and energy needed to start changing the hearts and minds of staff. A post-holder with the right organisational and leadership skills, who is respected by colleagues, is essential. It has been our experience that a passion for recovery values, and not simply a theoretical understanding of the principles, is pivotal in sustaining momentum.

We have also identified the essential role of supervision in supporting ward-based staff when introducing a new approach. Support whilst putting into practice changes in values and actions is key. The Staff Recovery Workbook contributed to this, but ongoing support is also necessary.

Finally, our experience to date has confirmed that culture change at a service level is not enough. It is necessary to examine the wider system and how this supports or undermines a recovery approach. For example, recent Department of Health documents clearly support a recovery approach (e.g. DoH, 2007) but this is not as evident from all parts of the system. Many service users in forensic settings require approval from the Ministry of Justice before taking escorted or unescorted leave from the hospital. A recovery approach encourages steps towards independence and positive risk-taking, allowing the individual to learn from their own mistakes, recognising the value of self-determination and hope (e.g. DoH, 2007). This approach, however, needs to be sensitive to the political climate in which it operates and the perspectives of Criminal Justice Agencies, and to find the means to enter into an open and collaborative dialogue with all aspects of service management.

It is also arguable, however, that a solution to the ongoing tension between public safety and the needs of the individual service user could come from recognition that the greatest public protection occurs when individuals take responsibility for managing their own risk. This requires that they can trust services to provide the help they need when they request it. This acceptance of service users' rights and responsibilities is at the heart of the recovery approach and could enhance risk management if understood and supported by the wider criminal justice system. While change at the widest system level is still needed, change at a local level can make a difference to service users' experiences, to give hope and illustrate that alternatives are possible. We have seen the hearts and minds of the members of our staff teams change, and as a result some of our service users have begun to think differently about their futures.

Acknowledgements

The authors wish to gratefully acknowledge the contribution of Kathy McAdam, Head of Forensic Occupational Therapy, who co-led the development of the Hatherton Centre Rehabilitation Framework with the author (SH). Also Dave Mason, Head of Forensic Nursing, who with Kathy McAdam was instrumental in the implementation of the framework across the service. Our thanks also to all the service users and staff who have contributed to the development of the framework and the Recovery Workbook over the years.

References

Allott, P., Loganathan, L. and Fulford, K. W. M. (2002) 'Discovering Hope for Recovery: A Review of a Selection of Recovery Literature, Implications for Practice and Systems Change'. *Canadian Journal of Community Mental Health*, 21(3): 13–34.

Anthony, W. A., Cohen, M. R. and Farkas, M. D. (1990) *Psychiatric Rehabilitation.* Boston: Boston University Press.

Barker, P. (1998) 'It's Time to Turn the Tide'. *Nursing Times*, 94(46): 70–73.

Carr, S. and McGowan, A. (2009) 'Introducing a Recovery Workbook for Service Users: An Evaluation of Staff Experience' paper presented to the International Association of Forensic Mental Health Services Conference June. Unpublished.

Davies, S. and Abbott, P. (2006) 'Forensic Rehabilitation'. In G. Roberts, S. Davenport, F. Holloway and T. Tattan (eds) *Enabling Recovery: The Principles and Practice of Rehabilitation Psychiatry.* London: Gaskell.

Deegan, P. E. (1988) 'Recovery: The Lived Experience of Rehabilitation'. *Psychosocial Rehabilitation Journal*, 11(4): 11–19.

Department of Health. (2005) *Creating a Patient-led NHS: Delivering the NHS Improvement Plan.* London: Department of Health.

—— (2006) *From Values to Action: The Chief Nursing Officer's review of mental health nursing.* London: Department of Health.

—— (2007) 'Best Practice in Managing Risk'. Published by Department of Health: London.

Goffman, E. (1968) *Asylums.* Hardmondsworth: Penguin.

Holloway, F. (2005) *The Forgotten Need for Rehabilitation in Contemporary Mental Health Services.* London: Faculty of Rehabilitation and Social Psychiatry, Royal College of Psychiatrists. http://www.rcpsych.ac.uk/pdf/frankolloway_oct05.pdf. Accessed May 2010.

Kielhofner, G. (1985) *A Model of Human Occupation: Theory and Application.* Baltimore. Williams and Wilkins.

Kissman, K. and Maurer, L. (2002) 'East meets West: Therapeutic aspects of spirituality in health, mental health and addiction recovery'. *International Social Work*, 45(1): 35–42.

Koslander, T., da Silva, A. B. and Roxberg, A. (2009) 'Existential and Spiritual Needs in Mental Health Care – an Ethical and Holistic Perspective'. *Journal of Holistic Nursing*, 27(1): 34–42.

McAdam, K., Mason, D. and Havers, S. (2009) *'More Than Care Planning'.* Paper presented to the Royal College of Nursing Mental Health Conference, Cardiff, March.

NIMHE. (2005) *Guiding Statement on Recovery.* National Institute for Mental Health in England. Available online at http://www.nimhe.org.uk. Accessed 30 September 2007.

—— (2007) *Mental Health: New Ways of Working for Everyone.* National Institute for Mental Health in England. Available online at http://www.nimhe.csip.org.uk/nww. Accessed June 2008.

Nolan, P. and Crawford, P. (1997) 'Towards a rhetoric of spirituality in mental health care'. *Journal of Advanced Nursing*, 26(2): 289–294.

Perkins, R. (2003) 'Paper presented to Stakeholder Day on User Involvement Conference', February 2003, South Staffordshire Healthcare NHS Trust.

Roberts, G., Davenport, S., Holloway, F. and Tattan, T. (2006) *Enabling Recovery: The Principles and Practice of Rehabilitation Psychiatry.* London: Gaskell.

Sainsbury Centre for Mental Health. (2009) *Implementing Recovery. A new framework for organisational change.* Position Paper. London: Sainsbury Centre.

Slade, M. (2009) *100 ways to support recovery. A guide for mental health professionals.* Rethink recovery series: volume 1. Available online at http://www.rethink.org/100ways. Accessed 5 October 2009.

Social Exclusion Unit. (2004) *Mental Health and Social Exclusion Report*. London: Office of the Deputy Prime Minister.

Vaggers, S. D., Nivarti, S. P., Hart, G. and Reynolds, J. (2008) *Integrating Spirituality into an Rehabilitation Framework at the Hatherton Centre*. Poster presentation at Royal College of Psychiatrists Forensic Faculty Meeting, Liverpool, February 2008.

Wing, J. K. and Morris, B. (1981) *Handbook of Psychiatric Rehabilitation Practice*. Oxford: Oxford University Press.

Working to Recovery Ltd. (2007) *In-House Training Programmes*. Available online at http://www.workingtorecovery.co.uk. Accessed 7 June 2007.

9 'Supporting recovery' and 'moving on' – the recovery approach applied to group intervention programmes in in-patient settings

Helen Miles

With: Tom Foulds, Sonia Griffin, Carol Guinan, Dr Tracy King, Anna Murphy, Kate Pellowe, Miriam Pucyutan, and service users from the Trevor Gibbens Unit, Kent Forensic Psychiatry Service.

Introduction

The concepts associated with 'recovery' are beginning to have a central importance in mental health services in the UK (Shepherd *et al.*, 2008), and this is increasingly so within forensic secure mental health services as well. This chapter will focus on one secure unit (Trevor Gibbens Unit, Kent Forensic Psychiatry Service) and specifically on how a recovery approach has become a central part of the rehabilitation programme. Descriptions of the process of the development of user-led 'recovery groups' will be presented, along with reflections made during the process by both mental health professionals and service users, and guidance for other forensic mental health services considering setting up similar group-based recovery interventions. Most importantly, in the course of our forensic secure unit's recovery journey we have come to realise that placing the service user at the centre of the development of the recovery model has been key to the successful implementation of a secure recovery approach within the forensic mental health services. We start with one service user's poetic reflections on recovery, written during one of the rehabilitation group interventions in mid-2008:

Recovery

> With the project of recovery
> I made an important discovery
> There's more to it than meets the eye
> At first I gave a shrug and then a sigh

Recovery, what does it really involve?
How would it unfold and evolve?
As I was asked I drew a sketch
What from my consciousness could I fetch
Like some of the others in the group
I selected words to make a pictorial soup
I managed to think of a list of six things
They would be attached to recovery by strings
And without being in the least bit rude
The ingredients of my soup include
Social inclusion and being healthier
Looking to the future and being happier
Hope and optimism and getting better
I savoured every single letter
The prospects make me smile
And the outcome looks so worthwhile
Recovery, I think you will find
Is simply an improvement in one's state of mind...

Starting the recovery journey in a forensic secure setting

As noted by Shepherd *et al.* (2008), *'one of the biggest obstacles to the implementation of recovery-orientated practice has been the lack of clarity and agreement regarding what it actually means in practice'.* Therefore when Kent & Medway NHS and Social Care Partnership Trust, the main stakeholder in the Kent forensic mental health services (or the Trevor Gibbens Unit: TGU), made a commitment to providing services that were recovery-focused, a core group of multi-disciplinary staff at the TGU met to consider what this actually meant in practice. One of the first observations made during this process was that it may be difficult for forensic mental health service users, who by definition have been detained for long periods of time in secure conditions, to achieve the local NHS Trust's primary aim of 'an individual taking control, making choices and developing a sense of self-worth and hope.' These initial discussions also noted that parts of our current practice (e.g. the Patients Council, a forum for service users to have their views heard on issues relating to their care and treatment, and the provision of Hucking Hill House Farm Day Therapeutic Programme) were already 'recovery focused', but not necessarily labelled as such.

Therefore, a few key decisions were made at this stage in the forensic service's recovery journey. First, that semantics were important. The recovery approach was framed as a philosophy, rather than a model, to reduce any fear amongst staff in the secure unit that it would be 'something new to learn', and subsequent resistance to implementation. Second, that given the prominence of the service user

Table 9.1 Recovery focus group results

	What recovery means to you?	What is your experience of recovery?	What are you doing at present to recover?
Group 1	– better person – hope – motivation – improvement in mental state	– right medication – groups – progress (e.g. more leave) – speaking with staff	– joining in groups – talking to staff – doing things you enjoy (e.g. art, music, pottery) – being in hospital
Group 2	– discovering a whole new world – becoming well	– having consistent and sensible thoughts – clear thoughts	– follow the care plan as much as possible – cooking, groups, walks, medications, healthy eating, exercise
Group 3	– coping – being well	– getting out in community – groups/therapeutic activities	– compliance with medications – helping others

perspective in the recovery literature (e.g. Deegan, 2001), any implementation of the recovery approach should consult with service users from the beginning. Consequently, the first step was to employ a focus group methodology across several time points and different wards within the TGU, to ask service users for their views about recovery. Table 9.1 outlines the main themes from this initial consultation process.

It can be seen that service users reported a mixture of 'wellness' and 'coping' with symptoms as their definition of recovery, and that group interventions or other therapeutic activities were viewed as an important part of their recovery processes. It was also noteworthy that service users had some clear ideas about recovery and were actively interested in being involved in the consultation and development process. Consequently, it was agreed that in order to 'embed' the recovery approach very decisively and clearly within the rehabilitation programme, a 'recovery group intervention programme' would be implemented within the different wards in the secure service. Andresen *et al.* (2006)'s model of the five stages of the recovery journey appeared to be a helpful way to conceptualise the framework and aims of these group interventions throughout the different stages of the service users' admission to the secure unit or their care pathway. This model is presented in Figure 9.1, with the TGU recovery groups at each stage mapped onto it.

Each of the different recovery groups will now be discussed in more detail in order to outline how the recovery approach was implemented within the group intervention programme in the different parts of the forensic secure service.

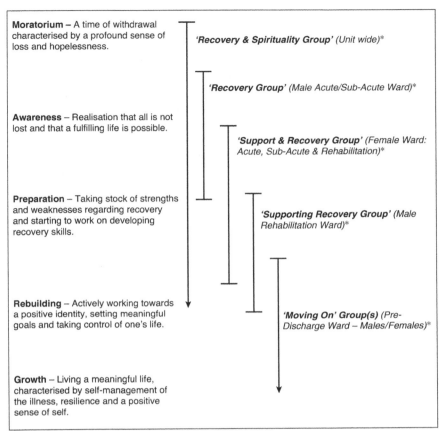

Moratorium – A time of withdrawal characterised by a profound sense of loss and hopelessness.

'Recovery & Spirituality Group' (Unit wide)*

'Recovery Group' (Male Acute/Sub-Acute Ward)*

Awareness – Realisation that all is not lost and that a fulfilling life is possible.

'Support & Recovery Group' (Female Ward: Acute, Sub-Acute & Rehabilitation)*

Preparation – Taking stock of strengths and weaknesses regarding recovery and starting to work on developing recovery skills.

'Supporting Recovery Group' (Male Rehabilitation Ward)*

Rebuilding – Actively working towards a positive identity, setting meaningful goals and taking control of one's life.

'Moving On' Group(s) (Pre-Discharge Ward – Males/Females)*

Growth – Living a meaningful life, characterised by self-management of the illness, resilience and a positive sense of self.

* The names of the recovery groups differ as they were chosen by the service users/staff working on each of the wards.

Figure 9.1 Andresen *et al.* (2006) Five stages of recovery and the associated TGU recovery groups

Recovery group interventions within forensic secure settings

Recovery in a forensic acute/sub-acute setting

The 'recovery group' within the men's acute/sub-acute wards was devised by the ward occupational therapist and nursing team leader, with additional support from other nursing staff and service users. It was held weekly in the afternoon, allowing a maximum number of service users to attend. The purpose was to provide an opportunity for service users to think about moving forward from the acute/sub-acute wards, often areas of the forensic mental health service where 'hope', a key component of recovery, is limited. The group format also encouraged service users to think about and identify the 'choices' available to them, to influence their recovery within the secure forensic setting. The theoretical framework of the group was primarily a client-centred approach, emphasising the therapeutic relationship (e.g. Pelau, 1952) and recognising the chaotic nature of change, often the only true constant (Baker, 1996) with acutely unwell individuals. Therefore, it aimed to support service users to become aware when small positive changes towards recovery are occurring, and identify pragmatic ways that they have learnt what works for them and why, so that they can begin to navigate their recovery journey. Other cognitive behavioural, narrative, psychodynamic or systematic models were also drawn upon as appropriate.

Specifically, it was recognised that the service users may not be familiar with the recovery philosophy, so group sessions began with a semi-structured didactic teaching component, after which service users explored and reflected upon the relevance of the topic to them. It was intended that the recovery philosophy would not only increase service users' ability to explore and develop an understanding of their experiences, but would also enable them to begin to take some personal responsibility for their recovery and gain some limited independence within the secure setting, as opposed to remaining powerless victims within the forensic mental health system. Examples of topics covered to date have included:

- What is recovery / moving on?
- Where do you want to be in future?
- What are your experiences of the forensic mental health system?
- Diagnosis – what does this mean?
- Personal responsibility
- Personal relationships and social inclusion
- Being a victim – fears and past traumas
- Acceptance
- Unusual beliefs we have about things

It is also intended that service users further on in their recovery through the forensic service may be invited to speak within the group in the future.

To date, the semi-structured approach to the group and service user involvement (e.g. in the preparation by one service user before each group of a 'recovery cake' to be shared within the group, choice of topics to be discussed, discussions led by service users) has been successful. Although there were concerns that a group format would not be appropriate with a population who were often still quite mentally unwell, the service users appear to have benefited from the sharing of their experiences and the opportunity to begin to consider recovery at an early stage in their admission to the forensic secure services. Consequently, the majority of the service users on the sub-acute ward, as well as some of those with appropriate leave from the acute ward, attended regularly. In terms of future directions, ways to increase service user empowerment and leadership of the group are being considered, which include nominating service users to prepare topics and facilitate the discussion.

Service user comments about the group are noted in the box below:

'I think that the NHS is still centred around containment rather than recovery. Staff need to catch up still.'

'I think that the Recovery Group is really helpful. There are things that you won't know like substances and how to cope and it helps you on the route to recovery by attending the group each week. Also because we are allowed to do the groups ourselves it helps to show what we have learnt and how far we are on our recovery. But in all, I would like to say that the group has been really helpful.'

Recovery in a forensic rehabilitation setting

The 'Supporting Recovery' group on the rehabilitation ward was the first recovery group intervention to commence within the forensic secure services, as it sat within the first clinical area to introduce the 'recovery philosophy'. Consequently, this group was more clearly defined and planned by staff then the previously discussed recovery group intervention. The specific aims of the supporting recovery group were defined as (1) to provide a supportive environment for service users to share experiences, reduce social isolation, and increase self-esteem and self-direction; (2) to increase service users' awareness of illness (physical/mental); (3) to increase service users' understanding of different treatment options; (4) to increase service users' understanding of relapse indicators; (5) to discuss the recovery philosophy and develop positive attitudes amongst staff and service users towards recovery; and (6) to explore positive ways that service users can continue their 'recovery journey' through the discussion of problems and the identification of solutions or coping strategies for the future.

The recovery group intervention consisted of a rolling programme of one-hour weekly, then fortnightly, afternoon sessions, held in comfy seats in the quiet lounge area and with refreshments provided. The group operated an open access policy, with service users encouraged to attend even if they missed previous sessions. This enabled the maximum number of service users to regularly attend. The group alternated psycho-educational structured sessions on a particular topic (facilitated by the psychologist, junior doctor and occupational therapist) with reflective unstructured sessions (facilitated by a non-ward-based psychologist and occupational therapist or nurse), the latter serving as an opportunity for service users to explore the relevance of the previous topic to themselves. Psycho-educational sessions included large group discussions, small group activities or exercises, case vignettes, identification of coping strategies, the use of patient leaflets and videos or newspaper articles, and drew on a variety of cognitive behavioural therapy (CBT), narrative and psychodynamic approaches, as required. Of note, the content of the psycho-educational group was often quite detailed and structured, which reflected the nature of the service user population within the rehabilitation setting, who were able to cope with a more intense, focused intervention.

Topics included:

- Psychotic symptoms (positive, negative or cognitive)
- Coping with low mood
- Dealing with diagnosis
- Different types of medication
- Psychology and occupational therapy
- The recovery philosophy
- Alcohol and drugs
- The stress-vulnerability model
- Dealing with stigma
- Positive recovery stories
- Managing stress
- Increasing self-esteem
- Future goals setting
- Relapse prevention

The group intervention was well received, with typically between 65 and 90 per cent of service users on the rehabilitation ward attending each week. Most of the service users readily grasped the concept of recovery and reported that they found it helpful to frame their admission as a 'recovery journey', as well as to begin to consider their next steps. It has also been found helpful to utilise noticeboards on the ward to display materials from the group, to further reinforce the recovery philosophy. A recovery art project developed out of interest in the recovery approach amongst some of the service users (see below). Of note, over time the group intervention became less structured and more similar to the group on the acute/sub-acute ward. This reflected increased service user involvement and suggests the importance of regularly reviewing rolling group intervention programmes and making appropriate adaptations as needed.

Service user comments about the group are shown in the box below:

> 'Having asked patients how they view the group I have summed up theirs and my view of the group: Before group (i.e. prison) some patients' experience of recovery would be to keep active, take meds but still be a little unwell. The group was a good chance to talk about issues such as psychosis and stigma. Also it was agreed that sharing problems with others was a beneficial experience. Some patients have also attributed their experiences of recovery to the stabilising effects of meds. Other patients believe that attending to hobbies and having a good staff/patient relationship can benefit recovery. Generally, the consensus amongst the patients who attend the group is that it can be a very helpful and interesting way to address peoples' mental health issues and can lead the way to a more active and rewarding role in life.'

'In this group, many different issues were discussed such as alcohol and drugs, the effects and the side-effects that they had on the individual. Medication was also looked at, the pros and the cons. The beneficial help they give and also what side-effects can do. Discussions on the possibility of relapse in the community and how to cope and stay out of hospital. Plus we talked about sections and life in the community. Also how courses in education and personal growth can help.'

'Patient Opinions of the Supporting Recovery Group: As required I have made a brief summary of patients' views on what they get from the supporting recovery group: 'An opportunity to get my views across'... 'Boredom/F**k All'...Conscience.'

As noted above, the rehabilitation ward also carried out a recovery art project as part of the rehabilitation programme. Art was chosen as a medium with which to explore recovery because creating artwork is inherently therapeutic and can bring about positive change to those who do it. The act of displaying art provides the artists and the community with awareness of the strength of creativity in the healing process. The recovery art project was a six-week project involving service users from the rehabilitation and pre-discharge wards. The objective of the project was to enable service users to have a deeper understanding about recovery and express this through creative works.

The project was made possible when the ward manager secured a small amount of funding from a local charity to fund a one-off session with a local art teacher in order to demonstrate acrylic painting techniques on canvas, as well as to purchase materials. The project lasted six weeks and was facilitated by the unit's occupational therapist. Service users were given the theme 'recovery' and asked to express what this meant to them through painting. The patients chose the best painting and an award was made. Paintings were then displayed in a service-wide exhibition, and remain as decoration on the walls of the rehabilitation ward to serve as a positive reminder of the expression of recovery by service users.

Service user comments about the recovery art project are given in the box below:

'A great chance to express feelings.'
'A good project threw up interesting ideas and concepts leading to recovery.'
'A journey from the darkness into the light.'
'A fascinating exhibition with great results.'

Figure 9.2 Recovery Art Project paintings from service users

Recovery within the Women's Unit

Within the forensic service, the women's ward meets the needs of service users, from the acute through the sub-acute to the rehabilitation phase of their admission. Consequently, the group intervention that was devised within this setting had to consider service users at all these differing stages of their recovery. Therefore, a brief version of the recovery group (10 sessions) for the men on the rehabilitation ward was devised and facilitated by multi-disciplinary staff as an open group to all women service users. Over the course of the sessions, the attendance fluctuated, although it was consistently at about 50 per cent. As in the recovery group interventions on the male wards, recovery principles were central, although the group was also psycho-educational, offering information (e.g. case vignettes, information leaflets and videos) on mental health issues relevant to the individual female service users. Group members were encouraged to reflect upon information material presented and to make this personally relevant. The staff to service user ratio was kept high in the women's group intervention in order that each group member could have this opportunity for individual reflection and to share their thoughts with facilitators, as well as to manage the sometimes challenging group dynamics appropriately.

The women's recovery group intervention was also found to provide a supportive environment, to foster a sense of peer support and enable ease of disclosure around mental health issues, to an extent that was perhaps more explicit with the women service users than the men. Consequently, themes relating to attachment and relationships were commonly present. As with the other group interventions on the men's wards, a strong emphasis was placed on involving service users in generating the discussion topics, which included:

- Decision-making and your role
- Aspects of psychosis
- The individual nature of symptoms
- Negative symptoms of psychosis
- Causes of mental illness
- Occupation and activity
- Stress management
- Relationships
- Medication and side-effects

Feedback on the group was positive (see box below) and service users reported that they had benefited from the group environment, particularly having the opportunity to listen to others' experiences and know that they were not alone in their recovery process.

'Thanks for an excellent group. I really feel I have learnt something new.'

'I enjoyed the whole group. It was rewarding. It showed me a lot about my mental health and how to overcome it. It's been great.'

'I really liked the stuff about living in the community and I found it surprising.'

'I think that listening to others' stories is really helpful.'

'They can give me all the therapy they want but I could still get ill again. I like this group because it will help me stay well and know what to do if I get unwell.'

Other feedback suggested that the group had helped service users to feel more positive about their own situation and better able to cope with their recovery. Of note, because the female service users responded well to the interactive elements of the group intervention, the next recovery group intervention will be practical sessions within which service users create their own personal recovery 'scrapbook'. This modification to the original approach again demonstrates the importance of ongoing flexibility in the delivery of recovery group interventions in order to match the needs of the service users attending them.

Recovery as 'moving on' from pre-discharge forensic settings

The 'moving on' group was devised to be the final stage in the recovery group programme and therefore takes place less frequently (i.e. monthly for one hour) on the men's and women's pre-discharge wards, again facilitated by multi-disciplinary staff. This recovery group intervention had aims more appropriate to the final stages of 'secure' recovery, such as (1) helping service users to utilise all available intra- and interpersonal resources to feel positive and in control of resettlement within the community, (2) consolidate treatment gains from time to time within the forensic unit, (3) setting of treatment goals for the future in addition to goals relating to areas of life important to recovery (e.g. employment, relationships, accommodation), (4) modelling appropriate acknowledgement of 'endings' after a long-term admission, within a forensic secure setting, and (5) fostering a greater level of self-efficacy and self-esteem in service users.

'Moving on' and coping with the final stage of recovery in a forensic setting before returning to the community therefore had a strong emphasis on relapse prevention and the development of appropriate recovery-orientated plans for the future. It was also acknowledged that this group should support service users to work through feelings of loss and discharge anxiety with regard to moving on from long admissions to the secure service, help orientate service users to changes in the community since they were last resident there, and address any practical skills necessary for moving on to the community. The recovery focus within the sessions stressed the importance of the personal meaning of moving on for each service user, with regular discussions about the recovery journey of each individual member and their progressions towards discharge. Central to the recovery approach within this group was the idea that, by pre-discharge, service users should have developed an idea of what helps them the most in terms of their own recovery, and sharing this will maximise their sense of empowerment and control for the future.

As with the other recovery group interventions, this group consisted of a balance of psycho-education and reflection, with the following topics chosen by group members:

– Fear and anxieties about moving on
– Experiences of being granted greater levels of freedom
– Forming new relationships and what to say about where you have been
– Hopes for the future
– Implications of conditions of discharge and Mental Health Act restrictions

In addition, outside agencies have attended the group to provide information relevant to service users at this stage in their recovery (e.g. Nacro, a crime reduction charity and Mind, a mental health charity).

Service user comments about the group are given in the box below, which again suggest that the group has been viewed as helpful by participants:

'The Moving On Group is open for discussion about moving on into the community and discharge. Different topics were discussed, such as life outside hospital. Coping whilst living in the community, the group is once monthly. It is constructive for the patient, returning into the community. This group is very helpful and has a good structure to it.'
'Learnt a lot…remember more in open groups…monthly is good.'

Recovery and spirituality throughout a forensic setting

Finally, a recovery and spirituality group intervention (of six one-hour sessions co-facilitated by the service chaplain and nurses) was set up service wide, following an internal audit which identified that issues around spirituality were an area of deficit within the therapeutic activities programme. Of note, participation in the group was lower than hoped, but this was suspected to be the result of the name of the group, as service users may have associated spirituality with religion, and therefore not perhaps considered the group as appropriate for them if they were not religious. Further explanation of the nature of the group intervention beforehand, and consideration of how recovery-based group interventions are advertised to service users, has therefore been taken up.

As with the other recovery group interventions within the forensic secure service, the format and the topics of discussion within the group were devised collaboratively with service users. These included:

- What is spirituality and what does it mean to you?
- Meaning, purpose, harmony and hope in life from internal and external sources
- Relationship and connecting meaningfully with self, others and a higher power (God)
- Who pulls the strings? Exploration of control in our lives
- Spirituality and coping
- Making changes for the future

Consequently, the aim of this group was slightly different from the other recovery group interventions in that it focused on one specific aspect of the recovery process – the role of spirituality – rather than multiple aspects. Future recovery group interventions could potentially focus on other aspects thought to be important to a particular group of service users (e.g. hope, control, empowerment, and so on). Of note, no particular belief system or structure was required to attend, only an interest in exploring spiritual concepts such as compassion, contemplation and appreciation of life in recovery.

This recovery group intervention was particularly reflective, and service users appeared to benefit from the time to pause and think about their own lives and personal belief systems, including how they coped in past difficult situations and used their spirituality in their recovery. Despite some of the service users experiencing residual psychotic symptoms and/or expressing unusual beliefs in this area, there was a noticeably high level of appropriate peer support, and participant satisfaction with the sessions was high. Moreover, this group intervention has highlighted the value of forensic mental health services being open to exploring the meaning of recovery in an alternative way to the traditional biopsychosocial model underpinning treatment and care.

Challenges and reflections

This chapter has attempted to outline the implementation of the recovery philosophy or model within forensic secure mental health services, in particular how a 'group intervention' format has introduced recovery at the centre of the group therapeutic activities or rehabilitation programmes. We have gained an appreciation of the importance of being flexible in approaching such an undertaking and in the process of devising group interventions, considering carefully service users' wishes, needs and levels of functioning, or phase of recovery.

All the authors of this chapter have found these recovery group interventions to be some of the most rewarding and interesting that they have facilitated whilst working in forensic mental health services and would argue that they are a positive and natural complement to the more structured group programme of psychological mental health or offending behaviour programmes and occupational therapy activities. These groups have specifically provided a good opportunity for service users to reflect upon and personalise the recovery philosophy as it has been implemented in the forensic secure service, and have resulted in them often having a better understanding of the recovery approach than some of the staff. Moreover, the groups have had secondary gains for some service users in providing an informal and 'safe' introduction to more structured groups (e.g. offending behaviour programmes), and reducing their anxiety about speaking in a group setting.

However, the last year or so since the implementation of the recovery group intervention programme has not been without its challenges, and any service considering setting up something similar should be mindful of these. For example, time dedicated to these activities can be difficult to fit around existing structured day programmes and there had to be some effort made by facilitators to organise the groups, as well as to promote their value to staff not directly involved. Moreover, the name of the group may have an impact on attendance. Where possible, we have tried to ensure that the name of the group is decided in collaboration with service users.

On reflection, we believe that the inclusion of the service user's perspective has been extremely important in ensuring the success of the recovery group intervention programme across the forensic secure service. At all stages, as far as possible within the forensic environment, service users have been involved in their development (e.g. time and location of group, topics chosen, format, provision of regular feedback about or evaluations of the groups, modifications to group structure in light of feedback, and so on), which has increased their ownership of the group and consequently their attendance and possible benefit from the group interventions. We would strongly advise other forensic secure services to include service users in their planning and development of similar recovery group intervention programmes in order to maximise their chance of success.

One of the other key challenges has been maintaining service user motivation and interest in the recovery groups throughout an often long admission within the forensic secure service. This has been achieved by varying the topics of the groups, having breaks between groups and utilising an open-door policy so that service users can attend groups as and when they are motivated to do so. This open-door policy has also ensured that service users who miss a session due to mental state deterioration or other issues are not excluded from future sessions. In addition, interest in the group sessions has been maintained by ensuring that the groups have been as interactive as possible, with a variety of different activities ranging from group discussions to videos, case vignettes, games, outside speakers, and so on.

It has also been important to allow service users in forensic settings opportunity to reflect upon their own experience of trauma around their offence and admission, as well as shame and guilt, and the impact of both their mental illness and offending behaviours upon themselves and others. These issues are a key part of 'secure' recovery or recovery in a forensic setting and the group interventions have aimed to give service users time to verbalise their own experiences at a pace that they are able to tolerate.

Consequently, in the development of the recovery group programme in the TGU, we have found that the group interventions may not immediately work 'over night' and perseverance on the part of staff facilitators has been important. Moreover, it has been found that regular peer-group supervision for all multi-disciplinary staff involved in the facilitation of the groups has been invaluable as a way to manage difficult group dynamics, discuss group processes, successes and difficulties, and share resources and 'recovery' materials to ensure consistency in the recovery philosophy across the forensic secure service.

Overall, a multi-disciplinary approach to the development and implementation of the recovery group intervention programme has been found to be the most useful, with representatives from all mental health professional disciplines within the forensic secure services having a role either in consultation, planning or facilitation of the recovery group interventions. The role of patience and key staff champions of recovery should also not be underestimated, as initially some staff and service users in forensic settings were often quite pessimistic about the relevance of recovery to them. However, over the course of the recovery group interventions (and basic recovery staff training), the recovery approach is now seen as meaningful and beneficial within the forensic secure service, evidenced within a recent local audit (Corlett and Miles, 2009).

In conclusion, recovery in forensic secure settings provides a new and interesting challenge to mental health services. Although it is made more difficult by the fact that forensic service users have the dual stigma of both a mental disorder and offending behaviour, our experience shows that by placing 'recovery' at the centre of the therapeutic or rehabilitation group programmes within forensic mental health services, the approach has value, meaning and usefulness in secure settings.

References

Andresen, R., Caputi, P. and Oades, L. (2006) 'Stages of Recovery Instrument: Development of a measure of recovery from serious mental illness'. *Australian & New Zealand Journal of Psychiatry*, 40: 972–980.

Baker, P. (1996) 'Chaos and the way of Zen: psychiatric nursing and the uncertainty principle'. *Journal of Psychiatric and Mental Health Nursing*, 3: 235–244.

Corlett, H. and Miles, H. (2009) 'An evaluation of the implementation of the Recovery Model in a Secure Forensic service'. *British Journal of Forensic Practice*, 12(4): 14–25.

Deegan, P. R. (2001) 'Recovery as a journey of the heart'. *Psychiatric Rehabilitation Journal*, 19: 91–97.

Pelau, H. (1952) *Interpersonal Relations in Nursing*. New York: Putnam.

Shepherd, G., Boardman, J. and Slade, M. (2008) *Making Recovery a Reality*. London: Sainsbury Centre for Mental Health.

10 The seesaw of recovery in women's secure care

Sarah Birch

In 2002 the Department of Health produced a document entitled 'Women's Mental Health: Into the Mainstream', which emphasised the role of socioeconomic, physiological and psychological risk factors in women's lives, including their experiences of violence and abuse. It highlighted the way that services have played a role in the re-enactment of trauma for women, so that previous life experiences, often involving violence and abuse, can be re-awakened and re-experienced. It spelt out a number of areas in which services for women could be improved, such as through the promotion of empowerment, choice and self-determination, placing importance on the underlying cause and context of a woman's distress, and valuing women's strengths and their ability to recover.

This document drew heavily on the theme of 'recovery', a term that arose from the user-led recovery movement, through which mental health service users expressed their dissatisfaction with the services they had received and highlighted the numerous ways in which their mental health difficulties in no way eclipsed their identity and their life skills. Writers such as Deegan (1994), Armstrong (1994) and Berman (1994) described their journey of recovery, which sometimes occurred despite the intervention of mental health services, emphasising the need for cooperation between service users and professionals, for respect, for an understanding of the uniqueness of the individual, and for the valuing of the experience and knowledge service users bring to their own recovery. More recently, recovery has been summarised as the steady process of empowerment: of a service user taking back control over, and responsibility for, their life and their treatment (CSIP *et al.*, 2007).

In addition, the document published in 2002 was a testament to the volume of research accumulated over the years demonstrating the role of gender in mental health, necessitating a different treatment approach which caters for the particular needs of women and understands the context within which their mental health difficulties have arisen. Since *The Female Malady* (Showalter, 1987), writers such as Russell (1994) and Busfield (1996) have all argued that women have not been listened to, that their 'symptoms' are reduced to biological substrates that have little evidence, and that more effort needs to go towards increasing the control women feel they have over their lives. Since 2002 there have been a number of documents that have explicitly recognised the importance of recovery as a set of guiding principles for women in the criminal justice system (see for example the Cortson Report, Home Office 2007), for the health-care aspects of women who have been the victims of violence (DoH, 2010), and for mental health care generally, with the publication of *New Horizons: Towards a shared vision for mental health* (DoH, 2009). Despite this increasing recognition, it remains to be clarified what the gender-specific recovery needs of women in secure services are, i.e. what it is that women need to recover (regain) or gain. This needs to be addressed given that the population of women in secure care is increasing (Dent, 2006), and that women in secure care are more likely to move up through levels of security due to staff difficulties in responding to their distressed behaviour (Scott and Williams, 2004). While Drennan and Alred (in this volume) have argued for a translation of the principles of recovery for a forensic setting, it may be that there needs to be a further translation that takes the needs of particular populations, such as men or women, into account.

Following the research and recommendations in *Women's Mental Health: Into the Mainstream* (Department of Health, 2002), a Women's Service was developed in the South East which sought to provide women with a different experience of mental health treatment that felt personally relevant, gender-specific, and caring in a real sense: in this way it sought to provide a women-centred, relational context to recovery, i.e. a place where relationships are used to provide the sanctuary that has often been missing in the lives of women who enter the criminal justice system, who have experienced domestic, social and personal vulnerabilities in their lives, as the Corston Report (Home Office, 2007) outlined. The women for whom the service was developed often attracted a diagnosis of personality disorder, had a long history of service use and had behaved aggressively towards themselves or others. Before the service opened, two documents were published: 'Personality Disorder Capabilities Framework' (NIHME, 2003) and the 'Ten Essential Shared Capabilities for Mental Health Services' (DoH, 2004). These further emphasised the principles of recovery in relation to personality disorder.

The women's service comprised a six-bedded secure unit and a six-bedded ward in the community. From the outset it took as the overall theoretical model one of attachment theory, whereby the relationships formed with the women took priority over everything else. This fits the 'best practice' more recently identified by Long, Fulton and Hollin (2008) for medium secure care for women. The staff were well trained in working with people with personality disorders, with self-harm, with issues arising from experiences of sexual and physical abuse, and with the recovery principles of empowerment and choice, hope, respect, individualised care, emphasising service users' strengths and areas of expertise in their own care, and the use of safe and supportive relationships to promote an ongoing recovery journey for the service user. There was a strong emphasis on staff support, which occurred in a range of contexts, from informal conversations with colleagues of all disciplines, through to weekly staff supervision groups and weekly staff forums where more business-related aspects of the service were discussed. As a clinical psychologist attached to both teams, I have had a largely consultative role in facilitating the staff supervision groups, attending staff forums and the weekly multi-disciplinary review meetings which provide the focal point for clinical decision-making. In this way it has been possible to witness and be a part of the way that the staff team, in conjunction with the women themselves, have struggled with the application of recovery principles in a secure service, with a client group who have for the most part a diagnosis of personality disorder.

During the previous six years of operation, the service has seen success in the form of reduced levels of deliberate self-harm, and a number of women, for whom secure care had been thought the only safe option, leaving secure care and progressing to community placements. Women have spoken of feeling nurtured and treated as individuals, and it has seemed as though the follow-up care they have continued to receive has helped them to feel that staff remain interested in their individual progress. The approach to self-harm of developing relational security meant that self-harm as a transitional object became less needed as clients felt that the relationships they had with staff and other clients gave them a feeling of safety which was a new experience for many (see for example Seager's concept of 'psychological safety', Seager, 2008). Women have found other ways to communicate their distress, and to tell their stories of trauma and loss. An evaluative study commissioned by the NHS Research & Development Programme on Forensic Mental Health, which included the secure unit, documented a number of areas of good practice, including the emphasis on relational security and the high standard of gender-sensitive care provided (Parry-Crooke and Stafford, 2009).

There have of course been challenges for this service along the way. Despite being given many reasons to refrain from aggression towards themselves and others, some women have found it impossible to prevent themselves from continuing to behave in this way. Staff have found this difficult, and during supervision have asked themselves why it should be that a woman who finds herself in a place where she is cared for, respected, listened to and given more freedom than she might have received elsewhere would continue to want to 'bite the hand that feeds her', spoiling her own chances of progress towards the life she said she wanted. At times this response has been felt to be rejecting and disheartening, and it has been difficult to maintain a position of non-judgemental acceptance of the challenges that the women bring. This paper will present a series of case examples to illustrate some of these challenges, followed by a number of possibilities for why with some women the recovery approach as it has been applied has proved challenging, raising perhaps more questions than answers. These examples represent amalgams of real women, and are therefore not attributable to specific individuals who have been in the service. Towards the end of the paper a possible solution for each case example is offered, following on from the questions that were raised.

Mary spends three years on the unit and is expected to participate in the community activities of the unit. She is also given responsibility for maintaining her room. She has no physical health difficulties that would prevent her from performing these chores, but has a bipolar illness that means that for months at a time she is profoundly depressed, spending long periods of time in her bed, being incommunicative and not attending to any of her own physical health needs such as bathing or eating.

When this client came to us, it became apparent from her history that for all of her adult life she had lived with her mother, who controlled every aspect of her daily life, treating her as a child who was unable to make the most basic choices for herself. To be given the chance to make choices was to be given the opportunity to do everything she had never been allowed to do: within a recovery framework is could be said that the client needed to develop a sense of herself as an effective, independent person who did not need to wait for the decisions of others, but who could make her own choices. She needed to be given privacy for the first time, so that this sense of herself could develop without undue intrusion from others. The client appeared to want this for herself, and during the times when she was not depressed she was able to assert her need for independence and privacy. In a recent article, Slade (2009) described the process of coaching, whereby an individual is allowed to develop the capacity to be 'self-righting' rather than having a problem fixed by others.

In many ways Mary was able to make progress, when active, in making treatment choices such as asking for and receiving individual psychotherapy, writing her own care plans, developing relationships with staff and other clients, and being increasingly able to articulate her own needs. So why did this approach not lead to 'self-righting' when it came to maintaining her room? Was the approach providing the client with the care they needed? Was this client making a choice? Was the service being 'led by the individual' (Slade, 2009), and if so, was she being led along a path of recovery or on a treadmill of self-destruction? Did her room represent a 'pocket' of pathology (or healthy rebellion) that she needed to keep for herself? Was she being 'enabled' only to risk being stuck in squalor?

> Kath speaks of having a small piece of glass in her bedroom that she intends to use to harm either herself or others. She has a history of extensive self-harm, and a history of sexual abuse. She has not previously harmed others, although she has been verbally aggressive at times. She may be experiencing flashbacks of her childhood abuse, and her behaviour is childlike. In the past, on other units, she has been prevented from self-harming through the use of physical restraint, and her belongings have been removed from her and her room. She has spoken about how invasive this has been, and how she has felt that her distress has not been noticed or understood.

The unit takes the approach of working with self-harm, rather than against it, and acknowledging the feelings it seeks to communicate, while alternative coping methods are sought. In this instance, the woman has not harmed herself or others and the piece of glass remains in her room, like a literalised sword of Damacles (thus creating the situation of 'coercive bondage' noted by Fagin (2004), in which staff must hold the anxiety for the welfare of their client). The guidelines for medium secure care would dictate that the glass is forcibly removed immediately. But is there a way of empowering her, perhaps for the first time, to make a positive choice – to give up her means of repeating her abuse by choosing to hand in the piece of glass? Or are we acting in a way detrimental to her recovery by giving her the message that we are negligent of her need for safety and containment? Is this client likely to be in a state of dissociation that would prevent her from being able to make positive choices for herself?

> Joanna, who has been in the service for a number of years, is being encouraged to consider moving on into non-secure care. She feels the possible loss of security acutely, and speaks of wanting to live behind a locked door for the rest of her life. She has a history of serious violence and sometimes says that she is prepared to hurt someone again if it means that she will remain locked up. However, an important part of her treatment has been in helping her to distinguish between her need to hurt others and her need to make threats in order to communicate her distress, i.e. to distinguish between reasons for thinking and reasons for acting.

Staff see this client's current risk to others as low. It is clear that part of her identity is being 'dangerous' and yet she has shown no sign of behaving in a dangerous way towards others during her four-year stay on the unit. Is helping someone down the road to recovery at times a contradiction in itself? Should we accept her desire to remain locked up or act in the hope that she might feel differently when she finally experiences greater freedom? If we subscribe to her view are we giving up on her, as her family did when she was younger?

These challenges perhaps relate in part to the dilemma of promoting choice and responsibility for people who are restricted, from 'without' in legal and physical ways, and from 'within' in cognitive, emotional ways. Roberts *et al.* (2008) describe how people have been compulsorily detained for the purpose of restricting the choices they had been making in their lives, as such choices have been felt to be the outcome of 'morbid motivations'. This means that there is a limit, and there should be, on the extent of choices individuals in secure care can make. To act as though a women on a secure unit has unlimited choice is to deny both the reality of her current existence, and her potential destructiveness. This has long been the case for women in forensic settings who have been stereotyped as turning their aggression in on themselves rather than hurting others due to their innately caring natures. But these women *are* destructive to both themselves and others, in a variety of different ways, some of which are more subtly pernicious. Such women often have a limited cognitive ability to make other choices, and all are limited in the extent to which they can manage their emotions and emotional communication.

Further, for people who have attracted the diagnosis of personality disorder, there may be a further dilemma. The 'Recovery: A Common Purpose' paper notes that one of the ongoing debates about recovery centres around the concern that if mental health services adopt the approach it will lead to services being taken away (CSIP, 2007). This may be particularly pertinent for people with personality disorders, for whom services represent safety. Reder and Duncan (2001) call this the 'Care Conflict': actual experiences of abandonment, neglect or abuse as a child lead to the need for excessive dependency on others and a fear of being left. Individuals make a choice to forgo areas of responsibility, preferring to rely on services to make choices that have become, or have always been, too difficult for them to make themselves. For these people, moving out of secure care, or even progressing while in secure care, may therefore be an unacceptable goal.

In all three clinical dilemmas we see that although choice has been given to the client, in an overall atmosphere of warmth and trust, on each occasion the client struggles to accept responsibility, instead prioritising their position of physical and emotional dependency. By expecting the clients to do what they perhaps could not, the service inadvertently failed to promote recovery, tipping the balance of empowerment the other way so that too many choices could lead to failure. There will hopefully be increasing numbers of people with mental health difficulties being provided a service that is respectful, listening and acknowledging, that believes in their ability to change and provides the means for them to make choices and assume control. But this is recovery as antidote to organisational and social control: this is necessarily redressing a balance in the movement of power from one group of people to another. For the women in this service, it is necessary, but insufficient.

Recovery for women in a secure setting must be merely a starting point, a springboard from which an internal process of recognition and acceptance of oneself and one's choices can begin, with the recognition that women in secure services frequently present with complex, care-seeking behaviours that have a detrimental effect on the care they receive (Macmillian and Aiyegbusi, 2009). That women with mental health difficulties need choices in their recovery is moot: the women described here needed nurture, acknowledgement, respect and all those elements of an environment that is good enough, but they kept needing it, and would continue to do so still more as mental health staff pushed them towards an independence they could not imagine. Roberts *et al.* (2008) describe the tension between enabling choice and saying 'no': the dilemma between 'embracing the dignity of risk' (Deegan, 1994) and providing a service user with nothing more discouraging than 'chances to fail' (Munetz and Frese, 2001). In relation to women with a diagnosis of personality disorder, the tension becomes more profound as the client struggles with a compulsion to take risks with her own health and sometimes that of others, until the compulsion gives way to a belief that instead it is possible to make choices. This might mean that for women with a personality disorder diagnosis, an important step on the path to recovery would be the realisation and/or acceptance that there are alternative ways to express distress and receive support, and that this can occur without the need to cling to the service wholeheartedly for fear of being left with no support at all.

So how can this tension of empowerment and containment, as it might be termed, be managed? How can the springboard of a woman's recovery be developed? It is perhaps a question of logistics: when, where, why and how much? Taking the latter point, if each step towards recovery represents a step towards independence, then the process must be piecemeal, with each piece allowing the opportunity to consider whether negative power (i.e. how clients exert others to take control for them) can be replaced by the positive power of relying on oneself: the slow separation from the service as caregiver. Deegan (1994) writes that

> recovery is not a sudden conversion experience. Hope does not come to us as a sudden bolt of lightning....I began in little ways with small triumphs and simple acts of courage.

Roberts *et al.* (2008) refer to Schwartz's (2004) finding that 'abundant choice makes for misery' and suggest that small choices are more significant in promoting wellbeing.

The question of when is also fundamental. The women in the service might be argued to have personality difficulties because they were not given ample opportunity to develop safe, secure relationships in their infancy and childhood. Until they have developed a dependency on services and the people in them (or in other words, a 'secure base' – Bowlby, 1988), which is restorative, they will not be able to relinquish this dependency in order to find greater independence. The women's service clearly understood the women's need for a nurturing environment; the length of time that this environment would continue to be necessary for some women to is easy to underestimate.

So in considering each aspect of treatment within a recovery framework we must ask, is this expectation/request/idea too extensive, too great a step? Does it leapfrog over a midway point where a client could rest and recoup? We must ask ourselves why we might be wanting to promote a particular aspect of recovery. Is this our agenda, our idea of what is best for a client? Is it realistic, or even necessary? Is dirt, for example, a sign of independent choice or a plea for intervention? If we attempt to remove all possible means to cut are we creating a feeling of safety that is specious and yet helps us to manage our own anxiety? Are the five-metre fences more uncomfortable for us than for the client? Do we really want this client to recover, and do we really think they can? Do we really think we have the ability to help them? Are we working with these women in appraising and developing the most helpful responses to the risk they present?

We must think about the stage or pre-stage of recovery of our clients. Does recovery equal abandonment? Is it tantamount to non-existence without the confirmation of another? (Consider, for example, Livesley (2003), who describes the difference between 'normal' and disordered personality in terms of the coherence and consistency of self-schemas.) We should consider who is best placed to take responsibility in this situation: how can the responsibility be shared between client and staff? What effect will this have on the client and their relationship to help? We may have given a client the opportunity to move forward in their recovery, but do they have the ability at the current time? If not then perhaps we are not facilitating recovery but becoming another obstacle in its way.

And all these questions need to be posed within a gendered framework, so that we are asking ourselves not just how women might recover and what this might look like from each individual woman's point of view, but whether particular objectives, such as living independently, working, managing finances, living without fear, feeling able to make choices about the use of one's body, and so on, might constitute long-term goals that have hitherto not been thought possible in the social context of their lives. The complex factors that women are more likely to bring to their recovery, such as their relationship with their children, their relationship with their own mother, and how this influences how they see themselves as a mother, must form an additional layer to the landscape of recovery. Further, there are questions about the gendered impact of psychiatric medication on women's bodies, about the ways in which their menstrual cycle affects their mental state (or not), about their sexuality, ethnicity and culture, and so on. I am not wishing to argue that these factors exist solely in relation to women, but rather that the ways in which they pertain to women as opposed to men needs to be borne in mind.

The three case examples presented at the beginning of this chapter have been an attempt to articulate the dilemmas faced by the committed and skilled staff team working with these women. The following vignettes are an attempt to respond to some of these dilemmas. At times, it has felt as though our attempts to help our clients have failed. But more objectively, as Slade (2009) writes, it could be said that failure represents an act of engagement in the process of recovery. So this must not be disheartening, but expected, and used to help a client find different ways of progressing in their journey. As Deegan (1994) puts it, within a recovery framework we have the *'opportunity to try and to fail and to try again'*. Bassett and Repper (2005) put this in an interactive context in what they call 'hope-inspiring relationships', where failure does not dispel hope in a client's recovery.

> Mary has spent three years on the unit and seems to struggle with the motivation to clean her room. Staff try to speak to her about this, and, although reticent, over time she is able to describe how the dirt and neglect of her room both symbolise the grime of her depression and act as a rebellious counterpoint to it. Attempts are not made to persuade her to clean her room, as staff know from experience with Mary that this will be heard as 'nagging' and responded to by further withdrawal. However, the neglect is noticed, and commented upon, and efforts are made to help Mary identify one part of her room that she might like to have clean, no matter how small. She chooses

her bed linen, so that her bed can be a place of sanctuary that could grow, nudging the dirt further towards the corners of the room.

Kath speaks of having a piece of glass in her bedroom that she intends to use to harm either herself or others. She is offered staff time, which she accepts, and gradually her thoughts of self-harm diminish. But she keeps the glass in her room, and refuses to hand it in voluntarily. Staff weigh up the risks, and decide that given her lack of history of violence towards others, and her ability to utilise the support that is given to her, they will refrain from taking the glass against her will unless her risk indicators change. Over the next few weeks, with minor incidents of self-harm, Kath begins to share her feelings about herself following her sexual abuse. Shortly before the end of a successful admission, she comes to the office door and hands in the glass.

Joanna, who has been in the service for a number of years, is being encouraged to consider moving on into non-secure care. She feels the possible loss of security acutely, and speaks of wanting to live behind a locked door for the rest of her life. The team work hard to help Joanna identify what she would want in a placement and she is able to specify the area and setting that would meet her ongoing needs for security. She shows signs of envying other clients who are moving onto low secure units, and eventually moves to a unit that is locked, but gives her more independence and choice.

Here we can see that the principles of recovery, such as empowerment and choice, hope, respect, individualised care, emphasising the service user's strengths and areas of expertise in their own care, and the use of safe and supportive relationships to promote an ongoing recovery journey for the service user, are being used in more nuanced ways, which take into account the limits of the system as a whole, including the vulnerabilities of the service user at any given time. As Drennan and Alred state in their introductory chapter to this volume, '*It is not only management but the clinical staff also who need to understand that a naïve interpretation of recovery principles could be hazardous to the public, to the service user themselves and even to their own professional careers*'. I would add that it can also be a mistake to conceive of recovery as a process that can occur without due respect and understanding of the gendered context and experience of people's lives.

I will end with the analogy in the title: that perhaps it is helpful to view recovery as a seesaw, with the client at one end and significant people in their life, including mental health staff, at the other. The position of the seesaw is negotiated with the client, perhaps using some of the questions above. At times the client will be in the 'up' position, where they are able to make positive decisions about their life (perhaps for the first time), while at others it will be the staff who need to do this in order to enable the client to work towards doing it for themselves. The goal will be achieving a balance, but it is the fact of being on a seesaw, where positions are not static and where the possibility of empowerment exists for these women, that enables recovery to begin.

References

Armstrong, M. (1994) 'Poem: Sounds of Songs'. In A. Spaniol and M. Koehler (eds), *The Experience of Recovery. Boston:* Center for Psychiatric Rehabilitation, Boston University.

Bassett, T. and Repper, J. (2005) 'Travelling hopefully'. *Mental Health Today*, November, p 16–18.

Berman, R. (1994) 'Lithium's other face'. In A. Spaniol and M. Koehler (eds), *The Experience of Recovery. Boston: Center for Psychiatric Rehabilitation, Boston University.*

Bowlby, J. (1988) *A secure base: clinical applications of attachment theory*. London: Routledge.

Busfield, J. (1996) *Men, women and madness. Understanding gender and mental disorder*. London: Macmillan Press Ltd.

Care Services Improvement Partnership, Royal College of Psychiatrists and Social Care Institute for Excellence. (2007) *A Common Purpose: Recovery in Future Mental Health Services* (Joint Position Paper 08). Leeds: Social Care Institute for Excellence.

Corston, J. (2007) *The Corston Report. A Review of Women With Particular Vulnerabilities in the Criminal Justice System*. London: Home Office.

Deegan, P. (1994) 'Recovery: the lived experience of rehabilitation'. In A. Spaniol and M. Koehler (eds), *The Experience of Recovery*. Boston: Center for Psychiatric Rehabilitation, Boston University.

Dent, E. (2006) 'The safer sex'. *Health Service Journal*, 116: 24–26.

Department of Health (2002) 'Women's mental health: into the mainstream. Strategic Development of Mental Health Care for Women', London: Department of Health. http://www.dh.gov.uk/publications

—— (2004) *The Ten Essential Shared Capabilities: A framework for the whole of the mental health workforce*, London: Department of Health. http://www.dh.gov.uk/publications

—— (2009) *New Horizons: Towards a shared vision for mental health*. London: Department of Health. http://www.dh.gov.uk/publications

—— (2010) *The Report from the Taskforce on the health aspects of violence against women and children. Responding to violence against women and children – the role of the NHS*. London: Department of Health. http://www.dh.gov.uk/publications

Fagin, L. (2004) 'Management of personality disorders in acute in-patient settings. Part 1: Borderline personality disorders'. *Advances in Psychiatric Treatment*, 10: 93–99.

Livesley, W. (2003) *Practical Management of Personality Disorders*. New York: Guilford Press.

Long, C., Fulton, B. and Hollin, C. (2008) 'The development of a 'best practice' service for women in a medium-secure psychiatric setting: Treatment components and evaluation'. *Clinical Psychology and Psychotherapy*, 15(5): 304–319.

Macmillian, S. and Aiyegbusi, A. (2009) 'Crying out for care'. In A. Aiyegbusi & J. Clarke-Moore (eds) *Therapeutic Relationships with Offenders: An Introduction to the Psychodynamics of Forensic Mental Health Nursing*. London: Jessica Kingsley.

Munetz, M. and Frese, F. (2001) 'Getting ready for recovery: reconciling mandatory treatment with recovery vision'. *Psychiatric Rehabilitation Journal*, 25: 35–42.

National Institute for Mental Health in England (2003) *Breaking the cycle of rejection: The Personality Disorder Capabilities Framework*. Leeds: NIHME.

Parry-Crooke, G. and Stafford, P. (2009) *My Life: In safe hands? Summary report of an evaluation of women's medium secure services.* London: London Metropolitan University.

Reder, P. and Duncan, S. (2001) 'Abusive relationships, care and control conflicts and insecure attachments'. *Child Abuse Review*, 10: 411–427.

Roberts, G., Dorkins, E., Woolridge, J. and Hewis, E. (2008) 'Detained – what's my choice? Part 1'. Discussion. *Advances in Psychiatric Treatment*, 14: 172–180.

Russell, D. (1994) *Women, Madness and Medicine.* Cambridge: Polity Press.

Schwartz, B. (2004) 'The tyranny of choice'. *Scientific American*, 290(4): 70–75.

Scott, S. and Williams, J. (2004) 'Closing the gap between evidence and practice: The role of training in transforming women's services'. In N. Jeffcote and T. Watson (eds), *Working therapeutically with women in secure mental health services.* London: Jessica Kingsley.

Seager, M. (2008) 'Psychological Safety: a missing concept in suicide risk prevention'. In S. Briggs, A. Lemma and W. Crouch (eds) *Relating to self-harm and suicide. Psychoanalytic perspectives on practice, theory and prevention.* London: Routledge.

Showalter, E. (1987) *The Female Malady: Women, Madness and English Culture.* London: Virago.

Slade, M. (2009) *100 ways to support recovery. A guide for mental health professionals.* Rethink Recovery Series, Vol 1. London: Rethink.

11 Recovery within a prison therapeutic community
Setting the scene

Michael Brookes

Introduction

The concept of recovery has largely been developed and applied in cooperation with those who experience mental health difficulties in community or mental health settings. And, as this book demonstrates, it is applicable to those detained in secure facilities. Yet the model has relevance too for assisting those detained in prisons, especially given that over 90 per cent of prisoners have one or more of these five psychiatric disorders: psychosis, neurosis, personality disorder, hazardous drinking and drug dependence (Bradley, 2009).

Applying the concept of recovery within a prison setting might initially seem to be slightly incongruous. Prisons were established to incarcerate those sentenced by the courts to a period in custody. Prisoners themselves are subject to the rules, procedures and regimes of the Prison Service. Their daily routines are prescribed by the governor of the jail in which they are held. To what extent then is it achievable to utilise recovery principles in such an environment? And is it possible for this to occur without it being perceived either as tokenism or as lacking in any real depth or purpose?

This chapter will explore recovery within one particular prison, HMP Grendon. HMP Grendon is a unique establishment situated in the Buckinghamshire countryside, where each of its wings functions as an autonomous therapeutic community. Moreover, if recovery is possible in any prison, then it ought to be achievable in this particular establishment given the remit it has and its place in penal history.

HMP Grendon

In the 1930s the prison authorities in England and Wales became increasingly aware of the need to better assist prisoners who presented particular difficulties to the prison authorities. The 1932 Report of the Departmental Committee on Persistent Offenders considered the need for psychiatric treatment of disturbed prisoners, while the 1939 East-Hubert report recommended that a special institution be built where prisoners could be treated using psychotherapeutic techniques. This proposal came to fruition with the opening of HMP Grendon in 1962.

Adopted as the treatment paradigm was the therapeutic community model. This has continued to remain as the central element within Grendon's regime and the basis of the group analytic psychotherapy offered. Each morning there is either a community meeting (two mornings a week) or small groups (three mornings a week, each group meeting with between six and ten residents/prisoners). The community meetings and small groups each last for ninety minutes.

Grendon is a Category B prison with the capacity to hold 240 men. There are six wings. Five of these are fully functioning therapeutic communities, the other an assessment/induction unit with a therapeutic community ethos. The five main communities have between 40 and 46 men residing in them. The assessment/ induction unit has space for 25 men. Grendon has no segregation unit. A multi-disciplinary team comprising a psychotherapist, psychologist, specialist group facilitator and uniformed prison officers, all of who are involved in the delivery of the therapy, form the community staff group.

Each of Grendon's main communities has been accredited. This follows a joint review by a team representing the Community of Communities[1] and the Prison Service. Accreditation validates Grendon's effectiveness in reducing offending behaviour through a process approved by the independent National Offender Management Service's Correctional Services Accreditation Panel. This is the same body which accredits the Prison Service's offending behaviour prog-rammes. Grendon, additionally, also has to meet the Community of Communities Therapeutic Community standards.

Therapeutic communities

It has been argued that recovery is not a new theory. Rather it represents a rediscovery of the 'moral treatment' practiced at the York Retreat (Roberts and Wolfson, 2004; Shepherd, Boardman and Slade, 2008) based on kindness, compassion, respect and hopes of recovery (Tuke, 1813). The emphasis of The Retreat, with the importance of the person, humane treatment, peer support and the capacity to bring about their own healing through their relationships with others, parallel the experiences of residents in therapeutic communities (Clark, 1974).

Treating differently some of those returning home from the Second World War battlefields was the inspiration behind the creation of therapeutic communities. In particular, this was through the work of Maxwell Jones at Mill Hill Emergency Hospital and the Belmont Social Rehabilitation Unit in South London, and of Tom Main, John Rickman, Siegfried Foulkes and Harold Bridger at the Northfield Military Hospital, Birmingham.

Main (1946), in an article subsection entitled 'A Therapeutic Community', considered that 'the Northfield Experiment is an attempt to use a hospital not as an organization run by doctors...but as a community with the immediate aim of full participation of all its members in its daily life and the eventual aim of the resocialization of the neurotic individual for life in ordinary society.'

Therapeutic communities emphasise respect for the individual alongside an expectation of normal behaviour arising in the context of general, social and peer encouragement. They offer healing and/or correcting through membership of an optimised social environment which is consciously designed to act as a therapeutic instrument. Therapeutic communities have proved particularly effective in treating those with personality disorders, including those of the anti-social and borderline types (Warren *et al.*, 2003). They provide complex, personality-disordered individuals with the skills, strategies and understanding to manage their responses to difficulties they face and, in so doing, establish a cycle of positive experiences that continually reinforces the new learning – though not without mistakes and setbacks occurring along the way.

The Community of Communities (2009) state that therapeutic communities embrace:

> A set of methods which aim to treat people suffering from emotional disturbance in a communal atmosphere. TC principles are based upon a collaborative, democratic and deinstitutionalised approach to staff–patient interaction. Highlighting this approach, patients are generally referred to as residents or members of the community. Traditional staff/staff and staff/member hierarchies are replaced by a more liberal, humane and participative culture.
>
> The Therapeutic Community offers a safe environment with a clear structure of boundaries and expectations where members have the opportunity to come to terms with their past through re-enactment within a treatment setting involving other members and staff. Group psychotherapy is integral to the treatment, but TCs also offer the individual experiences to awaken creative and social abilities. Members tend to learn much through the routine interactions of daily life and the experience of being therapeutic for each other. Through this psychosocial therapy the aim is to encourage members towards a better understanding of their previous behaviour and to enable them to improve their inter-personal functioning, first within the therapeutic community and ultimately in the wider community. Encouraging and reinforcing the notion of personal responsibility and sharing, members and staff meet together on a regular basis to discuss the management and activities of the community, to assist new members and to support leavers.
>
> Attendance is generally voluntary, and to benefit from participation in a TC, the member must be positively motivated to change his/her behaviour, to co-operate in group therapy and to accept the rules of communal living.

Therapeutic communities therefore aim to:

- Care
- Create a communal atmosphere
- Be collaborative and participative
- Value and respect each individual
- Be safe and have clear boundaries

- Enable emotional and personal development
- Have a multi-disciplinary approach

(Brookes, 2008)

Grendon's population

As of 31 December 2009, 90 per cent of Grendon's population were serving indeterminate sentences, 6 per cent determinate sentences of 10 years or more, and 4 per cent determinate sentences of less than 10 years. Of those serving indeterminate sentences, 48 per cent were serving life for murder, 26 per cent were discretionary life sentence prisoners, 4 per cent serving an automatic life sentence and 22 per cent an indeterminate public protection sentence. The majority were sentenced for acts of violence or for sexual offences.

23 per cent of Grendon prisoners are under the age of 30, 37 per cent are between 31 and 40, 30 per cent are between 41 and 50 and 10 per cent are over 50.

The mean scores on a number of psychometric measures administered to men upon arrival at Grendon show that the Grendon population is characterised by complex needs and psychological disturbance. For example, the mean Eysenck Personality Questionnaire-Revised (EPQ-R; Eysenck and Eysenck, 1991) neuroticism (N) score (14.6) for the prisoners at Grendon in December 2009 is significantly higher than the mean score reported in the EPQ-R manual for a normal male population sample (10.5) and is not significantly different to that for psychiatric patients seeking treatment for neuroses or personality disorders.

Newberry (2009) reported that Grendon receives prisoners who have significantly more previous convictions on average than prisoners in other Category B prisons, suggesting that they pose a higher level of risk in terms of reconviction. Findings concerning drug use draw attention to the dependency of prisoners; approximately half of new arrivals report that they have used opiates and/or cannabis on a frequent basis in prison prior to arrival. Two thirds of prisoners also reported experiencing abuse, with almost half of the population claiming that they had at least one previous suicide attempt.

An examination of scores on the Personality Assessment Inventory (PAI; Morey, 1991) by Newberry and Shuker (submitted) revealed that 36 per cent of prisoners who completed the PAI on reception (n=222) scored 70T or above on the Borderline Features (BOR) scale, indicating that they possess a number of features associated with borderline personality disorder. However, scores in this range do not necessarily indicate a diagnosis of BPD unless there are elevations on all BOR subscales (as individual features are common to other disorders). With regard to antisocial behaviour, a third of men had a score of 70T or above on the Antisocial Features (ANT) scale and the Physical Aggression (AGG-P) subscale indicating that many prisoners are impulsive, hostile, have a history of antisocial acts and are prone to physical displays of anger.

Shine and Newton (2000) found that Grendon prisoners' total score on the Psychopathy Checklist-Revised (PCL-R; Hare, 2003) was greater than those for prisoners in the high security estate. Jones and Shuker (2004) noted that a large proportion of the Grendon population (50 to 75 per cent) were identified as having dangerous and severe personality disorder during the Home Office's original calculations of DSPD men.

Within prison therapeutic communities it is not only offending behaviour that is addressed but also the impact of the individual's early years and other life experiences: school, work, relationships. It means that the disordered aspects of offenders' lives can be addressed, as well as their offending behaviour. This is especially significant given Grendon's population and means that mental health issues can be considered alongside offending behaviour needs. These mental health issues will, like offending behaviours, be discussed and considered within a group setting, not on a one-to-one basis.

Key recovery principles

Jacobson and Greenley (2001) viewed recovery as different to cure, better captured by the notion of healing, with the current interest in recovery being traced back to the publication of a major study by Harding *et al.* (1987). This demonstrated that mental illness did not bring about an inevitable deterioration. At this time personal accounts were also being published by those who had learnt to manage their mental illness (e.g. Houghton, 1982). Deegan's (1988) experience was that recovery for her became a way of approaching the day's challenges, a way of life, an attitude. A personal journey (Sheehan, 2002), depending far more on inner determination and confidence than on being treated by doctors (Coleman, 1999).

The 2005 NIMHE Guiding Statement on Recovery considered that 'recovery is what people experience themselves as they become empowered to manage their lives in a manner that allows them to achieve a fulfilling, meaningful life and a positive sense of belonging in their communities' (p. 2). Recovery is also self-directed, non-linear, active and ongoing, with no single path to recovery (Rethink, 2008). It is based on self-determination and self-management, with an emphasis on hope (Shepherd, Boardman and Slade, 2008). Most people who may be described as in recovery do not think about how they are changing in these terms. They are more interested in getting a job, making friends, living on their own, and getting their life back together (Davidson *et al.*, 2006). This is assisted by them connecting again with the social world that they were once a part of, along with possessing hope that recovery is possible, and feeling empowered through having a sense of autonomy and being able to act independently and to take personal responsibility for their lives and actions (Jacobson and Greenley, 2001). Required is the opportunity to make choices, which Roberts *et al.* (2008) consider to be an experience, a tension and dialectic in everyday life. Choice includes having an active role in their own care and treatment plan (Marin *et al.*, 2005).

The recovery approach also requires practitioners to act differently and to reframe treatment so that it is no longer looked at from the professional's perspective but from the person's perspective (Davidson *et al.*, 2006). Repper and

Perkins (2003) noted the importance of staff believing in the person's abilities and potential, attending to their priorities, accepting failures and setbacks as part of the recovery process, finding ways of sustaining hope and guarding against despair, acknowledging that the future is uncertain and understanding the importance of learning from experience. Perkins (2006) stressed the importance of 'hope-inspiring relationships'.

Borg and Kristiansen (2004) considered that the key practitioner characteristics were openness, collaboration as equals, a focus on the individual's inner resources, reciprocity, a willingness 'to go the extra mile', an encouragement of responsible risk-taking and a positive expectation for the future. Required are relationship skills, which include empathy, caring, acceptance and mutual affirmation. What is also helpful is for professionals to take a risk with someone (Berkins, 2006) and for risks to be shared rather than avoided (Roberts and Wolfson, 2004). This needs to be undertaken carefully in a society which is increasingly risk averse and where public protection is the predominant concern.

Recovery is also more likely to be successful if it takes place where a holistic approach is considered that includes psychological, emotional, spiritual, physical and social needs (National Institute for Mental Health in England (2005) fifth guiding principle for the delivery of recovery-orientated mental health services). NIMHE's third guiding principle is that service users are able to recover more quickly when their hope is encouraged, enhanced and/or maintained; life roles with respect to work and meaningful activities are defined; spirituality is considered; culture is understood; educational needs as well as those of families/ significant others are identified; socialisation needs are identified; and individuals are supported to achieve their goals.

Central to the recovery model is an approach that is person-centric, strengths-based and biographical, with a focus on personal meaning, growth, discovery and choice through considering distressing experiences in an understanding, value-centred, humanistic way and thereby encouraging transformation, self-management, self-control and personal responsibility – all within a social context (Roberts and Wolfson, 2004 citing Ralph *et al.*, 2002; May, 2004; Allott *et al.*, 2003). Recovery can therefore occur in the presence of continuing symptoms and disabilities, as the emphasis is on living a satisfying, hopeful and contributory life through changing attitudes, values, feelings, goals, skills and roles (Anthony, 1993).

Recovery for offenders at HMP Grendon

The above two sections demonstrate that there are strong parallels between the philosophy, principles and processes underpinning both the recovery model and therapeutic communities. Important within the recovery process and for those who reside within therapeutic communities is the opportunity for self-organisation. This includes the power to make decisions and to have some control over daily living arrangements (Appleby, 2006). It means that an individual's experience of whether something works or not is given precedence over theory or what has worked for other people (Care Services Improvement Partnership *et al.*, 2007).

To exercise control means that there must be an element of choice. Is it possible, though, for there to be choice within a prison environment? To some extent there is. Just as in wider society everyone has the choice of whether or not to conform to societies' norms, whether or not to get up each morning, how to arrange their finances, so prisoners can decide at what level they are prepared to conform with the prison regime. For example, whether or not to go 'on exercise', go to church, attend education, or to actively take part in their sentence-planning process.

This opportunity for prisoners to exercise choice and control is even greater within prison-based therapeutic communities. For example, to enter HMP Grendon, prisoners have to apply for a place. They, not prison staff, have to fill out an application form and say what their needs are. So, while Warner *et al.* (2006) could write that there is 'scant literature on choice for people in the criminal justice system, including prisoners, who we know experience very high levels of mental health problems' (p. 2) academic awareness about HMP Grendon is widely available (Gray, 1973; Gunn and Robertson, 1982; Morris, 2004; Sullivan and Shuker, 2010). Indeed, Grendon is probably the most researched prison in the country.

Through choosing to enter this distinctive prison establishment, prisoners can begin the recovery process envisaged by NIMHE (2005) 'of changing one's orientation and behaviour from a negative focus on a troubling event, condition or circumstance to the positive restoration, rebuilding, reclaiming or taking control on one's life' (p. 2).

Recovery principles and group-based psychotherapy are also closely related. Yalom (1995) identifies eleven therapeutic factors he considers important when undertaking group therapy. These include the installation of hope, altruism, the corrective recapitulation of the primary family group, the development of socializing techniques, imitative behaviour, interpersonal learning and group cohesiveness.

There is also a close relationship in delivering the recovery model with the delivery of the Good Lives Model (Ward, 2002). Like the recovery model, this is strength-based, emphasises personal responsibility and the establishing of an effective therapeutic alliance with the aim of enabling offenders to realise primary human goods, or goals, in ways that are socially acceptable and meaningful.

The Good Lives Model (Ward and Stewart, 2003; Ward and Brown, 2004; Ward and Marshall, 2004) was formulated to integrate aspects of treatment not well dealt with by the Risk-Needs-Responsivity approach (Andrews and Bonta, 2003; Andrews, Bonta and Wormith, 2006). Based on the assumption that offenders are essentially human beings with similar needs and aspirations to non-offending members of the community, important in the Good Lives Model is the development of a therapeutic alliance and motivating offenders to engage in the difficult process of changing their lives. Offenders do not need to abandon those things that are important to them, only to learn to acquire them differently.

Ward and Maruna (2007) considered there were at least ten groups of primary human goods:

(i)   Life (including healthy living and physical functioning)
(ii)   Knowledge
(iii)   Excellence in play and work (including mastery experiences)
(iv)   Agency (including autonomy and self-directedness)
(v)   Inner peace (freedom from emotional turmoil and stress)
(vi)   Friendship (including intimate, romantic and family relationships)
(vii)   Community
(viii)   Spirituality (in the broad sense of finding meaning and purpose in life)
(ix)   Happiness
(x)   Creativity

Brookes (2009, 2010) established that prison-based therapeutic communities provide an ideal environment in which these good lives goods can be achieved. Some of these goals can be provided within other prison establishments, but it is the holistic treatment environment of therapeutic communities that provides a setting in which all these goals can be achieved and integrated at the same time.

Treatment stages and the impact of Grendon

In recovery, Andresen, Caputi and Oades (2006) considered that there were five stages which individuals progressed through. First, a 'moratorium' period, a time of withdrawal characterised by a profound sense of loss and hopelessness. Second, an 'awareness', the realisation that a fulfilling life is possible. Third, a 'preparation' phase, taking stock of strengths and weaknesses and starting to work on developing recovery skills. Fourth, 'rebuilding' a positive identity, setting meaningful goals and taking control of one's life. Finally, 'growth', living a meaningful life, characterised by self-management, resilience and a positive sense of self.

This is similar to the five-stage career model for offenders in Grendon proposed by Genders and Player (1995), with these stages being:

Recognition – of problems and that at least some of the elements can be defined
Motivation – the desire to change
Understanding – the beginning of therapeutic activity with some idea of how the problems have arisen and how they are connected with other aspects of life
Insight – gaining an awareness of what has to be done or changed to bring some resolutions to problems
Testing – practicing new and alternative ways of coping

Ali (2008), in her investigation of the therapy experience of prisoners, found three major themes. The first related to the recognition, by men, of their need to change. The second concerned safety and factors relating to the environment, with the third being the importance of support networks.

The impact of Grendon and its contribution to prisoners' recovery is significant, even for those who might not complete therapy in the prescribed way. Mark Leech, now a successful author and businessman, who was voted out of Grendon, says in his lectures and in his book (Leech, 1993) that unless prisoners go to prisons like HMP Grendon where their criminality is examined, they will not have the opportunity he had to change their lives.

Frank Cook, a prisoner with a violent prison and community background, could write of Grendon that:

> The inmates were friendly and very talkative. The atmosphere was casual and everyone seemed very happy. It was a million miles away from the harsh regimes, violence and mass paranoia that I experienced in every other prison and it was completely unsettling at first. I was so used to confrontation that when people were pleasant to me, it was actually very disturbing. I wanted to hate so that I could be confrontational. I was comfortable with hostility but there was none at Grendon and it felt like there was a void in my life'.
>
> (Cook and Wilkinson, 1998, p. 53)

These experiences are shared by early Grendon residents. In Tony Parker's 1970 book about Grendon, 'Steve' is recorded as saying:

> Before, I was quiet, I couldn't talk, I never discussed problems with anybody – not my parents or Mary [his girlfriend] or anyone. But since I've come here and had this group therapy, it's helped me come out of my shell, it's made me accustomed to getting things off my chest. And listening to other people's problems too, I've found that very interesting, I've got involved with them and ready to give my own opinion if I think I have another point of view that might be of use. I think the groups are very good.
>
> (Parker, 1970, p. 11)

Criminologists and journalists have written that the therapeutic process 'tries to help the prisoner make sense of his life, to see how his criminal behaviour has been shaped by the circumstances of his childhood and the relationships he developed, both as a child and an adult. Here, responsibility is linked to an individual's reality' (Wilson, 1998, p. 125). For if men do not act responsibly then there are consequences. 'If someone has been acting up, missing therapy sessions, or failing to pull their weight, it is discussed and – if necessary – sanctions are decided. If all else fails they can be voted out of therapy' (Stanford, 2009).

Aitkenhead (2007) considered that 'Grendon deviates from the system in almost every single respect, but above all because it fundamentally believes that criminals can change' and that it is an 'extraordinary act of faith of redemption...founded to resurrect the humanity of violent, broken men, not as a means to an end but as an end in itself.'

The qualitative evidence that Grendon assists in changing behaviour, attitudes and levels of psychological functioning is encouraging. In respect of prison behaviour, Grendon's level of adjudications is low. Cullen (1994) found that the number of governor's reports at Grendon was amongst the lowest in the country. This had been the case for the previous thirty years. Newton (2006) reported similar findings. Grendon's adjudication rate was one fifth lower than that for closed prisons. This from a population whose number of governor's reports was previously seven times higher than what is was at Grendon.

Taylor (2000) found in his reconviction study that there was a reduction in the reconviction rate for violent offences and for sexual and violent offences among repeat sexual offenders. Reconviction rates were lower for prisoners who stayed at Grendon for at least 18 months.

Shuker and Newton (2008) noted that during the first 12 months of therapy there were statistically reliable and clinically significant mental health changes. For those who stayed longer than 12 months there was both an improvement in psychological wellbeing and a reduction in offence-related risk.

Using the Person's Relating to Others Questionnaire (PROQ), a measure of negative relating, Birtchnell, Shuker, Newberry and Duggan (2009) found there was significant progress in mean scores on a number of scales. This increased ability to relate to others, which occurred relatively early in the period of stay, was further improved during the next nine months. Thereafter, there was no deterioration in residents' capacity to relate to others.

Recovery and prison therapeutic communities

A dilemma facing managers of prison therapeutic communities is the extent to which decision-making responsibility can be devolved to residents. The democratisation process has to take into account centrally determined security procedures. These are regularly audited and an integral part of the prison service's performance management system. It means that these have to be adhered to and that exemptions and variations are not possible. Consequently, 'in a prison environment, the areas over which the Community can have legitimate influence are significantly reduced because of security restraints, some of which are mandatory' (Leggett and Hirons, 2007). This can create difficulties in meeting some of the Community of Communities (2006) democratic therapeutic community service standards. For example, in allowing all community members to use the kitchen to prepare shared meals (though health and safety requirements also impact on the ability to adhere to this standard). Limits are also placed on the extent to which community members can be involved in the process of agreeing the therapeutic community's operational policies and procedures, and in community members being responsible for identifying, maintaining and changing community rules. These limits mean that communities at Grendon can only be concerned with internal procedural matters, as these are outside the scope of nationally agreed prison service orders and instructions.

A similar difficulty exists when applying the recovery model in secure forensic settings. Some of the objections raised to Drennan and Alred (this volume), when they were leading discussions on the adoption of a recovery approach to forensic psychiatric rehabilitation, centred on the extent to which allowing patients more choice and decision-making as part of their daily experience would impact on, or compromise, the security of the environment.

There will always be restrictions within secure settings on how much responsibility can be devolved to service users. The key for clinical managers is how, working within these constraints, the environment can be shaped to give service users as much control as possible over the lives they live and the direction of their treatment. This also involves negotiation and agreement with managers responsible for other aspects of the institution's functioning, especially security managers. Cooperation is required to ensure that, wherever possible, procedures and routines are aligned with a therapeutic model that seeks to give as much responsibility as possible to service users.

Over the past seven years at Grendon much senior management time and energy has been committed to ensuring that there are good relationships between the clinical and security teams. As a consequence we have found that:

> good security at Grendon needs good therapy and good therapy (especially with the demographic characteristics and offence histories of Grendon's population) needs good security. So, rather than being mutually exclusive, good security and good therapy are in fact interdependent. If the security department is not committed to adjusting certain security procedures to reflect operating these within a therapeutic community culture, and if the clinicians and those involved in the delivery of therapy are not committed to ensuring a secure and safe environment, then Grendon's remit of operating a series of therapeutic communities within a Category B prison becomes increasingly difficult – if not impossible.
>
> (Brookes and Mandikate, 2009)

Encouragingly, following the last full announced inspection of HMP Grendon, the Chief Inspector of Prisons was able to record that 'the needs of security and therapy were appropriately balanced' (Ministry of Justice, 2009). She was also able to say, in respect of staff–prisoner relationships, that these 'were outstandingly good and reflected the close interaction required in the therapeutic process…This inspection reaffirmed Grendon's remarkable achievements with some of the system's most dangerous and difficult prisoners.'

Over and above local security/therapy issues, there are the demands of the host organisation. Grendon's governor, for example:

> must manage between, on the one hand, the expectations of the Prison Service, often expressed in the language of managerialism and, on the other hand, the principles of group psychotherapy, articulated in an adapted vocabulary of equality, democracy and autonomy.
>
> (Bennett, 2006)

Once these organisational constraints have been navigated as successfully as possible, the emphasis within the treatment programme or the treatment regime for the recovery model to be successful is to encourage the engagement of the service user in their personal recovery journey and to provide them with the opportunities to do this. This will enhance the meaning, purpose, success and satisfaction gained from engaging with the treatment programme, but also with their experiences of life. For the challenge presented by the recovery model is that 'recovery suggests a shift to the patient leading the process as far they can and drawing on service provider resources to do so' (Drennan and Alred, Preface to this volume).

In many ways this is similar to what therapeutic communities are seeking to achieve. And just as personal transformation is an important component within the recovery model so it is for therapeutic communities. The difference is that within the different therapeutic communities at Grendon, everything is geared to therapy being provided within the context of a group-based intervention. The recovery model tends to be geared to an individual approach, seeking to change the nature of the relationship between service providers and the individual service user – with the service user being the predominant driver of services required, rather than this being determined by the service provider. The nature of the therapeutic alliance within therapeutic communities is much more complex and involves all members of the multi-disciplinary staff team and all residents, though the strongest relationships will be with those who form part of the resident's 'small group'.

The ownership over the treatment process that the service user has in the recovery model can be greater than that which is possible for therapeutic community residents. Therapeutic community residents need to obtain group, wing and staff backing for prison work activity, jobs/roles within the community, and access to family days and other privilege events. Should it be considered that jobs/roles applied for are not suitable or the most appropriate one for the resident concerned, or if the individual is not showing commitment to the therapeutic process, then that backing will not be forthcoming. It means that the group and the community (staff and residents) have a key role in facilitating the direction of each individual's therapeutic journey, and that the individual needs to show commitment to the community and living with others. The focus cannot be solely on themselves and what they consider to be in their best interests.

Conclusion

The links between the recovery model and the therapeutic community approach are strong. This applies even within prison-based therapeutic communities. Belief in the possibility of change, and that this change should be resident-owned and led, is central to the process, though this is greater within in the recovery model. Residents of prison therapeutic communities need to consider others in the community and the community will help shape each individual's therapy plan and journey. They do this on the basis of wanting to assist and support each resident. The result is that strong community attachments develop, with residents being grateful for the help, support and encouragement offered by other residents.

Equally important is that the focus of the 'treatment' offered is on the individual need(s) (criminogenic, psychological, mental health, resettlement) of each resident/prisoner. It is the development of these individual treatment plans, combined with the increased control over how they live, that results in different lives being lived. As one Grendon resident has commented (Sullivan, 2007), 'it has changed my life. I have self-esteem and confidence. I would never have had this before. For the first time ever I have a voice.'

Note

1 A standards-based quality improvement programme for therapeutic communities in the UK and abroad, with a robust accreditation scheme ratified by the Royal College of Psychiatrists' Education Training and Standards Committee.

References

Aitkenhead, D. (2009) 'They have their minds opened up, dissected and put back together again'. *The Guardian.* 14 July 2009.

Ali, S. (2008) *Reflections: An investigation into the autobiographical accounts of prisoners' experiences of therapy in custody.* Unpublished MSc dissertation. London Metropolitan University.

Allott, P., Loganathan, L. and Fulford, K. W. M. (2003) 'Discovering hope for recovery from a British perspective'. *Canadian Journal of Community Mental Health*, 21: 13–33.

Andresen, R., Caputi, P. and Oades, L. (2006) 'Stages of recovery instrument: development of a measure of recovery from serious mental illness'. *Australian and New Zealand Journal of Psychiatry*, 40: 972–980.

Andrews, D. A. and Bonta, J. (2003) *The psychology of criminal conduct.* Cincinnati: OH: Anderson.

Andrews, D. A., Bonta, J. and Wormith, S. J. (2006) 'The recent past and near future of risk and/or need assessment'. *Crime and Delinquency*, 52: 7–27.

Anthony, W. A. (1993) 'Recovery from mental illness: the guiding vision of the mental health service system in the 1990s'. *Psychosocial Rehabilitation Journal*, 16: 11–23.

Appleby, L., Shaw, J. and Kapur, N. N. *et al.* (2006) *Avoidable Deaths: Five year report of the national confidential inquiry into suicide and homicide by people with mental illness.* http://www.medicine.manchester.ac.uk/psychiatry/research/suicide/prevention/nci.

Bennett, P. (2006) 'Governing a humane prison'. In D. Jones (ed.), *Humane Prisons.* Oxford: Radcliffe Publishing.

Berkins, K. M. (2006) *Implementing a recovery approach in policy and practice: A review of the literature.* http://www.scottishrecovery.net/Publications-Discussion-Papers/non-srn.html

Borg, M. and Kristiansen, K. (2004) 'Recovery-oriented professionals: Helping relationships in mental health services'. *Journal of Mental Health*, 13: 493–505.

Bradley, K. (2009) *The Bradley Report.* London: Department of Health.

Birtchnell, J., Shuker, R., Newberry, M. and Duggan, C. (2008) 'An assessment of change in negative relating in two male forensic therapy samples using the Person's Relating to Others Questionnaire (PROQ)'. *Journal of Forensic Psychiatry & Psychology*, 20(1): 1–21.

Brookes, M. (2008) *Directing Therapy at HMP Grendon: Learning by experience.* Paper Presented At The Association of Therapeutic Communities Windsor Conference, 8–11 September 2008.

—— (2009) 'The application of the Good Lives Model within the prison therapeutic community regime at HMP Grendon'. *Forensic Update*, 98, 12–15.

—— (2010) 'Putting principles into practice: The Therapeutic Community Regime At HMP Grendon And Its Relationship With The Good Lives Model'. In E. Sullivan and R. Shuker (eds) *Grendon and the emergence of therapeutic communities: Developments in research and practice.* London: Wiley.

Brookes, M. and Mandikate, P. (2009) *Adapting to increased security and audit requirements while still maintaining a therapeutic community culture – The experience at HMP Grendon.* Paper Presented At The ATC Windsor Conference 15–18 September 2009.

Care Services Improvement Partnership, Royal College of Psychiatrists, Social Care Institute for Excellence. (2007) *A common purpose: Recovery in future mental health services.* http://www.scie.org.uk/publications/positionpapers/pp08.asp

Clark, D. (1974) *Social Therapy in Psychiatry.* London: Penguin.

Coleman, R. (1999) *Recovery: An Alien Concept.* Gloucester: Hansell Publishing.

Community of Communities. (2006) *Service Standards for Therapeutic Communities* (5th Edition). http://www.rcpsych.ac.uk/PDF/Service%20Standards%20for%20Therapeutic%20Communities%205th%20Edition.pdf

—— (2009) *What is a Therapeutic Community?* http://www.rcpsych.ac.uk/pdf/What%20is%20a%20TC.pdf

Cook, F. and Wilkinson, M. (1998) *Hard Cell.* Liverpool: Bluecoat Press.

Cullen, E. (1994) 'Grendon: The therapeutic prison that works'. *Therapeutic Communities*, 14(4): 301–311.

Davidson, L., O'Connell, M., Tondora, J., Styron, T. and Kangas, K. (2006) 'The Top Ten Concerns About Recovery Encountered in Mental Health System Transformation'. *Psychiatric Services*, 57: 640–645.

Deegan, P. E. (1988) 'Recovery: the lived experience of rehabilitation'. *Psychosocial Rehabilitation Journal*, 11: 11–19.

East, W. N. and Hubert, W. H. de B. (1939) '*Report On The Psychological Treatment Of Crime'.* London: HMSO.

Eysenck, H. J. and Eysenck, S. B. G. (1991) *Eysenck Personality Scales (EPS Adult).* London: Hodder & Stoughton.

Genders, E. and Player, E. (1995) *Grendon: A study of a therapeutic prison.* Oxford: Oxford University Press.

Gray, W. (1973) 'The therapeutic community and evaluation of results'. *International Journal of Criminology and Penology*, 1: 327–334.

Gunn, J. and Robertson, G. (1982) 'An evaluation of Grendon prison'. In J. Gunn and D. Farrington (eds). *Abnormal offenders, delinquency and the criminal justice system* (pp. 285–305). Chichester: Wiley.

Harding, C. M., Brooks, G. W. and Ashikaga, T. *et al.* (2001) 'The Vermont longitudinal study of persons with severe mental illness: II. long-term outcome of subjects who retrospectively met DSM-III criteria for schizophrenia'. *American Journal of Psychiatry*, 144: 727–735.

Hare, R. D. (2003) *The Psychopathy Checklist-Revised* (2nd edition). Toronto, ON: Multi-Health Systems.

Home Office. (1932) *Report of the Departmental Committee on Persistent Offenders.* London: HMSO.

Houghton, J. F. (1982) 'First-person account: maintaining mental health in a turbulent world'. *Schizophrenia Bulletin*, 8: 548–552.

Jacobson, N. and Greenley, D. (2001) 'What Is Recovery? A Conceptual Model and Explication'. *Psychiatric Services*, 52: 482–485.

Jones, D. and Shuker, R. (2004) 'Concluding comments: A humane approach to working with dangerous people'. In D. Jones (ed.). *Working with dangerous people: The psychotherapy of violence.* Oxford: Radcliffe Medical Press.

Leech, M. (1993) *A Product of the System.* London: Victor Gollancz.

Leggett, K. and Hirons, B. (2007) 'Security and Dynamic Security in a Therapeutic Community Prison'. In M. Parker (ed.), *Dynamic Security: The Democratic Therapeutic Community in Prison.* London: Jessica Kingsley Publications.

Main, T. F. (1946) 'The hospital as a therapeutic institution'. *Bulletin of the Menninger Clinic*, 10, 66–70. Reprinted in Therapeutic Communities (1996) 17: 77–80.

Marin, I., Mezzina, R., Borg, M., Topor, A., Staecheli Lawless, M., Sells, D. and Davidson, L. (2005) 'The person's role in recovery'. *American Journal of Psychiatric Rehabilitation*, 8: 223–242.

May, R. (2004) 'Understanding psychotic experience and working towards recovery'. In P. McGorry and J. Gleeson (eds) *Psychological Interventions in Early Psychosis.* Chichester: Wiley.

Ministry of Justice (2009) *HM Prison Grendon: Report on a Full Announced Inspection 2 – 6 March 2009.* http://www.justice.gov.uk/inspectorates/hmi-prisons/docs/Grendon_PN_2009_rps.pdf

Moray, L. C. (1991) *Personality Assessment Manual professional manual.* Odessa: Psychological Assessment Resources.

Morris, M. (2004) *Dangerous and Severe: Process, Programme and Person: Grendon's Work.* London: Jessica Kingsley.

National Institute For Mental Health in England. (2005) *NIMHE Guiding Statement on Recovery.* London: DOH Publications.

Newberry, M. (2009) *Changes in the profile of prisoners at HMP Grendon.* Unpublished Prison Service Report.

Newberry, M. and Shuker, R. (submitted) *Personality Assessment Inventory (PAI) profiles of offenders at a therapeutic community prison and their relationship to Offender Group Reconviction Scale (OGRS) scores.*

Newton, M. (2006) 'Evaluating Grendon as a prison: Research into quality of life at Grendon'. *Prison Service Journal*, 164: 18–22.

Parker, T. (1970) *The Frying Pan.* London: Hutchinson & Co.

Perkins, R. (2006) 'First person: "you need hope to cope"'. In G. Roberts, S. Davenport, F. Holloway and T. Tattan (eds) *Enabling Recovery: The principles and practice of rehabilitation psychiatry.* Gaskell: London.

Ralph, R. O., Lambert, D. and Kidder, K. A. (2002) *The Recovery Perspective and Evidence-Based Practice for People with Serious Mental Illness: A Guideline Developed for The Behavioural Health Recovery Management Project.* http://bhrm.org/guidelines/Ralph%20Recovery.pdf

Rethink (2008) *A brief introduction to the recovery approach.* www.rethink.org/living_with_mental_illness/recovery_and_self_management/recovery

Repper, J. and Perkins, R. (2003) *Social Inclusion and Recovery.* London: Baillière Tindall.

Rivlin, A. (2007) 'Self harm and suicide at Grendon Therapeutic Community Prison'. *Prison Service Journal*, 17: 34–38.

Roberts, G. and Wolfson, P. (2004) 'The rediscovery of recovery: open to all'. *Advances in Psychiatric Treatment*, 10: 37–49.

Roberts, G., Dorkins, E., Wooldridge, J. and Hewis, E. (2008) 'Detained – what's my choice? Part 1 Discussion'. *Advances in Psychiatric* Treatment, 14: 172–180.

Sheehan, A. (2002) *Inspirations, A Photographic Record of Recovery*. London: NIMHE.

Shepherd, G., Boardman, J. and Slade, M. (2008) *Making Recovery a Reality*. London: Sainsbury Centre for Mental Health.

Shine, J. and Newton, M. (2000) 'Damaged, disturbed and dangerous: A profile of receptions to Grendon therapeutic prison 1995–2000'. In J. Shine (ed.). *A compilation of Grendon research*. Leyhill: HMP Leyhill Press.

Shuker, R. and Newton, M. (2008) 'Treatment outcome following intervention in a prison-based therapeutic community: a study of the relationship between reduction in criminogenic risk and improved psychological well-being'. *British Journal of Forensic Practice*, 10(3): 33–44.

Stanford, P. (2009) 'Is this Britain's most successful prison'. *The Independent on Sunday*, 8 March 2009.

Sullivan, E. L. (2007) 'Seeing beyond the uniform': Positive views of a prison through prisoners' eyes. *Prison Service Journal*, 173: 27–33.

Sullivan, E. and Shuker, R. (eds) (2010) *Grendon and the emergence of therapeutic communities: Developments in research and practice*. London: Wiley.

Taylor, R. (2000) *A seven year reconviction study of HMP Grendon therapeutic community*. London: Home Office Research Development and Statistics Directorate Research Findings No. 115.

Tuke, S. (1813) *Description of The Retreat*. Reprinted (1996) with an introduction by K. Jones. London: Process Press.

Ward, T. (2002) 'Good lives and the rehabilitation of offenders: Promises and problems'. *Aggression and Violent Behaviour*, 7: 513–528.

Ward, T. and Brown, M. (2004) 'The good lives model and conceptual issues in offender rehabilitation'. *Psychology, Crime & Law*, 10: 243–257.

Ward, T. and Marshall, W. L. (2004) 'Good lives, aetiology and the rehabilitation of sex offenders: A bridging theory'. *Journal of Sexual Aggression*, 10: 153–169.

Ward, T. and Maruna, S. (2007) *Rehabilitation: Beyond the risk assessment paradigm*. London: Routledge.

Ward, T. and Stewart, C. A. (2003) 'The treatment of sex offenders: Risk management and good lives'. *Professional Psychology: Research and Practice*, 34: 353–360.

Warner, L., Mariathasan, J., Lawton-Smith, S. and Samele, S. (2006) *A Review of the Literature and Consultation on Choice and Decision-making for Users and Carers of Mental Health and Social Care Services*. London: The Sainsbury Centre for Mental Health and the Kings Fund.

Warren, F., Preedy-Fayers, K., McGauley, G., Pickering, A., Norton, K., Geddes, J. R. and Dolan, B. l. (2003) *Review of Treatments for Severe Personality Disorder*. London: Home Office Online Publication 30/03. http://rds.homeoffice.gov.uk/rds/pdfs2/rdsolr3003.pdf

Wilson, D. (1998) 'Postscript'. In F. Cook and M. Wilkinson. *Hard Cell*. Liverpool: Bluecoat Press.

Yalom, I. D. (1995) *The Theory and Practice of Group Psychotherapy*. New York: Basic Books.

12 Embedding recovery into training for mental health practitioners

Helen Eunson, Suzanne Sambrook and Diane Carpenter

This chapter will explore how adult forensic services (Ravenswood House, Medium Secure Unit and Southfield, Low Secure Unit) in Hampshire Partnership NHS Foundation Trust [HPFT] have endeavoured to improve recovery training by embedding the values and principles into all training for mental health practitioners.

> 'I never teach my pupils; I only attempt to provide the conditions in which they can learn.'
>
> (Einstein)

Introduction

'Oh no, not more training' – as health-care practitioners, how many times have we heard, or said, these words? When these words are said does it really mean practitioners are not interested in developing their existing skills or learning new ones? In our experience, it is often said in frustration at the increasing demands on a practitioner's time to attend 'essential training' which, whilst important, does not always have a direct impact on our day-to-day engagement with service users. So perhaps practitioners are saying, 'Will this training actually help develop my clinical practice?' In the last 10 years how much training have we attended to learn how to 'deal with a fire', 'pick up a box correctly' or 'answer a telephone to maintain a corporate image'? Our intention is not to undermine the importance of essential training but to encourage services to keep a close eye on the training pendulum to ensure it does not swing away from clinical practice, and to ensure that the focus remains with the service user and their recovery. In contrast, how much training in the last 10 years have we attended which is recovery-focused? We propose that the balance has most likely shifted to 'essential training' due to society's increasing obsession with litigation and compensation – not something NHS managers are responsible for, but which they have to manage. With this in mind, our challenge has been to meet the need for essential training whilst keeping our pendulum firmly swinging towards clinical practice. Our overall aim was to make recovery intrinsic to what we do by providing training and

Box 12.1 The challenge...

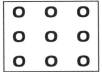

How did we join all the dots – using only four straight lines, which were joined together, and without lifting our pen off the paper? How would you do it?

support which promotes collaborative working whilst limiting time away from clinical practice. It was time to 'think outside the box' – but how?

Internationally, recovery-orientated practice has been discussed since the 1990s, and indeed the parallels are evident from as far back as the 1970s with the 'therapeutic community' (Shepherd *et al.*, 2008), so what has made us sit up and take notice now? Changes to clinical practice rarely happen overnight; more commonly they start with a few individuals (champions) who have a vision, and this was what began change in our service. There were many small discussions, and sharing of visions, but with the publication of 'Making Recovery a Reality' (Shepherd *et al.*) in 2008, the impetus was given to bring our champions together with key stakeholders to begin to consider how to embed recovery into practice and training. Noticeably, this represented a 'bottom-up' approach as our champions were, and still are, practicing clinicians. It was at this point that our recovery steering group was formed. As in many forensic settings, the 'traditional medical model' is common practice and can be perceived as one of the most challenging barriers to making recovery-focused services possible. We looked at the 10 Essential Shared Capabilities [10ESC] (NIMHE, 2004) to encourage multi-professional discussions about recovery and identify existing strengths in our service. We have also been clear that we do not refer to recovery as a 'model' as we have found this can be used to mean something we will 'do to' rather than 'do with' service users, the opposite of what recovery stands for. So we view recovery as a set of values and principles that we aspire to work with to promote joint thinking and inclusive practice to support service users in achieving their recovery.

We acknowledge that service development is not only about 'training' but also includes a cultural shift including service changes – delivery and job roles/ descriptions. Whilst there is movement, in a positive direction, within the service, through projects such as creating a capable teams approach [CCTA] (DoH, 2007) and experience-based design [EBD] (NHS, 2007), this chapter will address specifically our training developments.

Education, training or development?

Is there a difference between education, training and development, or, as in our experience, do health-care professionals tend to use these terms interchangeably?

Box 12.2

Learning style	Description	Examples
Visual	seeing and reading	Observation of practicing clinicians, literature
Auditory	listening and speaking	Induction, supervision, reflective practice groups
Kinaesthetic	touching and doing	Clinical Practice, in-house training programmes

Simply put, education is 'the process of acquiring knowledge and understanding'; training is 'the process of bringing a person to an agreed standard of proficiency by practice and instruction...'; development is 'the process of growing...' (Collins, 2003). All terms have close links to the principles of the Knowledge and Skills Framework (DoH, 2004), National Occupational Standards (NIMHE, 2003), 10ESC (NIMHE, 2004) and The Capable Practitioner (SCMH, 2001), whereby there is an expectation that competency or proficiency is achieved, or at the very least is being worked towards. Our view has been that each can be independent, but that linking all three together can be advantageous. Throughout this chapter we will use 'training' as the adjective to represent all terms. To enable us to plan our training we carried out a training-needs analysis which covered three specific areas: 1. skills and knowledge – what is needed to achieve our objective and what skills and knowledge do staff already have?; 2. learning styles – what are staff preferences – visual, auditory or kinaesthetic [VAK] (Petty, 2004) (box 12.2) – and what opportunities would there be to deliver training that encompassed each style?; and 3. trainers – who is best-placed to deliver training, and where and when should this be delivered? Our multi-professional training and development group took on these tasks and advised the recovery steering group.

Skills pledge

The skills pledge may seem a million miles away from recovery; however, it was this pledge that prompted the embryonic idea of altering the focus of our training. Leitch (2006) proposed the skills pledge to develop the workforce and, although it was voluntary, expected the public sector to lead the way. The purpose of the skills pledge is to develop the UK workforce and, as a minimum, to gain basic skills in language, literacy and numeracy, then to continuously extend staff skills. To support the skills pledge, the Department for Education and Skills [DfES] encouraged basic skills to be embedded into all education programmes to promote the value in everyday life. Post-compulsory education has embraced this and tends to use either dual-skilled trainers or joint working. As with all terms and departments, they develop and change; basic skills are also referred to as core and key skills, whilst DfES was split in 2008, with responsibilities for adults being met by Department for Innovation, Universities and Skills [DIUS], and then merged in 2009 to form the Department for Business, Innovation and Skills [BAS].

Hampshire Partnership NHS Foundation Trust made the skills pledge and our local champion saw the pledge and embedding basic skills as an opportunity to develop in-house training to support staff in ensuring they are 'fit for purpose'. The practice development nurse (who was also our multi-professional training lead) completed the post-graduate certificate in education, which gave her the knowledge and skills to embed basic skills into our in-house training programmes. This capability was used to start embedding other skills which we felt were imperative, e.g. recovery.

Embedding recovery into general training

When we first proposed the idea of embedding recovery into all our training it was met with apprehension and scepticism – not abnormal reactions to something new. One of our authors has skills and experience of embedding basic skills (discussed above in relation to the skills pledge) and therefore the confidence to start this new way to teaching recovery. We believed this would provide the opportunity for recovery to be kept high in staff thoughts and promote continuous reflection to improve clinical practice. The starting point was the training the author was already involved in: the two-year staff nurse development programme, HoNOS-Secure and CANFOR-S in-house training. The challenge was to embed recovery without it feeling tokenistic, and to build on the learners' existing skills and knowledge and encourage them to share their experiences.

Let us take CANFOR-S as a working example – this one-day training for mental health practitioners (Band 5 and above) has been in existence in our adult forensic services for over six years and whilst the lesson planning was structured it was not written down formally. The starting point was to identify the context, aims and specific objectives that the session was to meet; these were written into a formal lesson plan (Appendix 1). The next stage was to lay out the content of the session, giving consideration to time, resources, what elements meet the objectives, assessment and, most importantly, how and where in the teaching session recovery could be discussed. This may feel like the 'difficult' element, but when we believed recovery was 'a way of working' then it became more about giving time and thought to it than doing anything new in the teaching session. Appendix 1 identifies where recovery has been embedded. It is difficult to capture exactly what is said during these sessions, but examples of questions and answers/discussions are below. It is important to remember that the learners are qualified practitioners who in general have learning styles that are either 'interested learner' or 'involved learner', and therefore require a teaching style of 'motivator' or 'facilitator' (Grow, 1991).

Question 1: 'Thinking about the principles of recovery, how does the CANFOR-S needs assessment help build a meaningful and satisfying life?'

Answer/Discussion: 'It allows services users to express their opinions, and helps us (practitioners) to understand what is important to them.'

Question 2: 'Does CANFOR-S help you to encourage family/carer involvement?'

Answer/Discussion: 'It would be good to ask the carers to score a CANFOR-S – it might give us some more information or another insight, especially at the beginning or end of a service user's stay in our service.'

Question 3: 'Thinking about your role as the "professional", does CANFOR-S help you to reconsider what your role is?'

Answer/Discussion: 'I think completing this assessment together will help me, as primary nurse, to understand what he (service user) really needs instead of what we (health-care professionals) think he needs ... I observed my mentor completing this assessment with a service user and it was a surprise to hear their "sexual expression" was not being met – no one had thought it was important but actually when they started talking it explained a lot about how he had responded to particular staff. I was impressed that they started to discuss how this could be met and it was a significant part of the CPA discussions.'

Feedback from this session, and from other in-house training facilitated by the practice development nurse, has been overwhelmingly positive, with comments such as 'hadn't thought about recovery in this way, it was nice to discuss what we're doing every day', 'I liked hearing how others have actually got on when trying to be recovery focused', and 'It's reminded me it's what I do'. However, there have been comments made that remind us as trainers that not every health practitioner agrees with recovery in secure settings – 'What's the point, they (service user) don't have any choice, they have to be here cause they're sectioned' – and our challenge is to continue the training and discussions to encourage the sceptics to believe that recovery has a valid place in forensic services. Choice does not mean getting everything our own way – life is full of restrictions but also full of choices. We have also found that embedding recovery in training challenges and stimulates participants; it informs discussion and debate, and ultimately invites reappraisal through reflection on practice.

Other areas where we have embedded recovery are:

Induction: All new staff are introduced to recovery values and principles during their secondary induction training. This is delivered every four months by multi-disciplinary staff and service users.

One-to one supervision: During professional/clinical supervision there is encouragement for supervisees to reflect on their practice and identify how they can further support recovery.

Reflective practice groups for clinical staff: Opportunities are given for groups (particularly ward-based teams) to reflect on their practice and share examples of when and how recovery is being supported, as well as the inevitable challenges associated with this approach.

Group supervision for non-clinical staff: Opportunities to identify how their roles support service users and their recovery journey.

Star wards (Jenner, 2006): This is an initiative the service has implemented, the main focus of which is to enhance service users' daily ward experiences.

Staff meetings: Nurse Governance Forum, Psychological Therapies, Occupational Therapy, Clinical Governance and Unit Management meetings, which all keep 'recovery' on the agenda through discussions, reflections and specific presentations.

Specific recovery training

'[The role of the profession is in] offering their professional skills and knowledge, while learning from and valuing the patient, who is an expert-by-experience.'

(Roberts and Wolfson, 2004)

'The most powerful evidence for recovery…lies in the narrative accounts of individuals rather than in changes in the severity of symptoms.'

(Shepherd et al., 2008)

Starting point

To both prompt and support local development, the steering group invited members of the Scottish Recovery Network to talk to us about their implementation of recovery-based practice into forensic services. Both professionals and service users attended and found the information inspiring; they were encouraged to believe that forensic services and recovery were indeed compatible.

A further boost to the growing interest in recovery was for a group of thirty multi-professional staff to attend a three-day training programme provided by 'Working to Recovery Ltd', a specialist company run by Ron Coleman and Karen Taylor, which focuses on working with health professionals to understand recovery and to promote inclusive ways of working. It was a provocative and challenging three days for the multi-professional group who attended, but it allowed everyone to express their views, expectations and anxieties, and to agree on a goal. Out of this came a plan which could then be presented to management teams to get the support needed to further develop recovery-based working. These two events gave impetus to the steering group and laid good foundations from which to develop.

Involving the service user

A key component to any training which supports recovery-based values is inclusion. Training which only involves professionals giving information to other professionals is a one-sided endeavour. In line with recovery ideals, training needs to be a shared process which values the experience of the service user alongside the theoretical knowledge of the professional. Recovery-based training has several strands, one of which is balancing the empiricism of evidence-based practice with the experience-based knowledge of service users. A full understanding of the nature of recovery and the challenges faced by service users, and hence what would constitute effective help and support, can only be appreciated by hearing their stories and understanding their perspectives. Increasingly, these narratives are becoming part of both research dialogues and everyday practice (Faulkner and Morris, 2002) as ways of developing services. However, in forensic settings this may present a unique challenge. Forensic services have a dual function – negotiating the sometimes opposing needs of rehabilitation and security. The service users are present because of detention under the Mental Health Act, hence they are often unwilling 'consumers' of forensic services. Alongside this is the notion of recovery, i.e. building a meaningful life which allows choice and inclusion, based on the strengths of the individual. Furthermore, there is an often implicit, but nevertheless powerful, set of beliefs and attitudes that forensic patients are different, that they may be unable to collaborate because of their offence-related histories and behaviours, and that any collaboration should be viewed with suspicion (Maltman, Stacey and Hamilton, 2008). Effective, values-based, collaborative training could provide the appropriate forum to challenge these attitudes whilst at the same time equipping staff with the knowledge needed to provide effective services. Recovery and risk management are not mutually exclusive, and developing collaborative services, that value the individual regardless of their past, will support not only the development of a meaningful life for the service user, but a greater understanding of risk and the need for risk management. Involving service users in training is an effective way of changing attitudes and bridging gaps, perceived and actual, between staff and service users.

The following account describes the experience of bringing collaborative, recovery-oriented training into a traditional adult forensic service.

Awareness training

The first step is ensuring that the workforce has a good understanding of the recovery approach. Because of the traditional nature of the service and the need to work on culture change, it was important to include all disciplines. A series of presentations was planned. Initially these were professionally led. Presentations were made at medical education meetings, psychological therapy service meetings, and clinical ward manager/charge nurse away days. These presentations included definitions and principles of recovery, details of government drivers towards recovery and outlines regarding ways of working. Ample opportunity was allowed for discussion and questions. These set the scene but also highlighted the difficulties in changing a culture where the prevailing ethos was one of expert/patient to that where professionals were more like coaches or 'partners' – where clinicians are there to be 'on tap, not on top' (Shepherd *et al.*, 2008). The vexed question of 'choice' was also a hotly debated subject, with comments that detained patients could not be given choices. This led to a literature review and a small research project looking at how choice could be incorporated effectively into a forensic environment.

From here, a short introduction to recovery was developed which could be rolled out across both forensic units (medium and low secure) to all staff, clinical and non-clinical. Initially, the plan was to invite service users to come along to the training session. However, after the first session it was clear that the most important aspect of the training was not the knowledge (or education) – which could be given in a handout – but the comments of the service users who were able within the sessions to give their views on the ideas expressed in the training outline. They were able to talk about what recovery meant for them, how their illness had affected them and what helped (or hindered) their recovery journey. Subsequent sessions were planned with service users, who became an integral part of the awareness training programme. Staff feedback was overwhelmingly positive. Comments from the service users involved suggested that they had found this process helpful both in building relationships with staff and in feeling understood and listened to.

Evidence to assess attitude change was collected by asking staff to complete a brief questionnaire before and after the session (Recovery Attitudes Questionnaire, Borkin *et al.*, 2000). This questionnaire has nine statements with which people rated their level of agreement or disagreement on a five-point Likert scale. Statements include items such as 'All people with serious mental illness can strive for recovery' and 'Recovering from mental illness can occur without help from mental health professionals'. Scores range from 9–45, with lower scores indicating positive recovery attitudes. The mean for the accumulated scores prior to the awareness training was 19.2; after training this was reduced to 17. The shift was not statistically significant but was in the right direction. Considering that this was a brief training, the results were viewed as positive. It was interesting to note that those attending the training had quite positive recovery attitudes to start with, with scores ranging from 15–24. Comments from the attendees indicated that they appreciated the views of the service users, which deepened their understanding of the recovery process.

The original awareness programme was based on the outline in the 'Making Recovery a Reality' document (Shepherd *et al.*, 2008), which suggested that recovery training should focus on the components of the process of recovery, including:

- Finding and maintaining hope
- Re-establishment of positive identity
- Building a meaningful life
- Taking responsibility and control

The final outline for the awareness training included the following topics:

- A brief history of the recovery approach
- Service user definitions of recovery
- The recovery cycle

- Recovery themes and principles
- 10 Essential shared capabilities for mental health practice (NIMHE, 2004)
- How to work in a recovery-oriented way
- Hope-inspiring strategies
- Collaborative working
- Self-management, including Wellness Recovery Action Plans (WRAP, Copeland, 2000)

Building on awareness

Several training initiatives have developed following the initial awareness programme. These have included a service user-led training session on how to help when someone has an urge to self-harm. This was presented to staff on the women's ward, and led to the development of collaborative care plans. The service user developed both the materials and the presentation, with help from her primary nurse, and later presented this at a local service user conference.

A further development has involved ex-service users coming back to the units to talk about their experiences of secure services. These presentations have been to staff and current service users. Feedback is largely focused around the inspiring of hope – that people can develop independent lives beyond secure services.

Alongside the developments in involving service users in training for staff has been the development of service user forums within both units. These provide ongoing support and encouragement to service users to become more confident in their own recovery, and are described more fully by Anita Bowser in her chapter on service user involvement.

Trust commitments

Hampshire Partnership NHS Foundation Trust, like other trusts, has a business plan which includes their mission statements, one of which is 'To provide excellent services which promote recovery, independence and wellbeing'. Further to this the Specialised Services Directorate (which includes Adult Forensic Services) have a Strategic Goal 'to enhance the quality of life for patients, service users and carers' and a Specific Objective 'to further develop user and carer involvement across the Directorate'. We acknowledge that words are easy to say, but this is the start of a true commitment to recovery approaches. Additionally, a Trust-wide Recovery Strategy is under consideration, which will add impetus to the already growing commitment to and development of recovery-based services. Embedding recovery into all aspects of training and development across the Trust will be a challenge, but one which has in a small way begun with the work presented here.

The future

It's time to go back to our challenge – joining those dots and thinking 'outside the box' – how did we do?

Box 12.3

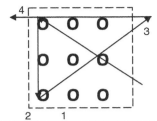

1 = Our starting point

2 = Service User involvement

3 = Embedding recovery into training

4 = The 'unknown' future

Although our starting point (1) was 'inside the box' we quickly agreed that for this challenge to work we needed to change the 'solid lines' to become 'permeable' so we could go outside the box and the 'norm'. The next point (2) enabled us to get service users involved in our awareness training, followed by point (3), embedding recovery into all training, and onto point (4), which is yet unknown. Our view is that like everything in life, it develops and grows, and is sometimes unimaginable until we get closer to achieving the unknown.

'Thinking outside the box' is a perspective we have needed to adopt consistently. We have been constantly presented with challenges in developing thoroughgoing recovery-oriented training plans. This has required openness, an inquisitive attitude and a willingness to take risks to develop new responses that creatively meet the needs of the service users at the heart of our services.

Appendix 1

CANFOR-S Lesson Plan

Name of trainer	Date and start/end times	No. on register	Location, inc. room	Course, subject and level

CONTEXT: summary of the background factors which influence your intentions for this lesson – including the group's characteristics and the course situation

The Camberwell Assessment of Need [CAN] is an evidence-based assessment measure which assesses the health and social needs of people with mental health problems. The Forensic CAN [CANFOR] is an assessment that highlights what can be frequent problem areas for forensic mental health service users. There are three versions: a clinical version, a research version and a short version [CANFOR-S], which is a one-page version suitable for routine clinical use.

The Care Programme Approach [CPA] is a framework used within mental health and requires clinicians, in collaboration with service users, to assess needs. CPA meetings are held at least every six months with each service user in adult forensic services.

This training is required to ensure qualified mental health practitioners can carry out effective assessments with service users. The training has been delivered in-house for six years by Helen Eunson, Practice Development Nurse.

All learners come together specifically for this training and whilst some learners may know/work with each other there may be some learners who have never met. All learners are professionally qualified and have already achieved a Diploma. Some learners will be developing their academic ability to Degree level and beyond.

TEACHING AIMS: A list summarising your intentions for the lesson, showing its main purposes and expressed in terms of the teaching events planed

Introduce learners to CANFOR-S and enable them to use it within the CPA process.

LEARNING OBJECTIVES: Assessment criteria for the lesson – what you will check learners can now do to indicate how successful learning has been.

The learners will be able to:
1. State what CANFOR-S is
2. Identify Needs
3. Explain why we assess Needs
4. **Identify how recovery values and principles are supported during and following a CANFOR needs assessment**
5. Correctly carry out a Needs assessment
6. Construct a CANFOR-S report suitable for CPA purposes

EMBEDDED SKILLS: as relevant, state which embedded skills will be developed or supported the most within this lesson.

Recovery through discussion and reflection, literacy and language through reading of vignettes and writing CPA reports.

Content	Time	Content	Teaching activity	Learning activity	Resources required	Assessment activity	Objective no.
Introduction	0915	Registration				Signed in	
	0930	Welcome Introductions	Exposition [Exp]	Listening, Q&A	Flip chart and pens	Questioning	
		Housekeeping			PowerPoint [PP] / OHP		
		Expectations		Boardstorm		Boardstorm	
		Introduce the lesson **aims and objectives**	Group Discussion [GD], Boardstorm, Exp	Listening, Q&A		Questioning	

Development	0950	Introduce Camberwell Assessments	Exp	Listening, Q&A	PP/OHP	Questioning	1
	0955	Exercise 1 – Define and identify Needs including concepts within mental health	GD, Boardstorm, Exp	Boardstorm, GD, feedback	Flip chart and pens, PP/OHP	Boardstorm, Questioning, GD	2
	1045	Break					
	1100	Recap	Exp, GD	Listening, Q&A	PP (if required)	GD, Q&A	1 & 2
	1110	**Why and how we assess needs**	Exp, **GD, Q&A (recovery)**	Listening, Q&A feedback	PP	Questioning	3 & **4**
	1120	Scoring	Exp, GD	Listening, Q&A	PP, score sheet	Questioning	**5**
	1130	Exercise 2 – vignette	Exp, **paired discussion (including recovery), practice and role-play**	Listening, Q&A, Individual Scoring, Paired Discussions, Feedback, GD **(share recovery discussions)**	PP, vignettes, score sheets, CANFOR-S book	Feedback, GD	**4** & / 3, **4** & 5
	1230	Lunch					
	1300	Re-cap	Exp, GD		PP (if required)	GD, questioning	
	1315	**Context within CPA including writing CPA reports**	Exp, GD			Boardstorm, GD / Feedback, GD, CPA reports, questioning	**4** & 6
	1415	Break	Exp, **GD, Q&A (recovery)**	Listening, Q&A	PP, flip chart and pens, handout		
	1430	Exercise 3 – vignette	Exp, **GD, paired discussions (including recovery), practice and role-play**	Listening, Q&A, individual scoring, paired discussions, feedback, GD **(share recovery discussions), CPA report**	PP, vignettes, score sheets, CANFOR-S book, flip chart and pens	GD, Q&A	4, **5** & 6
	1600	Recap					
	1630	Review aims, objectives and expectations					

References

Borkin, J., Steffan, J., Ensfield, L., Krzton, K., Wishinick, H., Wilder, K. and Youngarber, N. (2002) 'Recovery Attitudes Questionnaire: Development and Evaluation'. *Psychiatric Rehabilitation Journal*, 24: 95–102.

Collins (2003) *Concise Dictionary and Thesaurus Dictionary* (3rd edn) HarperCollins Publishers: Glasgow.

Copeland, M. E. (2000) *Guide to Developing a WRAP – Wellness Recovery Action Plan*. (http://www.mentalhealthrecovery.com)

Department of Health (2004) *The NHS Knowledge and Skills Framework (NHS KSF) and the Development Review Process*. London: HMSO.

—— (2007) *Creating Capable Teams Approach*, HMSO: London.

Faulkner, A. and Morris, B. (2002) *Expert paper on 'User Involvement in Forensic Mental Health Research and Development'*. NHS National Programme on Forensic Mental Research and Development.

Grow, G. O. (1991) 'Teaching Learners to be Self-Directed'. *Adult Education Quarterly*, 41(3): 125–149 2006.

Hampshire Partnership NHS Foundation Trust (2008) *Trust Business Plan*. HPfT: Hampshire.

Jenner, M. (2006) *Star Wards*. London: Bright. (http://www.starwards.org.uk)

Leitch (2006) *Prosperity for all in the global economy – world class skills*. Retrieved from http://www.hm-treasury.gov.uk/leitch.

Maltman, L. Stacey, J. and Hamilton, L. (2008) 'Peaks and Troughs – an exploration of patient perspectives of dangerous and severe personality disorder assessment (Peaks Unit, Rampton Hospital)'. *Personality and Mental Health*, 2(1): 7–16.

National Institute of Mental Health England [NIMHE] (2003) *National Occupational Standards for Mental Health*. London: NIMHE.

—— (2004) *The Ten Essential Shared Capabilities – A framework for the whole of the mental health workforce*. London: NIMHE.

NHS Institute for Innovation and Improvement (2007) *Experience Based Design*. Retrieved from http://www.institute.nhs.uk.

Petty, G. (2004) *Teaching Today* (3rd edn). UK: Nelsons Thorne Ltd.

Roberts, G. and Wolfson, P. (2004) 'The rediscovery of recovery: open to all'. *Advances in Psychiatric Treatment*, 10: 37–49.

SCMH (2001) 'The Capable Practitioner'. London: Sainsbury Centre for Mental Health. Retrieved from http://www.scmh.org.uk.

Shepherd, G., Boardman, J. and Slade, M. (2008) *Making Recovery a Reality*. Sainsbury Centre for Mental Health.

13 Recovery evaluation

The Scottish Forensic Services

Helen Walker and Dave Langton

Introduction: recovery in Scottish context

The publication of the *Delivering for Mental Health* (Scottish Executive Health Department, 2006a) Action Plan for Services and the report on the review of mental health nursing in Scotland – *Rights Relationships and Recovery* (Scottish Executive Health Department, 2006b) – have been two of the most influential documents to shape the mental health services in Scotland in many years. The most recent publication, *Towards a Mentally Flourishing Scotland: Policy and Action Plan* (Scottish Government 2009–2011), has laid further emphasis on empowering service users to own their recovery journey. There has been an expectation that these influential documents, with their various initiatives, would make a real impact on the way services are delivered, and consequently improving the patient experience. Our focus here is to explore how the measurement of 'recovery' in Scottish health services has been approached and used to meaningfully inform future service development. Perspectives from those both receiving and delivering services, and the views of carers, are important, and various approaches are necessary to contribute to the overall picture.

In Scottish health services generally, formal and informal evaluation has already contributed significantly to the implementation of the recovery approach. However, the key initiatives that relate directly to the evaluation of the recovery approach in the Scottish Forensic Services are valuable in that they have unique features arising out of our particular setting and the multi-faceted data that had been, or is, in the process of being collected. We will begin with an overview of the Scottish Recovery Indicator (SRI) as this provides a bedrock on which other initiatives can build. The development and implementation of the Scottish Recovery Indicator has had a significant impact on services. We will describe how the Scottish Forensic Service took up the SRI, and make an initial assessment of its impact. We will move on to an evaluation of values-based practice, using survey methods in order to demonstrate how we have generated baseline data on staff attitudes. We will also provide an overview of two formal evaluations of multi-modal interventions used to enhance recovery in service users using orthodox research methodologies.

The development of the Scottish Recovery Indicator

Following the appointment of a new Chief Nursing Officer for Scotland in 2004, a review of mental health nursing was undertaken. The initial scoping exercise offered an opportunity for service users, carers and clinicians to contribute to the discussion, with a view to them shaping the future services together. One of the many actions from the review (Scottish Executive Health Department, 2006b) was the commissioning of a tool that could be used to measure recovery. As part of this work, NHS Education for Scotland (NES) and the Scottish Recovery Network (SRN) were asked to review and revise existing tools appropriate for use in Scotland. The outcome of this was the creation of the Scottish Recovery Indicator (SRI), which is itself based on a tool called Recovery Oriented Practice Index (ROPI), developed by the New York State Office for Mental Health (Davidson *et al.*, 2008).

A pilot was carried out in five health boards across the country, between 2007–2009; the indicators were then reviewed, revised and relaunched for general use by September 2009. With this revision, the SRI has evolved into a tool which measures services against aspirational statements about recovery-focused practice; as such it should be seen as a mental health service development tool to help services ensure that their activities are focussed on supporting the recovery of the people who use their services. The use of the tool assists services to consider recovery-related issues such as inclusion, rights, equality and diversity. It also helps services to evaluate how well the ethos of recovery is embedded.

The SRI comprises nineteen indicators in eight parts, each of which is rated 1, 2, 3, 4 or 5 based on a judgement as to adherence to the indicator, where 1 is no adherence and 5 is full adherence:

PART 1: Meeting Basic Needs comprises two indicators. The first covers basic needs and is scored having considered references to assessments and care plans. The second covers the services provided to meet basic needs and is scored having considered the views of service providers, service users and ex-service users.

PART 2: Personalised Services and Choice comprises three indicators. The first indicator considers the extent to which the service identifies personal choice as fundamental to its work. The second indicator covers care plans and asks if they contain personal set goals, and the third asks how varied services provided are, in order that individual needs and preferences can be met. All are scored following consideration of care plans, service publications and interviews, as above.

PART 3: Strengths-based Approaches comprises three indicators. The first indicator asks whether assessments identify and explore strengths. The second indicator asks if care planning integrates strengths into goals and the third indicator asks about the information the service provides in respect of strengths-based approaches. All are scored following consideration of assessment documentation, together with information provided by the service in its policies and procedures.

PART 4: Comprehensive Service comprises one indicator, which seeks to establish the range of services available within, and accessible by, the service. The services required to achieve a full score are as follows, which is agreed following interviews, as above:

- Medication
- Vocational/employment
- Alcohol and drug misuse
- Talking therapies
- Family/social system based treatment
- Trauma services
- Staying well
- Health improvement

PART 5: Service User Involvement/Participation comprises two indicators. The first concerns service policies and procedures and how these promote service user involvement; the second is concerned with how services promote service user involvement throughout service planning. All are scored using interview data and consideration of how service information, policies and procedures promote involvement.

PART 6: Social Inclusion and Community Integration comprises two indicators which are both service-related. The first asks how services make efforts to involve extended support networks in care and treatment whilst the second asks how services provide a range of responses to promote inclusion. The indicators are scored following consideration of care plans and following interviews with providers and service users.

PART 7: Advance Planning comprises two indicators. The first is an assessment as to whether the service encourages advance planning and the second is an assessment of the service's policies and procedures for encouraging people to participate in their own care even under compulsion. The indicators are scored following consideration of care plans and interviews with providers and service users.

PART 8: Recovery Focus comprises four indicators, which assess attitudes towards recovery within the service. The first indicator is an assessment of how care plans link goals to life roles, activity and relationships; the second asks if services use recovery-oriented practice; the third asks if staff training in recovery is routine and the fourth asks if supervision is provided to staff following recovery-focussed principles. Once again, analysis of written care plans and interview data are used.

Forensic services use of the Scottish Recovery Indicator

The State Hospital is the only high secure mental health facility for Scotland. The service established a local steering group to drive forward the recovery agenda and to further support the implementation of values-based practice training.

A pilot of the SRI was carried out in this forensic setting during 2010 as part of the national implementation of the tool by a member of the recovery steering group.

Key issues to emerge

For the SRI to be meaningfully completed in a clinical area, full clinical team participation was required, together with the involvement of the service users in that clinical area. The estimated time taken to complete the evaluation was around 75 hours, with additional time required to prepare the clinical team in advance of the audit.

Although the tool appeared relatively easy to use and was set out in a way that was 'user friendly', the preparation phase was quite complex. Definitions of each aspect required a degree of interpretation and a 'judgement call' as to whether the materials available in the record met the required standard. For example, the requirement that there was an assessment and ongoing review meant that the assessor had to decide which documents and processes constituted an assessment review. What constitutes evidence was also a 'judgement call'. For the purposes of the pilot, 'written data and interviews' were taken as relevant evidence. Additional aspects of collecting evidence also proved a challenge at times due to the nature of the information clinicians recorded following clinical interactions. It became clear that there was no expectation that the individual clinician recording an interaction with a patient would routinely record the level of patient participation in their encounter. This meant that many aspects of recovery-oriented practice, required as evidence within the SRI, were not readily available in the documentary evidence that clinicians maintained of their work. This proved quite frustrating as the evaluator for the pilot was well aware in her own clinical area of recovery-oriented practice, but for the purposes of the SRI this was anecdotal evidence without explicit written evidence. This necessitated low scores on certain items. An example is provided in Box 13.1 below.

Box 13.1 Sample result from the SRI item relating to service user participation / involvement

Scenario

The person doing the SRI assessment has witnessed the patient and member of staff sitting down together and discussing his care plan at length, yet there is no mention of collaborative discussion in his progress notes. The patient has not signed his care plan prior to it being submitted for his biannual case review with the multi-disciplinary team. When the patient is asked whether his care plan was discussed with him he cannot remember if it was discussed or not and responds, 'I'm not sure, but I don't think so.'
   Score =1

The most important dimension of the SRI identified for initial improvement was that of service user involvement/participation. The tool helped to identify that involvement needed to increase i.e increased patient-focussed interventions (as opposed to interventions generated by clinicians) and self-generated goals in relation to the service users' own care plans. There was also a need to document this type of activity as legitimate clinical and service data, and therefore a need to encourage clinicians and clinical teams to record this aspect of their work more accurately, as the example above illustrates.

As a result of reviewing the pilot, the steering group agreed the need for a culture shift away from the conventional rehabilitation model currently in operation, towards a recovery approach. This subtle but significant shift was considered to be a key element in bringing about greater involvement of patients in their own care.

The other key area to emerge as a focus for targeted intervention was the issue of staff attitudes in relation to recovery. Anecdotes emerged in which it was clear that the attitudes of staff ranged from welcoming, to indifference, to quiet indignation. Statements such as, 'recovery is nothing new', 'we've been doing this for years' and 'it's just a new word for rehabilitation' were not uncommon. This highlighted the need for greater understanding of what recovery really meant before there would be any possibility of a cultural shift taking place.

In summary, while undertaking the SRI requires a substantial service commitment, our initial findings suggested that using the tool could lead to significant improvements in practice. In adhering to the principles that underpin recovery, the SRI has been developed in a way that promotes ownership and responsibility. While supporting organisational level changes, the tool also helped to generate conversations within clinical teams about recovery-supporting environments and person-centred approaches.

Current use of the SRI is 'optional' within health boards in Scotland. Despite this there is government expectation, through the Strategy for Mental Health, that a recovery orientation to services will be evidenced in some form, and each health board is required to both accept this and act upon it. The health boards are also required to submit progress reports every six months, identifying steps taken towards achieving success in relation to each of the actions set out in the national action plan, and the implementation of the SRI is included within this.

Surveys of values-based practice

In addition to the SRI, baseline data was gathered in relation to staff attitudes towards both recovery itself and training in values-based practice, using survey methodology. Two examples of such practice are highlighted below, the first on a national and the second a local level.

National survey

In tandem with the implementation of the recovery agenda, the Scottish Government sought to invest in the development and delivery of training materials, in addition to evaluation of the training process. Survey methodology was used in the study entitled 'Evaluation of the Impact of the Dissemination of Educational Resources to Support Values-Based and Recovery-Focussed Mental Health Practice' (MacDuff *et al.*, 2010). NES commissioned this significant piece of work on behalf of the government and set the following objectives:

- To explore perceptions and experiences of the trainers who delivered the training programme, in addition to exploring the perceptions of the learning achieved.
- To explore the experience of the training, both for trainers and for participants on the receiving end of the training.
- To examine the methods used to disseminate and cascade the training/ learning, in addition to examining the success and challenges associated with implementation – including analysis of organisational barriers and opportunities and sustainability.
- To evaluate the extent to which people learn from participants.

The overall approach was informed particularly by: the stakeholder involvement perspective of Guba and Lincoln (1989); the exploratory case study methods suggested by Yin (1994); and Robert Stake's early work on congruence between intention and enactment (1977). Within this context, qualitative methods were the primary means used for building understanding (review of policy, education and practice literature, and use of interviews/focus groups), but the study also at times used questionnaires with a view to achieving breadth of coverage.

A number of conclusions were reached, and recommendations listed. The study established that a quarter of all mental health nurses had received training in values-based practice over a two-year period. A minimum of two days' training was accepted, and recommended as future good practice. There was evidence of collaboration in both the delivery and the receipt of training with service users, across agencies and across disciplines. The aspiration to effect culture change has required training with significant facilitation of experiential learning in many health boards. The challenge for those committed health boards was not only to expand delivery of values-based training, but more fundamentally to support sustainable related practice development. Findings also showed that a number of boards had led the way in developing and testing mechanisms to support the training and future practice (e.g. use of team reflection/clinical supervision, Personal Development Plans and action learning sets), however the Mental Welfare Commission survey indicated that many services had not instituted follow-up support and mentoring processes. It was suggested that 'situated power', service priorities and embedded culture of place (i.e. 'the way things are done round here') will be key influences on any embedding of the espoused values into practice. Some boards have shown how leadership can influence this. Moreover, many participants in the study expressed optimism at the way in which the 10 Essential Shared Capabilities (which form the basis of the values-based practice training programme) have become incorporated as the basis for pre-registration nurse education.

It was evident that the evaluation provided significant insights into processes and impacts for those involved in the initial cascade of this educational initiative, and some early insights into the experiences of the larger body of mental health workers who received training. There were some promising indications of development around patient involvement, personalised care planning and positive risk-taking in particular. Tension persisted between the need to train sufficient staff to achieve critical mass and the need to ensure sufficient depth of engagement to optimise enactment of the espoused approaches. The challenge for researchers is how best to apprehend the influence of the educational experience on practice (Macduff *et al.*, 2010).

Forensic Services survey

A second survey was undertaken at the State Hospital as part of a post-graduate research project (Greenfield, 2010). This project sought to determine the attitudes towards recovery of health practitioners providing care for mentally disordered offenders in a high secure hospital. The intention was also to examine the attitudes of participants who have undergone training in 'values-based practice' and compare them to the participants without training. Finally, to establish if there was a significant difference in attitudes towards recovery in relation to the length of time employed within the hospital.

The survey method was used, distributing a self-administered questionnaire to all staff with patient contact (350), including predetermined statements that participants would respond to by selecting from a five-point Likert scale. The questionnaire was based on that developed by Hardiman and Hodges (2008) to determine differences in professional attitudes towards recovery. The researcher included three additional questions, making nineteen items in total, in order to gain insight into attitudes which could be perceived as specific to the high secure environment.

Key findings from this research indicated that there was little difference in attitudes of nursing staff whether they had attended the one-day values-based training or not. This is consistent with other evaluations of short training courses and reflects the need for sustained follow-through, with individual coaching and mentoring and team-based reflective practice. There were no obvious differences in attitudes towards recovery, as defined by age or length of service. One particularly interesting point to note in relation to nursing attitudes was the improvement with level of seniority. A clear pattern emerged whereby nursing assistants (Band 3) appeared to have more negative attitudes than enrolled nurses and staff nurses (Band 4 and Band 5) and senior charge nurses (Band 7) had the most positive attitudes. This important piece of work has provided the organization with baseline data on staff attitudes. It is anticipated that further training and educational initiatives will be adjusted and refocused in view of these outcomes.

Formal evaluation of recovery-oriented interventions

Differing approaches to evaluation are expected and ought to be actively encouraged, because each method will generate findings of value to different people. Anecdotal evidence in forensic services support the argument that formal evaluation, and in particular randomised controlled trials, continue to be the method favoured amongst medical staff, whereas alternative methods seem to be broadly accepted across all other disciplines. Here we describe a well-established clinical intervention designed to promote 'clinical recovery' and present data from the earlier pilot study. The revised research design used in the new study was heavily influenced by the participating patients. The rationale for this was that the patients would be in the best position to detect changes that might occur for themselves or others through participation in a particular intervention.

The Coping With Mental Illness Programme[1] has been delivered every year in the State Hospital, Scotland since 1996. The patients have hugely influenced both the programme itself and the way in which outcomes are measured. The programme developer actively encouraged the patients to take ownership of the programme, primarily because it would be of little benefit if it was not providing information that was relevant to their recovery. The current Randomised Controlled Trial (RCT) builds on findings from the early pilot study, completed in 2005 by the first author (HW).

An eighteen-month pilot study was carried out whereby a consecutive case sample (treatment group) was formed using a 'no treatment' comparison group (control group). Pre, post and six-month follow-up assessments were carried out throughout the research. A range of outcome measures were used, including two measures of knowledge: a self-report assessment tool – Forensic Assessment of Knowledge Tool (FAKT) – and the Understanding Medication Questionnaire (MacPherson *et al.*, 1995). Other measures were used to establish level of insight (Schedule for the Assessment of Insight (SAI), David, 1990) and assess mental state (Positive and Negative Syndrome Scale [PANSS], Kay, 1987). Results from this pilot study (n=48) indicated that there were no statistical differences between the treatment- and control-group scores on any assessment prior to the commencement of the intervention, indicating a well-matched sample group. However, all four of the assessments showed statistically significant changes post-group. The treatment group showed an ability to improve knowledge and retain information about psychosis, which may account for their improved mental state and level of insight (see Table 13.1 below). Despite methodological limitations and a small sample group, this project provided an early indication of the positive value of this psycho-education programme in a forensic setting.

The primary outcome of the current trial is improved insight/self-awareness into illness. Secondary outcomes include improved knowledge, mental health and relationships with staff, social functioning, willingness to communicate and collaborate with others. The trial started in 2009 and is being undertaken across four forensic settings, one high secure (The State Hospital [TSH]), two medium secure (Orchard Clinic [OC] and Rowanbank Clinic [RC]) and one low secure (Leverndale).

Table 13.1 Comparison of treatment versus control group scores pre-group and at six-month follow up

Assessment tool	Treatment mean	Control mean	t	Level of significance
FAKT pre	24.93	23.59	0.424	0.674
FAKT 6m	34.39	22.77	3.038	0.005*
MacPherson pre	16.48	14.40	0.957	0.344
MacPherson 6m	20.48	15.54	2.038	0.050*
PANSS pre	42.70	48.44	−1.865	0.070
PANSS 6m	38.58	45.38	−2.122	0.042*
David pre	9.82	7.56	1.420	0.164
David 6m	12.40	9.21	2.153	0.039*

During the trial, patients referred to the CWMI Programme will be approached and asked to be involved in the measurement of the effectiveness of this psychoeducation programme for patients.

The Coping with Mental Illness Programme, in keeping with its roots in psychosocial interventions (PSI), is located within the person-centred tradition. Person-centred theory is one which starts from a process theory of authenticity, not from a theory of disorders (Mearns *et al.*, 2006). In accordance with this, it is accepted that all participants in the programme bring with them their own ideas, experiences and opinions. The experiences of all participants are viewed as authentic and their opinions are heard in an open-minded and collaborative spirit. The teacher/student relationship will be informed by 'care' or 'therapeutic relational' principles. This provides the medium for learning to occur and for the patient to experience success and to build on his or her knowledge. The notion that this patient group benefits from an individual and holistic approach, that we must respect each individual's understanding of their own experience, and that patients should be acknowledged as experts in their own experiences, is in line with the pivotal report by The British Psychological Society, *Recent advances in understanding mental illness and psychotic experiences* (The British Psychological Society, 2000). This idea has been further reinforced by Kingdon and Turkington (2005), who report, 'Individualising psycho-education helps people feel listened to and understood, and this approach adds to its effectiveness'. The purpose of this programme is to engage with patients who suffer from psychosis and/or other mental illness, plus (possibly, but not always) cognitive difficulties or educational difficulties within a relational framework. The aim is to raise awareness about their illness and to help them to adopt a lifestyle which will help them to stay well, reduce the risk of relapse and subsequent increased risk, and facilitate recovery.

The authors were aware of a number of other key philosophical underpinnings that are currently driving delivery of twenty-first-century health care, and highlight throughout the programme the importance of:

1.   Ensuring that a strong message of recovery is delivered and that a recovery focus is maintained in the approach at all times.

2. Building on the individual's strengths and resilience.
3. Ensuring a values-based approach to care (e.g. in keeping with the principles of *Rights, Relationships and Recovery*, the report of mental health nursing in Scotland (SEHD, 2006b)).
4. Ensuring that facilitators are also cognisant of the significant role that 'spirituality' can play in an individual's life and in their ongoing journey of recovery.

The CWMI programme consists of three modules:

- Module 1, Foundation, includes: Introduction to the Programme, Understanding mental illness and personality disorder, Stigma & Myths, Looking at 'symptoms' of psychosis, *What's caused my illness?* and how the brain works, Reflecting on the 'symptoms' of psychosis, Looking at mood difficulties, Reflecting on mood difficulties, Anxiety, Post-Traumatic Stress Disorder (PTSD).
- Module 2, The Legal System, includes: Risk assessment and planning, Legal issues around admission, Legal issues around discharge and appeal, Coping with assessment for moving on.
- Module 3, Coping Skills and Recovery, includes: Coping with 'highly charged' atmospheres, Looking at treatment, Relapse and 'early warning' signs, Problem-solving, Difficulties relating to people, Recovery, Families and mental illness, Reflecting on living with schizophrenia.

All participants in the trial are in-patients between the ages of 18 and 65, have a diagnosis of one of the psychoses, and are required to be able to function in a group setting. Patients are excluded if they have a primary diagnosis of Learning Disability or are too unwell to take part, as decided by the Responsible Clinician – using their clinical judgement. The programme offers a combination of didactic (information-giving) sessions and behavioural (problem-solving) sessions. The group are encouraged to become involved in open discussion during each session and are issued with information relating to the session and supplementary reading material at the close of each session.

At the outset of the trial all participating organisations agreed to the following process of participant selection. Referrals would be received for the group through the customary route, the group facilitator (the local Principal Investigator [PI]) would wait until there were adequate numbers of participants for two groups and then random selection would take place. Each PI would be randomly allocated to a group, following instructions they received at the beginning of the process in a sealed envelope. Half of the participants would be allocated to the experimental group, and the other half to a (waiting list) control group. All participants would eventually take part in the CWMI psycho-education programme – the control group would simply have to wait until the first group has been completed and then engage in the intervention.

Data collection has been ongoing since February 2009 and will continue over the course of three years. A battery of psychometric tests is carried out immediately before and after the psycho-education groups, and again at a six-month follow-up. The breadth of assessment reflects discussions with a large number of patients (who had previously attended the group), highlighting how difficult it was to decide 'what makes the biggest impact on you as a person receiving information'. They were keen to reflect the importance of what their understanding of illness was and 'show somehow that knowing more about your illness – or your diagnosis – helps you regain control of yourself and your life'. The reality of knowing more does, however, create tension for some patients, and they can become quite despondent about their future. In order to capture the impact of this particular experience, certain assessment tools have been selected. The instruments in use are designed to measure: insight (David, 1990; Markova *et al.*, 2003), mental health symptomatology (Kay, 1987), side-effects of medication (Day, Wood, Dewey and Bentall, 1995), knowledge of psychosis (Walker, unpublished), social behaviour (Reed and Woods, 2000), anxiety and depression (Snaith and Zigmond, 1994; Addington and Addington, 1993), self-esteem (Rosenberg, 1965), quality of life (Martin and Allan, 2007), locus of control (Jomeen and Martin, 2005) and level of intellectual functioning (Wechsler, 1999). It is intended that findings generated from this study will be published in peer-reviewed journals.

An interview will also be carried out between the Chief Investigator (HW) and project participants, prior to and following on from attendance at the group. This interview will be used to gather information to complete a Repertory Grid and elicit the participants' impressions of what has changed as a result of attending the group.

As far as possible – and in keeping with the patients' explicit requests – assessment tools are self-rated, rather than clinician-rated. This highlights the 'measure of control' the participant has in reporting the impact accurately and from their viewpoint. So despite the fact the evaluation is a randomised, controlled trial, and not a design that immediately evokes recovery orientation, in this instance the patients are still heavily influencing the direction and the outcome. On occasion it is deemed useful to use more than one instrument on the same subject; in the aforementioned study two tools are used to measure insight (David, 1990; Markova *et al.*, 2003) – the former is clinician-rated and the latter participant-rated. It will be of particular interest to compare results from both to see how well the clinicians' views match with the patients'.

It is obvious that differing approaches are being, and will continue to be, used to measure recovery. The next account differs somewhat radically from the randomised controlled trial previously described; instead this evaluation adopts a qualitative methodology. Laithwaite and Gumley (2007) argue that a person's recovery from psychosis involves more than a reduction in symptoms. It involves the entire self, bringing all components of physical, emotional, mental and spiritual aspects of themselves into their experience of life (Forchuk *et al.*, 2003).

Recovery After Psychosis (RAP) and self-esteem

In addition to the large-scale study described above, the Scottish Forensic Service supported smaller qualitative studies of recovery in high secure settings. Laithwaite and Gumley (2007) has found a small yet growing amount of qualitative research into the experience of people with psychosis, recognising qualitative methods as particularly useful to explore perceptions and experiences of the relationship between individuals' behaviour in the context of their social environment. She describes qualitative research in psychosis as helping to bring about a greater understanding of people's experiences, and the meanings they attach to these experiences. Furthermore, she informs us of the processes involved in these experiences. Such knowledge and understanding is important if we are to gain a greater knowledge of the factors and processes involved in recovery from psychosis.

Prior to the study undertaken by Laithwaite and Gumley (2007), they could find no published studies into the experiences of people with psychosis in maximum security settings. The importance of understanding recovery in this particular population is critical to helping the development of interventions, to lower risk and to inform risk management. Their study presents a user's perspective on being a patient in a high security setting and the factors he/she considers important in his/her recovery. A grounded theory approach to analysis (Strauss and Corbin 1990) was used. The methodology was also influenced by the social constructionist revision of grounded theory (Charmaz, 1990) which recognises the roles of the researcher's perspective in the generation and development of theory.

Thirteen participants were involved in the study. All took part in taped interviews, lasting between 60 and 90 minutes, which were in-depth, unstructured and open-ended. The open-ended nature of the interviews, without any set agenda, was considered to facilitate collaboration and enable the participant to have control over the discussion. A list of all emerging codes was compiled, in conjunction with memos and field notes made by the researcher, to produce analytical categories of initial descriptive codes. Consistent with Dey (1999), theoretical sufficiency was preferred to theoretical saturation (Glaser and Strauss, 1967; Strauss and Corbin 1990) as the aim of the study.

Participants spoke about their relationships and a 'changing sense of self' in terms of two broad categories of experience: their 'past experiences of adversity and recovering in the context of being in hospital'.

The sub-categories drawn from each of these are highlighted below:

- Past experiences of adversity: parental break-up and loss, feeling rejected and worthless, relationships with significant others, perspective on past selves.
- Recovering in the context of being in hospital: frightening versus safety, feeling entrapped, the importance of relationships, development of trust, coping, and valued outcomes.

Broadly speaking, findings of research emanating from the user's perspective (Laithwaite and Gumley, 2007) suggested that recovery from psychosis did not require remission of symptoms but involved minimising, managing and overcoming the effects of being a 'patient in the mental health system': adverse experiences such as loss, disruption in family relationships, peer relationships, loss of valued social roles, and the loss of a sense of self as an autonomous and meaningful contributor to society.

A second study was undertaken by Laithwaite *et al.* (2009) in order to evaluate the effectiveness of a recovery-group intervention based on Compassionate Mind training, for individuals with psychosis. The objective of the study was particularly focussed on improving depression, to develop compassion towards the self and promote help-seeking behaviour. Laithwaite *et al.* (2009) suggest that recovery in the forensic high secure population is not just about reduction of symptoms or distress, but reduction and management of the risk of violent offending. It is therefore important that the therapies that have been researched in general mental health settings are adapted and piloted with this population. A recovery programme that draws on Compassionate Mind theory (Gilbert, 2005) is attractive as it has a developmental perspective that focuses on the effect of disrupted attachment histories on the current functioning of the individual, and their ability to respond to self-criticism, self-soothe and modify distress. Hence a programme that focuses on developing a compassionate understanding of those vulnerabilities may promote recovery and help-seeking behaviour, and in turn reduce the risk of violent reoffending.

Results were based on outcomes from three groups run in the high secure facility in Scotland. The Recovery After Psychosis (RAP) programme consisted of three modules:

Module 1: Understanding psychosis and recovery.
Module 2: Understanding compassion and developing the ideal friend.
Module 3: Developing plans for Recovery after Psychosis – this part of the programme involved the development of a RAP plan (focussing on triggers, early warning signs, use of safety behaviour, action plans and agreed coping strategies). The information was used to create a compassionate letter, which involved participants writing a letter to themselves (as written by their ideal friend). This letter contained encouragement and support in relation to how to respond to obstacles and how to seek help in the future.

A within-subjects design was used. Participants were assessed at the start of the group, mid-group (after five weeks), at the end of the programme and at a follow-up six weeks later. Three group programmes were run over the course of a year. Nineteen participants commenced the intervention and eighteen completed it.

Results revealed significant effects on the Social Comparison Scale (SeCS, Neff, 2003), the Beck Depression Inventory II (Beck *et al.*, 1996), the Other As Shamer Scale, the Rosenberg Self-Esteem Measure (Rosenberg, 1995) and the Self-Image Profile for Adults. Significant effects were not found on the Self-Compassion Scale, the Robson Self-Concept Questionnaire or the Self-Image

Profile for Adults. Significant effects were found on the general psychopathology scale from the Positive and Negative Syndrome Scale (Kay, 1987) at the end of the group, and this was maintained at follow-up. Significant effects were not found on the PANSS positive, negative or depression scales. Conclusions from the study (Laithwaite, 2009) indicated that group intervention based on the principles of compassionate-focussed therapy for this population were effective.

Importance of evaluation

The concept of recovery in forensic settings is arguably still in its infancy. Differing approaches to evaluating and improving our understanding of the patient's recovery journey are evident throughout this chapter. Encouragingly, the evidence presented here indicates a willingness to gather evidence to support recovery, but with this comes the realisation of the associated barriers in current practice. The biggest hurdle in forensic settings continues to be the inability to strike a reasonable balance between working in partnership and maintaining adequate levels of security. The 'fear factor' associated with giving away any element of control and decision-making to the patient remains evident. In order to shape future progress it will be essential that clinicians continue to explore new ways of working, and share findings. Our belief is that the impact of recovery-based practice is yet to be seen in forensic settings. Despite the attempts of a handful of enthusiastic researchers, the impact has yet to be fully explored – to date we have simply 'scratched the surface' and further outcome studies are essential if we are to truly understand recovery.

Acknowledgements

A number of people contributed to the development of this chapter and deserve our gratitude. We would like to extend our thanks to all patients who aided the discussion in relation to the development of the research protocol for the RCT. Thanks also must be extended to Patricia Coia, Yvonne Murray and Frank Greenfield, who have individually contributed greatly to the gathering of data.

Note

1 Developed by Dr Jenni Connaughton (Consultant Psychiatrist), supported by one of the authors (HW) and Patricia Cawthorne (Clinical Nurse Specialist).

References

Addington, J. and Addington, D. (1993) 'Premorbid functioning, cognitive functioning, symptoms and outcome in schizophrenia'. *Journal of Psychiatry and Neuroscience*, 18: 18–23.
Beck, A. T., Steer, R. A. and Brown, G. K. (1996) *Manual for the Beck Depression Inventory-II*. San Antonio Tx: The Psychological Corporation.

Becker, D. R., Torrey, W. C., Toscano, R., Wyzik, P. F. and Fox, T.S. (1998) 'Building recovery-oriented services: Lessons from implementing individual placement and support (IPS) in community mental health centres'. *Psychiatric Rehabilitation Journal*, 22(1): 51–54.

Borkin, J. R., Steffen, J. J. Ensfield, L. B. Krzton, K. Wishnick, H. Wilder, K. and Yangarber, N. (2000) 'Recovery Attitudes Questionnaire Development and Evaluation'. *Psychiatric Rehabilitation Journal*, 24(2): 95–102.

Butler, R. J. and Gasson, S. L. (2004) *The Self-Image Profile for Adults (SIP-Adult)*, Haricourt Assessment.

Charmaz, K. (1990) 'Discovering chronic illness: Using grounded theory'. *Social Science and Medicine*, 30(11): 1161–1172.

David, A. S. (1990) 'Insight and psychosis'. *British Journal of Psychiatry*, 156: 798–808.

Davidson, L. (2003) *Living outside mental illness: Qualitative studies of recovery in schizophrenia*. New York: University Press.

Davidson, L., Rowe, M., Tondora, J., O'Connell, M., Staeheli, J. and Lawless, M. (2008) *A practical guide to recovery-oriented practice: tools for transforming mental health care*. New York: Oxford University Press.

Day, J. C., Wood, G., Dewey, M. and Bentall, R. (1995) 'A self-rating scale for measuring neuroleptic side effects. Validation in a group of schizophrenic patients'. *British Journal of Psychiatry*, 166: 650–653.

Dey, I. (1999) *Grounding Grounded Theory: Guidelines for qualitative inquiry*. San Diego: Academic Press.

Forchuk, C., Jewell, J., Tweedell, D. and Steinnagel, L. (2003) 'Reconnecting: The client's experience of recovery from psychosis'. *Perspectives in Psychiatric Care*, 39(4): 141–150.

Glaser, B. G. and Strauss, A. L. (1967) *The discovery of grounded theory: Strategies for qualitative research*. Chicago, IL: Aldine.

Gilbert, P. (ed.) (2005) *Compassion: conceptualizations, research and use in psychotherapy*. London: Bruner-Routledge.

Greenfield, F. (2010) *Compassion: conceptualizations, research and use in psychotherapy*. London: Bruner-Routledge.

Guba, Y. and Lincoln, E. (1989) *Fourth Generation evaluation*. London. Sage.

Hardiman, E. R. and Hodges, J. Q. (2008) 'Professional Differences in Attitudes Toward and Utilisation of Psychiatric Recovery'. *Families in Society*. 89(2): pp. 220–227.

Haro, J. M., Novick, D., Suarez, D., Alonso, J., Lepine, J. P., Ratcliff, M. and SOHO Study Group. (2006) 'Remission and relapse in the outpatient care of schizophrenia: three-year results from the Schizophrenia Outpatient Health Outcomes study'. *Journal of Clinical Psychoharmacology*, 26(6): 571–578.

Jomeen, J. and Martin, C. R. (2005) 'A psychometric evaluation of form C of the Multi-dimensional Health Locus of Control (MHLC-C) Scale during early pregnancy'. *Psychology, Health and Medicine*, 10(2): 2002–214.

Kay, S. R. (1987) 'The Positive and Negative Syndrome Scale (PANSS) of schizophrenia'. *Schizophrenia Bulletin*, 13: 261–276.

Kingdon, D. G. and Turkington, D. (2005) *Cognitive Therapy of Schizophrenia*. Hove: Lawrence Erlbaum Associates Ltd.

Laithwaite, H., Gumley, A. I. and Benn, A. (2007) 'Self-Esteem and psychosis: A pilot study investigating the effectiveness of a self-esteem programme on the self-esteem and positive symptomatology of mentally disordered offenders'. *Journal of Behavioural and Cognitive Psychotherapy*, 35(5): 569–577.

Laithwaite, H. and Gumley, A. (2007) 'Sense of Self, Adaptation and Recovery in patients with psychosis in a Forensic NHS setting'. *Clinical Psychology and Psychotherapy*, 14: 302–316.

Laithwaite, H., Gumley, A., O'Hanlon, M., Collins, P., Doyle, P., Abraham, L. and Porter, S. (2009) 'Recovery after Psychosis (RAP): A comparison focussed programme for individuals residing in high security settings'. *Behavioural and Cognitive Psychotherapy*, 37: 511–526.

MacPherson, R., Jerrom, B. and Hughes, A. (1996) 'A Controlled Study of Education About Drug Treatment in Schizophrenia'. *British Journal of Psychiatry*, 168: 709–717.

Markova, I. S., Roberts, K. H., Gallagher, C., Boos, H., McKenna, P. J. and Berrios, G. E. (2003) 'Assessment of insight in psychosis: a re-standardization of a new scale'. *Psychiatric Research*, 119: 81–88.

Martin, C. R. and Allan, R. (2007) 'Factor structure of the Schizophrenia Quality of Life Scale Revision 4 (SQLS-R4)'. *Psychology, Health and Medicine*, 12(2): 126–134.

Mearns, D., Elliott, R., Schmid, P. F. and Stiles, W. B., (2006) 'The challenge of schizophrenia'. *Person-centred and Experiential Psychotherapies*, 5(3): 153–154.

MacDuff, C., Gass, J., Laing, A., Williams, H., Coull, M., Addo, M. and McKay, R. (2010) *An Evaluation of the Impact of the Dissemination of Educational resources to Support Values-Based and Recovery-Focussed Mental Health Practice*. Robert Gordon University. http://www.nes.scot.nhs.uk/media/440374/final_report_mar_10.pdf.

Neff, K. D. (2003) 'The development and validation of a scale to measure self-compassion'. *Self and Identity*, 2(3): 223–250.

Pekkala, E. T. and Merinder, L. B. (2002) 'Psychoeducation for schizophrenia'. *Cochrane Database of Systematic Reviews*, Issue 2, 2002. Cochrane Database of Systematic Reviews, Issue 4, 2009 (Unchanged).

Reed, V. and Woods, P. (2000) *The Behavioural Status Index; a 'life skills' assessment for monitoring therapy in health care*. United Kingdom: Psychometric Press.

Rosenberg, M. (1965) *Society and the adolescent self-image*. Princeton: Princeton University Press.

Scottish Executive Health Department. (2006a). *Delivering for Mental Health: The Mental Health Delivery Plan for Scotland*. http://www.scotland.gov.uk/Publications/2006/11/30164829/0.

—— (2006b) *Rights, Relationships and Recovery: National Review of Mental Health Nursing in Scotland*. http://www.scotland.gov.uk/Publications/2006/04/18164814/0.

Scottish Government. (2009) *Towards a mentally flourishing Scotland action plan (2009–2011)*.

Snaith, R. P. and Zigmond, A. S. (1994) 'Hospital Anxiety and Depression Scale (HADS)'. *Acta Psychiatrica Scandinavica*, 7: 361–370.

Stake, R. (1977) 'The countenance of educational evaluation'. In: D. Hamilton (ed.) *Beyond the numbers game*, pp. 146–155. Basingstoke: Macmillan Education.

Strauss, A. and Corbin, J. (1990) '*Basics of qualitative research: Grounded theory procedures and techniques*'. Newbury Park, CA: Sage.

The British Psychological Society. (2000) *Recent advances in understanding mental illness and psychotic experiences: A report by the British Psychological Society Division of Clinical Psychology*. Leicester, UK:BPS. http://www.bps.org.uk.

Wechsler, D. (1999) *The Wechsler Abbreviated Scale of Intelligence (WASI)*., San Antonio, USA: The Psychological Corporation.

Yin, R. (1994) *Case study research: design and methods*. 2nd edition. California: Sage.

14 Evaluating recovery at a forensic mental health service using the Developing Recovery Enhancing Environments Measure (DREEM)

Elina Baker, Zeffa Warren, Alexis Clarke, Emma Laughton, Elaine Hewis and Jason Fee

In this chapter we will describe the process of using the Developing Recovery Enhancing Environments Measure (DREEM) on the Medium Secure Unit at the Devon and Cornwall Forensic Mental Health Service. We will describe the events and conditions that led to the decision to carry out this work and reflect on what we learnt from both the process and the outcome of the evaluation.

Setting the scene

The forensic service consists of four in-patient units for men of working age: a 30-bed medium secure unit (incorporating a 12-bed acute assessment ward and an 18-bed rehabilitation ward), a 14-bed low secure unit, a 10-bed open rehabilitation unit and a 16-bed open unit for men with a borderline or mild learning disability. The service has a rural location in Devon, at some distance from other local mental health services, and serves a population drawn from a large geographical area, both rural and urban, although there is a lack of ethnic diversity.

The Devon recovery journey began in earnest in 2003 with a conference hosted by Recovery Devon, an affiliation of mental health workers from a variety of agencies, people who use services and carers. Three members of staff and three service users from the forensic service attended the conference, where they were introduced to the recovery ideas and principles. The presentation of Roberts and Wolfson's paper 'The Rediscovery of Recovery: Open to all' (2004) also set out a vision of how recovery approaches could be adopted by mental health services. Following this, the first author became involved with Recovery Devon, building connections with other local services and professionals who were working to develop the recovery agenda across Devon. In the wider context, this led to a commitment by Devon Partnership NHS Trust to 'putting recovery at the heart of everything we do'. Maintaining this connection was influential in and supportive of a number of recovery-related initiatives at the forensic service.

From the outset, we have recognised that introducing recovery ideas to the forensic service would present challenges. However, all of us who have sought to do so have felt that the nature of the service should not be a barrier to adopting a recovery-based approach. This belief was later endorsed in the Care Services Improvement Partnership 2007 position paper on recovery, which stated that 'there should be no "recovery free zones"' (CSIP *et al.*, 2007, p. 22). In seeking to put recovery into practice we have run a number of training courses, co-facilitated by people who have used services, introduced a recovery group for service users (Baker *et al.*, 2006), carried out a project to promote a more collaborative approach to ward rounds (Baker, 2005) and introduced recovery ideas to supervision and clinical discussions. As a consequence, interest in and awareness of recovery ideas began to grow amongst senior clinicians and service managers.

As a next step, we wanted to introduce a more comprehensive and strategic approach to adopting recovery-based practice. In order to do this, we needed to evaluate the extent to which this was already happening and to identify areas where development was both a priority and a possibility. We took a proposal to the service governance meeting, where a number of concerns were expressed: in particular that the service would inevitably perform badly against recovery principles and that it may not be possible to implement a recovery approach within a forensic setting, as promoting service user autonomy might be in direct conflict with the need to prioritise public protection and risk management. Despite this, it was ultimately felt that it was 'better to know' how the service was performing and that the project would help people at all levels of the service to think about what might be possible in a range of areas. There was also recognition that the proposal would support the service in engaging with the Trust's commitment to recovery.

Getting started

The first step was to assemble a multi-disciplinary project group of people with an interest in recovery to decide how the evaluation should be carried out. There were representatives from clinical psychology, psychiatry, occupational therapy, social work, nursing, chaplaincy and advocacy. At our first meeting we looked at the available tools, including the DREEM, which had been used to evaluate the local rehabilitation service. We decided to invite members of their project group to discuss the experience with us and to give us guidance on our own evaluation.

From this discussion, we learnt that the DREEM was carried out at the rehabilitation service as part of a pilot study conducted by NIMHE of recovery evaluation measures (Dinnis *et al.*, 2007). The DREEM was chosen for this pilot as it was thought to be the most promising of an emerging group of recovery sensitive measures (Campell-Orde *et al.*, 2005). It therefore seemed that the DREEM would not only meet our needs but also give us the invaluable opportunity of comparing our data with a non-forensic service that was already attempting to operate according to recovery principles.

We were inspired by the way in which the rehabilitation service had carried out their evaluation in a 'recovery-based manner', collaborating with people who used services at every step of the process. We contacted the service user group who had been involved in the rehabilitation service project for advice on the basis of their experience of using DREEM. They recommended using the DREEM as the basis for an interview rather than giving it out as a questionnaire. We therefore contacted a number of local service user organisations in order to recruit people with experience of using services to act as interviewers. We hoped that this would help our service users to be more open, that they would value the opportunity to discuss their experiences with people who could identify with them and that the service user interviewers might provide role models of recovery. We offered to pay interviewers £10 per hour, in accordance with the Trust policy for involving service users. We also secured funding from Rethink to pay service users who were interviewed £10 to recognise the value of their contributions.

Revising the DREEM

The DREEM (Ridgway and Press, 2004) is a self-report questionnaire that was designed to evaluate mental health services in relation to recovery. It was developed in the USA from first-person accounts of the process of recovery and a review of practices that promote recovery. It has been edited for use in England. The DREEM consists of seven components, some of which ask about the individual's personal process of recovery. We decided to use only those components which reflected the operation of the service: Elements of Recovery Services, Organisational Climate and two of the Final Questions.

The Elements of Recovery component asks people to rate the importance of 24 areas to their recovery. It then has three sub-questions, asking them to rate the performance of their service on activities associated with each of these areas. The Organisational Climate component asks people to rate the service on 14 qualities that support recovery. All ratings are made on a five-point scale from 'strongly disagree to strongly agree'. The Final Questions are open-ended and provide an opportunity for people to say in their own words how they feel the service could be more supportive of people's recovery.

We felt that the wording of some items on the DREEM was complicated and potentially ambiguous and this was also reflected in the feedback from the interviewers from the rehabilitation service (Dinnis *et al.*, 2005). We therefore revised the questionnaire to try and make it more accessible. We then asked some users of the forensic service to review the items and further changes were made on the basis of their comments. We also developed a set of guidance notes for interviewers to help with explanation of difficult terms (e.g. discrimination, spirituality).

We recognised that in order to deliver recovery-based practice we needed to engage staff in reflecting on the meaning of recovery and the ways in which it could be achieved. We therefore decided that it would be useful to have a measure of staff attitudes as well as service user experience and to follow the example of the rehabilitation service in asking members of staff to complete the DREEM.

In order to make it easier for staff to know how to respond, we amended the DREEM to produce a staff version of the questionnaire.

Carrying out the project

We took on a psychology graduate as a volunteer research assistant to recruit participants, assist with the interviews and analyse the data. We hoped that having someone independent of the service doing these tasks would enable both service users and staff to be open and honest in their responses. Two service users from external service user groups expressed an interest in carrying out interviews. In order to prepare them for this role, we ran a three-hour workshop, which was also attended by the service user representatives who had carried out the DREEM at the rehabilitation service. This was used to discuss the purpose of the project, to explore how the DREEM could be used as the basis for an interview, to practice interviews in role play and to address and problem-solve any concerns that were raised, including explanations of difficult terms. We made some further revisions to the DREEM as a result of this process.

We distributed the staff version of the DREEM through the internal post to all members of staff. They were returned anonymously to the research assistant, who sent non-respondents a reminder letter after the deadline.

The research assistant approached all the service users individually and offered them the opportunity to participate. On the acute ward, the research assistant liaised with the nursing staff about whether they thought the service user would be able to participate and whether it would be safe to carry out the interview. No-one was excluded on these grounds. Service users were offered the choice of being interviewed by the research assistant or an external service user and with the support of a member of staff or an advocate. Many expressed no preference and approximately half were interviewed by the external service users. Responses were returned to the research assistant.

We felt it was important to capture the reflections of the service user interviewers, who had many thoughtful and thought-provoking comments on their experience of the service and both the process and the content of the interviews. We developed a short questionnaire to obtain their feedback and used this in evaluating the project.

Results

We sent out 69 questionnaires to staff and 18 were returned, giving a response rate of 26 per cent. During the interview process, 29 service users were resident on the unit. Of these 20 completed an interview, giving a response rate of 69 per cent.

Elements of Recovery

We converted the ratings that people gave to the importance of each Element of Recovery into a numerical scale, from -2 (strongly disagree) to 2 (strongly agree).

We then calculated a mean rating for staff responses and service user responses. We also converted the ratings given to the three performance items associated with each element in the same way and an overall mean rating of performance for each element was calculated for staff responses and service user responses. We then compared staff and service user ratings of importance and performance using Mann Whitney U tests to see if there was a statistically significant difference.

The mean importance ratings of each Element of Recovery for staff and service users are shown in Table 14.1. There were statistically significant differences between the staff and service user ratings of the importance of the following Elements: hope (U (20, 13)=69, p=0.024), knowledge (U (20, 14)=62.5, p=0.006), meaningful activities (U (19, 13)=131, p=0.022) and help in a crisis (U (19, 14)=83.5, p=0.047), with staff rating all these Elements as more important than service users.

The mean performance ratings of each Element of Recovery for staff and service users are shown in Table 14.2. There were statistically significant differences between the staff and service user ratings of performance on meaning in life

Table 14.1 Mean staff and service user ratings of importance of Elements of Recovery

Element of Recovery	Staff	Service users
Identity	1.70	1.20
Meaning in life	1.67	1.40
Hope	1.85*	1.20*
Knowledge	1.29*	0.15*
Self-management	1.50	0.94
General health	1.54	1.30
Active in own recovery	1.57	1.40
Having rights upheld	1.62	1.35
Peer support	1.38	1.35
Meaningful activities	1.77*	1.16*
Community involvement	1.29	1.47
Personal relationships	1.42	1.35
Build on strengths	1.50	1.32
Developing new skills	1.36	1.00
Basic needs met	1.46	1.60
Sense of control in life	1.50	1.30
Spirituality	1.29	0.68
Social roles	1.21	1.37
Challenging stigma	1.43	1.00
Facing new challenges	1.21	1.00
Role models	1.43	0.75
Help in crisis	1.64*	1.37*
Sexuality	1.36	1.21
Staff who care	1.43	1.47

Those elements where a statistically significant difference (p<0.05) between staff and service user ratings was found are marked with asterisks.

Table 14.2 Mean staff and service user ratings of performance for Elements of Recovery

Element of Recovery	Staff	Service users
Identity	0.71	0.26
Meaning in life	0.63*	0.14*
Hope	0.65	0.64
Knowledge	0.79	0.21
Self-management	1.63	0.25
General health	0.46	0.59
Active in own recovery	0.01	0.05
Having rights upheld	1.27*	0.29*
Peer support	−0.08	0.15
Meaningful activities	0.42	0.70
Community involvement	−0.53	−0.53
Personal relationships	0.19	0.02
Build on strengths	0.50	0.46
Developing new skills	−0.06	0.21
Basic needs met	0.65	0.64
Sense of control in life	0.50	0.25
Spirituality	0.65*	−0.14*
Social roles	−0.51	0.00
Challenging stigma	0.52	0.20
Facing new challenges	0.29	0.51
Role models	−0.06	0.18
Help in crisis	0.60	0.42
Sexuality	−0.42	−0.49
Staff who care	0.52	0.55

Those Elements where a statistically significant difference ($p<0.05$) between staff and service user ratings was found are marked with asterisks.

(U (19, 16)=84, p=0.024), having rights respected and upheld (U (19, 16)=53, p=0.001) and spirituality (U (19, 15)=78, p=0.008). Staff ratings of performance were higher on all these Elements.

As many Elements of Recovery were given low ratings and there were many significant differences in staff and service user ratings we decided to focus on the Elements that were given the five highest importance ratings by staff and service users. We then identified Elements that were given a performance rating of less than 0.5 by service users as areas for improvement. We chose this cut-off to take account of the tendency for users of mental health services to rate services positively (Stallard, 1996) and to reflect items where the majority of respondents had made negative or neutral ratings. These Elements are shown in Table 14.3. The areas where the mean service user achievement rating was below 0.5 are marked with asterisks.

Organisational Climate

We converted the ratings given to each of the items on the Organisational Climate scale in the same way as the Elements of Recovery.

Table 14.3 Five highest-rated Elements of Recovery for staff and service users and mean service user achievement rating

Staff	Mean SU achievement rating	Service user	Mean SU achievement rating
Hope	0.64	Basic needs met	0.64
Meaningful activities	0.70	Staff who care	0.55
Identity (person not patient)	0.26*	Involved in community	−0.53*
Meaning in life	0.14*	Meaning in life	0.14*
Help in a crisis	0.42*	Active in own recovery	0.01*
Self management	0.25*		

The mean staff and service user ratings of the Organisational Climate items are shown in Table 14.4. As we made final amendments to the service user questionnaire after the staff questionnaire was sent out, staff were asked to rate whether the service was safe and attractive as a single item, but for service users this was separated into two separate items. There were significant differences between staff and service user ratings of the following items: hopeful environment (U (19, 19)=111.5, p=0.043), enough resources (U (19, 19)=100.5, p=0.018), opportunities for meaningful involvement (U (19, 19)=50, p=0.00), making people feel valued and respected (U (18, 19)=103, p=0.039), creative and interesting things going on (U (19, 19)=88, p=0.006) and providing real choices (U (19, 19)=48.5, p=0.00). All these items were rated more negatively by staff.

Table 14.4 Mean ratings of Organisational Climate items

Item	Service users	Staff
Promotes learning and growth	0.88	0.21
Hopeful environment	0.53	−0.16
Inspiring and encouraging	0.29	−0.26
Caring staff	0.53	0.89
Enough resources	−0.37	−1.10
Meaningful involvement	0.74	−0.42
Helps people feel valued	0.39	−0.37
Helps people have positive contact	0.61	0.11
Attractive	0.5	−0.68
Safe	−0.63	
Welcoming staff	0.24	0.37
Creative and interesting things happen	0.63	−0.26
Provides choices and opportunities	0.68	−0.53
Asks for feedback	0.37	0.28
Uses feedback	0	−0.32

Responses to Final Questions

We grouped the responses together into themes for each of the Final Questions.

Question 1 *What are one or two of the most important things this service and its staff can do to support people in their recovery?*
The themes that emerged from the responses included having staff who were available to talk and listen to service users about their difficulties. This was linked with an identified need for more staff and more talking therapies. Positive staff attitudes were also frequently identified, and in particular relating to service users as individuals rather than in terms of their diagnosis or offence. Both service users and staff also identified the importance of involving service users in their care, especially through giving them information. Staff responses reflected a theme of being realistic with service users and service user responses reflected a desire for honesty from staff. Other commonly identified themes were: helping service users to develop skills that would enable them to live independently in the future, increasing service user involvement in the community, especially through better links with outside organizations, and supporting service users to improve their physical health.

Question 2. *Do you have any other comments or ideas that could improve the service?*
The most frequently identified theme related to resources and funding, with both staff and service users feeling that the physical environment in particular needed to be improved. A separate theme was created to account for the large number of staff and service users identifying a need for higher staffing levels. This was also linked to other themes around service user leave, which enabled therapeutic access to outdoor space and meaningful activities, and provision of talking therapies. Positive staff attitudes were again identified as being important, with service users wanting to be taken seriously and have their perspective on their difficulties valued. Building links with the community to facilitate social inclusion was also identified by both staff and service users.

Reflecting on the results

Comparison with the rehabilitation service

Although concerns were raised in the governance meeting that, due to its function, the forensic service would not perform well in relation to recovery principles, our comparison with the performance of the rehabilitation service was better than we had expected. We again used 0.5 as a cut-off for satisfactory performance on the Elements of Recovery and found that performance was the same in many areas: Table 14.5 shows how the services compared. There were many elements where both services did not achieve the cut-off. This may reflect how difficult it

Table 14.5 Comparison of Elements of Recovery rated above and below 0.5 by service users at the forensic service and rehabilitation service

Both services above 0.5	Both services below 0.5	Forensic service above 0.5, rehabilitation service below	Rehabilitation service above 0.5, forensic service below
Hope	Knowledge about problems	Having your basic needs met	Identity
Meaningful activities	Being active in your own recovery		Meaning in life
General health	Having your rights respected		Self-management
Taking on new challenges	Community involvement		Peer support
Having staff who care	Personal relationships		Building on strengths
	Spirituality		Developing new skills
	Taking on valued social roles		Having control over your life
	Challenging stigma		Having help in a crisis
	Providing role models of recovery		
	Sexuality		

is to achieve recovery-based practice in in-patient mental health services, irrespective of the level of security.

We were struck in particular by some differences between the services, which we will now discuss in more detail.

Engagement with recovery ideas

In looking at the overall pattern of responses we wondered if some of the findings reflected a lesser awareness of, and engagement with, recovery ideas at the forensic service. The rehabilitation service obtained responses from all of their staff. This reflects their approach of asking staff to respond during a team development day rather than using a postal survey. However, the response rate amongst staff at the forensic service was even lower than would be expected from a postal survey. One possible explanation is that only those staff who felt recovery principles to be relevant responded to the survey at the forensic service.

The rehabilitation service found no significant differences between their staff group and their residents in importance ratings of the Elements of Recovery, whereas there were significant differences on four Elements in the forensic sample, with a clear trend for service users to rate most Elements as less important. We wondered if this meant that users of the rehabilitation service were more in touch with recovery ideas than our service users.

The rehabilitation service found significant differences between staff and service users on ratings of performance on eight Elements, whereas this was only found on three in the forensic service. However, staff ratings of performance were generally lower in the forensic service, with several Elements having mean ratings below zero or being lower than the mean service user rating, which did not occur in the rehabilitation service results. We thought that this might reflect staff feeling disempowered or unable to deliver recovery ideas in the forensic setting. The users of the forensic service, in rating services higher than staff, may have had lower expectations or different understandings of the role of services than this group of staff, and consequently been more positive about the service's performance.

Hope

Both services scored above our cut-off for satisfactory performance on Hope. However, in comparing the qualitative data, we noticed some interesting differences in the way that people talked about hope. Staff at the rehabilitation service felt that holding hope for people was very important and users of the rehabilitation service identified that hope was central to someone's recovery journey. However, users of the forensic service identified a need for staff to be realistic and honest with them and the staff identified a need to balance service users' goals with public protection. This suggests an awareness at the forensic service of the greater restrictions that may be faced by people with an offending history and this may make it harder to focus on hope. In trying to understand how, given this difference, both services had achieved a rating above the cut-off, we wondered whether users of the forensic service might have lower expectations about what was possible for them and the extent to which the service should hold hope.

Meaning in life and identity

One of the areas where the forensic service did not perform as well as the rehabilitation service was in supporting people to have meaning in life. This in particular stood out for us, as it was also one of the areas that was given the highest importance ratings by both staff and service users, and there was a significant difference between staff and service user ratings. There was also poorer performance at the forensic service on supporting people in developing a positive sense of identity, as a person rather than a patient. This was also one of the items with the highest importance ratings from staff and came through as being valued by service users in the qualitative data.

While forensic service users will have more limited access to opportunities and communities that may support their sense of personal meaning and positive identity (e.g. families, faith communities, open employment) it should still be possible to develop practice in this area, although more creative or imaginative solutions may need to be found. Slade (2009) identifies a number of practices that could be included or adapted in the secure setting, such as using assessment to amplify strengths, access to spiritual or uplifting experiences and introducing different ways of understanding unusual experiences. The latter were all incorporated to some extent in our recovery group (Baker *et al.*, 2006). Given the breadth and individuality of the concept of a meaningful life, this is something that would need to be explored individually with service users. Staff may need additional support and training to engage with service users around such issues, which may be very different from the traditional focus of forensic mental health services on reducing symptoms and managing risk.

Being in control

The forensic service also compared unfavourably to the rehabilitation service on self-management and having control over your life. We wanted to consider these together as both are related to ways that it may be possible for people to take up an active stance. The extent to which forensic service users can have control over their lives is particularly likely to be limited by the need for the service to prioritise risk management and public protection. However, we feel that it should still be possible to develop practice in this area. For example, service users played key roles in initiating and delivering our project to review the ward round process, which resulted in service users being invited to be present throughout meetings to review their care (Baker, 2005). There are likely to be other strategies that can maximise the involvement that forensic service users have in decisions about their care or how the service is delivered.

Encouraging service users to develop skills in self-management may also help them to feel more in control and like active partners in their care. While being in the forensic service will also limit people's access to resources and environments that support their wellness (e.g. natural environments, sports facilities, complementary therapies) it should still be possible to find ways of introducing new techniques and experiences. As part of our recovery group, we organised sessions with an aromatherapist, an environmental arts therapist and a mindfulness practitioner, which were well received (Baker *et al.*, 2006). These and other interventions to support self-management should therefore continue. Introducing self-management systems, such as Wellness Recovery Action Plans (Copeland and Mead, 2004), which contain a crisis planning tool, could also help improve service users' experiences of help in a crisis, another area where performance was poorer than at the rehabilitation services and which received high importance ratings from staff.

Meeting basic needs

The only area where the forensic service performed better than the rehabilitation service in relation to our cut-off was having your basic needs met. This may reflect different expectations at the two services about which needs should be met by staff and which the service users should be able to fulfil for themselves.

In a service with greater access to the community, where the aim is social inclusion, service users may be expected to take greater responsibility for accessing community resources to meet basic needs autonomously. This would be more difficult to achieve at the forensic service and the presence of social workers as integrated members of the multi-disciplinary team rather than a community-based resource may mean that staff take on more responsibility for meeting basic needs.

Organisational Climate

We were surprised to find that more Organisational Climate items received below-zero ratings from staff than from service users. This seems to bear out our thinking that staff may feel unable to put recovery ideas into practice and that service users may have low expectations of what the service should offer. As performance was generally poor on the Organisational Climate scale, we decided to focus on areas where both staff and service users rated the service negatively.

Neither staff nor service users felt safe in the service. As service users will often have been admitted following violent or aggressive acts, it is to some extent inevitable that people will be aware of risk and that incidents will occur. However, this suggests a need to explore in more detail what has made people feel unsafe and to think about what improvements could be made. It may be that this is linked to the identified lack of resources, which seemed from the qualitative data to be related to low staffing numbers and the physical environment. While addressing resourcing issues may be a complex task and involve high levels of organisational commitment and change, collaboratively identifying ways that both staff and service users could be made to feel safer within the existing resources may be possible, and would also address the perception that the service does not make use of the feedback it gets. We hope that the process of undertaking the DREEM and identifying priorities for change could also go some way towards addressing this issue.

Priorities for change

Several different aspects of our results suggested that there may be limited awareness of recovery ideas, or belief in being able to use them, among both staff and service users at the forensic service. The first step could therefore be to find ways of introducing recovery ideas, with the key message that recovery is possible and applicable in all settings. There would need to be opportunities to explore the challenges and dilemmas around putting recovery into practice in the secure setting, and ongoing opportunities to review practice in relation to principles.

We have already discussed most of the areas that we identified as key areas for improvement. We have not yet touched on being involved in the community, which is perhaps the area that would be most challenging for a secure service to address, given the restrictions which are required in order to manage risk. However, the qualitative data suggests the possibility of greater links with community organisations and we wonder whether this might be an idea where creativity and innovation could achieve more recovery-based practice, perhaps through finding ways of bringing the community into the hospital.

The other areas for improvement all indicate a more specific staff-training agenda. In particular, supporting staff in developing skills in valuing people's own perspectives on their difficulties, identifying strengths and exploring and developing what constitutes a meaningful life would be important. Additionally, building staff knowledge and awareness of self-management strategies, including psychological approaches, would be beneficial. This could also inform the more widespread use of crisis plans, which could be routinely incorporated into care planning and review.

Reflecting on the process

We used the feedback from the service user interviewers to reflect on the strengths and weaknesses of the project. Many of the limitations that we identified are common to other surveys of user experiences of mental health services (Baker, 2003). The project attempted to evaluate the service as a whole, and many respondents, and the service user interviewers, identified that different ratings would be made in relation to different aspects of the service (such as interactions with different staff groups), resulting in some cases in an overall neutral rating. Service users may also tend not to feel able to be critical of services. We attempted to address this, by using interviewers who were independent of the service and, in some cases, who had experiences of using services themselves. The service user interviewers felt that this had enabled respondents to be more open, although there was still a concern that some answers reflected what was desirable or acceptable to say. Further, the areas that the study asked about reflected the priorities of the service and not necessarily those of the service users themselves. Though the contents of the DREEM are based on service user accounts, it is noticeable that user ratings of importance tended to be lower than staff ratings. This could suggest that the Elements of Recovery may not have adequately captured what the users of the forensic service felt was most important to their recovery, and this needs further exploration. The service user interviewers identified that a more qualitative approach could have yielded data that was more reflective of service users' concerns and experiences. One of them pointed out that relying on quantitative data has been criticised for attempting to 'simplify complex human experience to the point where it has no meaning' (Allen, 2007).

As we got the impression that recovery ideas may be unfamiliar to both staff and service users of the forensic service, it may have been difficult for them to respond to questions about what is important to recovery in a meaningful way. The service user interviewers reported that the process of engaging in the interview had stimulated thought in some service users about the meaning of recovery and their own potential to recover. They also felt that they may have provided a positive role model of recovery, to which users of the forensic service did not often have access. We hope that the use of the DREEM could have been a first step in introducing the key principles of recovery to the service and that engaging in the project will have encouraged both service users and staff to reflect on recovery in a new way. An alternative, and perhaps more recovery-orientated, approach could have been to engage service users and staff in a collaborative process of discovery about recovery ideas. This would have allowed further exploration of complex issues, such as the tension between maintaining hope and being honest and realistic. The response to the DREEM does, however, indicate that such a process could be valuable, through giving us a sense of our starting point. Carrying out the DREEM has served to put recovery firmly on the agenda of the forensic service and, following the project, a staff member from the service contributed to a more detailed exploration of recovery and compulsory treatment (Roberts *et al.*, 2008).

The service user interviewers raised concerns that evaluating the service against recovery principles would be a 'lip service' exercise and would not result in any positive change. The results of the project have been presented and discussed with service users and the team responsible for clinical governance on the medium secure unit and there is a commitment to attempting to develop practice in the areas identified for improvement. The quantitative data obtained from the DREEM can therefore provide a baseline of service functioning and we hope that repeated administration in future will enable progress in relation to recovery-based practice to be monitored.

The aim of this project was to evaluate a forensic service against recovery principles that have developed out of an understanding of how people regain a meaningful life following mental health difficulties. We did not give much consideration to whether there might be different or additional processes involved in moving on from a history of offending or high-risk behaviour. There has been some associated research into the narratives of people who have desisted from offending (Maruna, 2001) which could contribute to an extended understanding of recovery for people using forensic mental health services. Further research in this area could help to develop a measure of services that support recovery from offending, which would make a valuable supplement to the DREEM for forensic services.

Acknowledgements

Paul Blakesley, Chris Harper, Simon Harrison, Caroline Jacob, Ray Lancaster, Rita Luxa.

References

Allen, C. (2007, 28 March) 'Form of torment'. *The Guardian.*
Baker, E. (2003) 'Service user views on a low-secure psychiatric ward', *Clinical Psychology Forum*, 25, 11–13.
—— (2005) 'Working together to improve ward rounds'. *Clinical Psychology Forum*, 152: 9–12.

Baker, E., Luxa, R. and Warren, Z. (2006) 'Introducing a recovery group to a forensic psychiatric service'. Retrieved 26 March 2008 from http://www.recoverydevon.co.uk/html/downloads/Group-Evaluation.pdf.

Campbell-Orde, T., Chamberlin, J., Carpenter, J. and Leff, H. S. (2005) *Measuring the promise: A compendium of recovery measures*, Volume II. Cambridge, MA: The Evaluation Centre at HSRI.

Care Services Improvement Partnership, Royal College of Psychiatrists and Social Care Institute for Excellence. (2007) *A Common Purpose: Recovery in Future Mental Health Services*. London: SCIE.

Copeland, M. and Mead, S. (2004) 'Wellness Recovery Action Plan and Peer Support'. Peach Press: Vermont.

Dinnis, S., Roberts, G., Hubbard, C., Hounsell, J. and Webb, R. (2005) *The Russell Clinic Survey: Implementing the Developing Recovery Enhancing Environments Measure – DREEM*. Retrieved 26 March 2008 from http://www.recoverydevon.co.uk/html/downloads/DREEM%20-%20Russell%20Clinic.pdf.

—— (2007) 'User led assessment of the recovery orientation of a rehabilitation service using DREEM'. *Psychiatric Bulletin*, 31: 124–127.

Maruna, S. (2001) *Making Good: How Ex-Convicts Reform and Rebuild Their Lives*. Washington, DC: American Psychological Association.

Ridgway, P. A. and Press, A. (2004) *Assessing the recovery commitment of your mental health service: a user's guide to the Development of Recovery Enhancing Environments Measure (DREEM)*. UK Pilot Version.

Roberts, G., Dorkins, E., Wooldridge, J. and Hewis, E. (2008) 'Detained: what's my choice?' *Advances in Psychiatric Treatment*, 14: 172–180.

Roberts, G. and Wolfson, P. (2004) 'The Rediscovery of Recovery: Open to all'. *Advances in Psychiatric Treatment*, 10: 37–49.

Slade, M. (2009) *100 Ways to Support Recovery: A Guide for Mental Health Professionals*. London: Rethink.

Stallard, P. (1996) 'The role and use of consumer satisfaction surveys in mental health services'. *Journal of Mental Health*, 5: 333–348.

Index